Charlotte Brontë

Twayne's English Authors Series

Herbert Sussman, Editor

Northeastern University

TEAS 541

CHARLOTTE BRONTË
By courtesy of the National Portrait Gallery, London.

Charlotte Brontë

Diane Long Hoeveler and Lisa Jadwin

Twayne Publishers

New York

Twayne's English Authors Series No. 541

Charlotte Brontë
Diane Long Hoeveler and Lisa Jadwin

Twayne Publishers
1633 Broadway
New York, New York 10019

Library of Congress Cataloging-in-Publication Data

Hoeveler, Diane Long.
    Charlotte Brontë / Diane Long Hoeveler and Lisa Jadwin.
        p. cm. — (Twayne's English authors series ; TEAS 541)
    Includes bibliographical references and index.
    ISBN 0-8057-4513-0 (alk. paper)
    1. Brontë, Charlotte, 1816–1855—Criticism and interpretation.
2. Women and literature—England—History—19th century.
I. Jadwin, Lisa.   II. Title.   III. Series.
PR4169.H64 1997
823'.8—dc21   97-7226
                                                                                        CIP

10 9 8 7 6 5 4

Printed in the United States of America

*This book is dedicated to our husbands,
David Hoeveler and Steve Derné*

Contents

Preface

In 1979 Charlotte Brontë's literary prominence underwent a dramatic resurgence. Sandra Gilbert and Susan Gubar published their ground-breaking critical study *The Madwoman in the Attic,* and in the process they highlighted the dual images of Jane Eyre and Bertha Mason Rochester as the victors and victims of a submerged women's literary tradition. Six years later Gilbert and Gubar made the controversial decision to reprint the entirety of *Jane Eyre* in the Norton anthology entitled *Women's Literature: The Tradition in English* (1985), the standard textbook used in university and college women's literature courses for the past decade. These two critical developments, in addition to the continuing production of film versions of *Jane Eyre,* have combined to increase Charlotte Brontë's visibility and importance as a figure of substantial importance in the revised and expanded literary canon of nineteenth-century British female writers.

Because of the increase in critical studies published on Charlotte Brontë's novels and juvenilia during the past 20 years, most of which are informed by the new feminist, historicist, and materialist methodologies, the coauthors of this volume offer a critical reassessment of Charlotte Brontë's novels, juvenilia, poetry, and letters that emphasizes those new critical approaches.

Finally, we wish to thank our editor, Professor Herbert Sussman of Northeastern University, for both his patience and his critical astuteness.

Chronology

1848 July, Charlotte visits Smith, Elder in London to reveal the identity of Currer Bell. September, Branwell dies; December, Emily dies.

1849 May, Anne dies. October, Smith, Elder publishes *Shirley*.

1852 Charlotte rejects Arthur Bell Nicholls's marriage proposal; her father disapproves of her intention to marry his curate.

1853 January, Smith, Elder publishes *Villette*.

1854 April, Charlotte finally accepts Arthur Bell Nicholls's marriage proposal; June, she marries him.

1855 31 March, Charlotte, possibly pregnant, dies.

1857 Smith, Elder publishes Elizabeth Gaskell's *Life of Charlotte Brontë*. Smith, Elder publishes *The Professor*.

1860 April, *Cornhill Magazine* publishes Charlotte's unfinished story *Emma*.

Chapter One
"Fact Is Often Stranger Than Fiction": Biographers on Charlotte Brontë

Public interest in Charlotte Brontë's life began with the publication of *Jane Eyre* in 1847, when readers began immediately to speculate about the identity of the mysterious Currer Bell and his putative brothers Ellis and Acton. Brontë's concealment of her identity would later help incubate such rumors as the one that arose in response to her impassioned dedication of the second edition of *Jane Eyre* to the novelist William Makepeace Thackeray: it was whispered that the "autobiographer" of *Jane Eyre* was actually a former governess of Thackeray's young daughters and that the novel was an account of her romance with her erstwhile employer.[1]

> Isolated from London, Charlotte Brontë could have no idea that Thackeray's personal life bore an unhappily close resemblance to that of Mr. Rochester. He too had a mad wife to whom he was shackled for life—and malicious London gossips whispered that *Jane Eyre* must be written by his mistress. An embarrassed Thackeray finally wrote to Currer Bell via Mr. Williams [the publisher], gently outlining his family circumstances. Charlotte was quite mortified by the consequences of her innocent blunder, telling Mr. Williams in a letter of 28 January 1848, "Well may it be said that fact is often stranger than fiction! . . . The very fact of his not complaining at all and addressing me with such kindness . . . increases my chagrin."[2]

Writers' lives have always seized the interest of readers and biographers who want to acquaint themselves with the creator of a beloved text. Upon *Jane Eyre*'s first publication, Brontë's life attracted immediate attention; where information was lacking, the public simply constructed a story that attempted to explain and thus contain the effect of an excessively passionate utterance. After Brontë's death, less than a decade later, the novelist Elizabeth Gaskell moved immediately to secure the Reverend Patrick Brontë's permission to write his last surviving daughter's life, thus inaugurating a tradition of Brontë biographies that has persisted without interruption into our own time. Yet the many biographies of Brontë present conflicting views of their subject. The Gaskell school of biography presents Brontë as a dutiful, suffering Victorian daughter; the tradition inaugurated by E. F. Benson depicts her as a neurotic, vindictive malcontent. Some writers, beginning with the novelist Mary Augusta Ward, have been idiosyncratic, attributing Brontë's development to a particular aspect of her ancestry or character. In the last half of the twentieth century, such biographers as Inga-Stina Ewbank, Winifred Gérin, and Lyndall Gordon have tended to present Brontë as a pioneering feminist heroine.

In Brontë's lifetime, the status of female writers was slowly changing: it was becoming increasingly socially acceptable for a woman to write fiction. Yet in an era when female writers began to outpublish male writers,[3] the poet laureate Robert Southey assured the young Charlotte Brontë in 1837 that "literature is not the business of a woman's life, and it cannot be."[4] Fifteen years later, E. S. Dallas was more permissive, arguing that "women . . . have a talent for personal discourse and familiar narrative, which, when properly controlled, is a great gift, though too frequently it degenerates into a social nuisance."[5] In 1852, G. H. Lewes went so far as to say that because "love is the staple of fiction," then "of all departments of literature, fiction is one to which by nature and circumstances women are best adapted."[6] Seldom, however, were critics unambivalent about women as writers. Such debates persisted well into the twentieth century. In 1929, Virginia Woolf undercut her famous assertion that "a woman must have money and a room of her own if she is to write fiction" with the observation that "it is fatal for a woman to lay the least stress on any grievance; to plead even with justice any cause; in any way to speak consciously as a woman."[7]

Brontë understood this dilemma only too well. She struggled throughout her life to reconcile her life as a woman—a life that required her to be a dutiful, retiring helpmeet—with her life as a writer, which required her to be bold, assertive, and ambitious. Biographies of Brontë have reflected this division and have alternately excoriated, deified, rationalized, romanticized, and justified her. Often she has been treated as an anomaly whose unconventional desires and attitudes threatened or succeeded in preventing her adjustment to Victorian standards of proper womanhood. As Catherine Hamilton, author of *Women Writers: Their Works and Ways* (1892), argues,

Happy women, whose hearts are satisfied and full, have little need of [literary] utterance. Their lives are rounded and complete, they require nothing but the calm recurrence of those peaceful home duties in which domestic women rightly feel that their true vocation lies.[8]

Logically, Hamilton's assertion suggests, a woman who writes must be unhappy, unsatisfied, incomplete, not at peace—in short, not feminine.

Traditionally, biographies of "women of genius" have often focused disproportionately on their subjects' ability or failure to conform to cultural norms, whereas biographies of men have embraced eccentricity as the prerogative of greatness. Brontë's biographers have often attempted to reduce Brontë to an acceptable female stereotype: the crazed, sexually repressed spinster; the neurotic depressive; the front for her brother's literary productions; the enraged political agitator. Biographers have attempted to outdo one another, to set the record straight, enlisting Brontë's life as an arena for political and cultural debates.

The achievements of nineteenth- and twentieth-century feminist movements have intensified the battles. As Brontë biographer Rebecca Fraser has said, "The lost continent of the mores and taboos hedging women round in the mid-nineteenth century has surfaced, and the sort of constraints under which the woman writer worked, and the inimical way in which she was perceived" have recently given us a clearer picture of the "different landscape" of the female writer's life.[9] Revisionist biographies of Brontë, seeking to redress the distorted impressions of earlier ages, have presented Brontë's iconoclasm as heroic and implicitly feminist. A balanced approximation of the actual Brontë—the complex and often contradictory person and writer—has eluded biographers who have attempted to reduce her to type.

Certainly Brontë's nonconformity has helped stimulate the mythologies that have arisen to explain her. Her reclusiveness, introversion, loneliness, and emotional intensity marked her as different even during her own lifetime. The pseudonym she retained throughout her adult life served not simply to protect her briefly from misogynistic attacks by critics but to ensure her privacy in Yorkshire, where she could live relatively undisturbed by the bustling competition of the London literary marketplace. She was aware enough that the combination of intense passion and introversion that facilitated her work was exceptional to confide to Southey, "I carefully avoid any appearance of preoccupation and eccentricity which might lead those I live amongst to suspect the nature of my pursuits."[10] Even to her best friend she felt it necessary to say, "*I am not like you*. If you knew my thoughts, the dreams that absorb me, and the fiery imagination that at times eats me up, and makes me feel society, as it is, wretchedly insipid, you would pity and I dare say despise me."[11] A person who felt and desired intensely, who balanced a literary career with a series of menial jobs, who watched illness destroy her beloved mother and five siblings, who endured years of loneliness before marrying, and who died prematurely at 39, Brontë led a dramatic and often tragic life.

Three ancillary issues have bedeviled Brontë biographers. First, the biographical basis of her novels has led biographers to equate Brontë's life with the "lives" of her first-person narrators. This mistake has been exacerbated by Brontë's own blurring of the line. The subtitle "An Autobiography," for example, has led generations of readers of *Jane Eyre* to equate the "editor" Currer Bell with Charlotte Brontë.

Second, Brontë's life has often been paired with that of each of her siblings, particularly Emily and Anne. Writers have tended either to conflate the writers as a pair or trio or to define them artificially in opposition to one another. The complexity of Brontë's aesthetic and emotional relationships to her siblings, who during her apprenticeship as a writer were her coauthors and closest confidantes, defies such reduction.

Finally, the primary materials on which biography is based have been unreliable or inaccessible to many generations of biographers. Brontë's letters and unpublished manuscripts are scattered throughout the Western world, forcing biographers to travel to collections, some of which have been lost or destroyed. Biographers have relied heavily on Brontë's letters to outline her life, but as Tom Winnifrith and Edward Chitham have argued, "the fact that [Brontë] wrote most of [her letters] to her rather dull and conventional friend, Ellen Nussey, and the fact that all letters, especially those written to Ellen Nussey, have been badly edited and inaccurately dated, have inevitably distorted our knowledge of the Brontës."[12] The extremely tiny size of the unpublished juvenile manuscripts has also made transcription challenging. All of these issues have encouraged biographers to speculate and mythologize in an attempt to enlarge our understanding of Brontë.

Nineteenth- and Early-Twentieth-Century Biographies

Brontë's contemporaries began formally to speculate about her life even before it was over. Their public and private comments about her often reveal more about their own attitudes than about Brontë herself. After reading *Villette,* William Makepeace Thackeray, the "titan" to whom Brontë dedicated the second edition of *Jane Eyre,* derided Brontë in a private letter:

> The poor little woman of genius! The fiery little eager brave tremulous homely-faced creature! I can read a great deal of her life as I fancy in her book, and see that rather than have fame, rather than any other earthly good or mayhap heavenly one she wants some Tomkins or another to love and be in love with. But you see she is a little bit of a creature without a pennyworth of good looks, thirty years old I should think, buried in the country and eating up her own heart there, and no Tomkins will come. You girls with pretty faces and red boots (and what not) will get dozens of young fellows fluttering about you—whereas here is one a genius, a noble heart longing to mate itself and destined to wither away into old maidenhood with no chance to fulfil the burning desire.[13]

Here Thackeray equates Brontë with a caricatured version of *Villette*'s Lucy Snowe and implicitly condemns Brontë's novels as wish-fulfillment fantasies designed to compensate for a miserable, manless life. Ironically, of course, Thackeray was wrong: Brontë had in fact received and rejected numerous marriage proposals, preferring to remain single rather than settle for a man she did not love. A year after publication of *Villette,* Brontë married a longtime suitor.

Magazine articles about Brontë began to appear as early as the late 1840s, less than two months after her death, and it was not unusual to see an article like the one in *Sharpe's London Magazine* in 1855, "A Few Words about Jane Eyre," which was filled with speculations about Brontë's life and personal relationships.[14] By June 1855, the Reverend Patrick Brontë was sufficiently concerned about the public's demand to know about his daughter that he asked Elizabeth Gaskell to write Charlotte's official biography, a work that would become one of the greatest biographies in English literature.[15]

Elizabeth Cleghorn Gaskell met Charlotte Brontë during a shared visit to the estate of Sir James and Lady Kay-Shuttleworth in 1850. Gaskell had already achieved literary success with *Mary Barton* (1850); she would go on to produce *Ruth* (1853), *Cranford* (1853), and *North and South* (1855), all fictionalized accounts of laborers' lives in working-class Manchester. Gaskell cultivated the shy Charlotte Brontë assiduously, and eventually the two novelists became intimate enough to visit one another's homes. Though Gaskell and Brontë shared many political and

aesthetic concerns, they were temperamentally different; Gaskell was as
ebullient and socially adept as Brontë was melancholy and ill at ease
among strangers. Alan Shelston indicates that their friendship was "as
much a combination of opposite as of like minds; paradoxically it is a
tribute to its strength that it should have developed in the face of such
disparities." Shelston hypothesizes that the writers were united by two
bonds: their shared religious faith, which had at its base a commitment
to duty, and the fact that "from the earliest stages of their friendship,
Mrs. Gaskell saw in Brontë the living epitome of all the qualities with
which she had invested her fictional heroines."[16] Though married to a
Unitarian minister and the mother of four daughters, Gaskell admired
in Brontë qualities she herself lacked.

Gaskell's biography dominated public perception of Brontë for several decades. Like an effective fiction, it dramatized Brontë's life and
environment, giving a particularly good feel for setting, and transformed its subject into a convincing character. It also inaugurated a persistent binary tradition in Brontë biography and criticism by dividing
Brontë into two people—Charlotte Brontë the Victorian woman and
Currer Bell the Victorian writer:

> Charlotte Brontë's existence becomes divided into two parallel currents:
> her life as Currer Bell, the author, her life as Charlotte Brontë, the
> woman. There were separate duties belonging to each character—not
> opposing each other, not impossible, but difficult to be reconciled. When
> a man becomes an author, it is probably a mere change of employment
> to him. He takes a portion of that time which has hitherto been devoted
> to some other study or pursuit. . . . But no other can take up the quiet,
> regular duties of the daughter, the wife, or the mother, as well as she
> whom God has appointed to fill that particular place . . . nor can she
> drop the domestic charges devolving on her as an individual, for the exer-
> cise of the most splendid talents that were ever bestowed. And yet she
> must not shrink from the extra responsibility implied by the very fact of
> her possessing such talents. She must not hide her gift in a napkin; it was
> meant for the use and service of others.[17]

Gaskell rationalizes Brontë's nonconformism by restricting it to her
writing life. "Charlotte Brontë the woman," Gaskell argues, was
absolutely conventional: she was a long-suffering, dutiful, moral, spiritual Victorian heroine. "Currer Bell the author," on the other hand, personified the unspeakable traits Brontë's critics deemed "coarse," "rebellious," and angry. The domestic metaphor Gaskell employs to describe

Brontë's responsibility not to hide her writerly gifts "in a napkin" gives a sense of the way Gaskell recuperates the dutiful "Charlotte Brontë the woman" at the expense of the unruly "Currer Bell the author." Gaskell reinforces the split and devotes little discussion to Brontë's works, consequently eliding much evidence of Brontë's deviations from the norm of proper Victorian womanhood. Guided perhaps by the adage "If you can't say something nice, don't say anything at all," Gaskell presents us with a Charlotte Brontë who more closely resembles Elizabeth Gaskell than was perhaps true.

A second central element of Gaskell's mission was to defend Brontë against those who had persecuted her and her family during her lifetime. She criticizes the most notorious of these offenders, the Reverend William Carus Wilson, administrator of the Clergy Daughters School at Cowan Bridge, where Elizabeth and Maria Brontë died in the typhus epidemic. Wilson is caricatured as Mr. Brocklehurst in *Jane Eyre*. Gaskell also has harsh words for Thomas Newby, the exploitive publisher of Emily's and Anne's novels, for Lydia Robinson, Branwell's supposed lover, and for Elizabeth Rigby, Brontë's severest critic. Both the family of William Carus Wilson and Lady Scott, formerly Mrs. Robinson, brought suit against Gaskell's publishers, and unsold copies of the first two editions were removed from the shelves and eventually replaced by a later edition. Gaskell's solicitors later offered a public retraction of some offending passages. The third edition, amended and improved by suggestions from such friends of Brontë's as Mary Taylor, compensated for these changes by providing new material.[18]

Gaskell's biography of Brontë had three lasting effects: it was instantly popular and well received by readers and reviewers, and it was controversial, plagued by threatened and actual lawsuits from those who felt libeled by it. Though unsold copies of the first and second editions were removed from the shelves, the taint of libel remained, causing both Gaskell's *Life* and Brontë's novels to sell extremely well thereafter. Third, the biography effectively established Brontë's literary reputation for the remainder of the century.

Tributes and evaluations quickly followed Gaskell's biography. In May 1871, Ellen Nussey, Brontë's longtime friend, wrote a reminiscence refuting critics' allegations that Brontë was irreligious.[19] George Smith, Brontë's longtime publisher, alienated by her representation of him as John Graham Bretton in *Villette,* generated a short memoir, "The Brontës," for the *Cornhill Magazine.* In this faintly retributive critical piece, Smith elevates Emily at Charlotte's expense and distinguishes Charlotte as "intense" but lacking the breadth that indicates true genius. Still angry about Brontë's presentation of him in *Villette,* Smith ranks Brontë's final novel far below *Jane Eyre.*[20]

At this point, Brontë biography merges so thoroughly with Brontë criticism that the two genres become one. During the last quarter of the nineteenth century, a series of reactive critical reappraisals attempt to situate Brontë in the canon. Once again, Brontë's emotionalism and nonconformity condition critical appraisal. Romantics tend to respond positively to Brontë, whereas classicists, with their more rational, pragmatic orientation, tend to denigrate her. Her life and works are compared, usually unfavorably, to the life and only surviving novel of her sister Emily. Mrs. Oliphant, in an 1877 jubilee-year article entitled "The Literature of the Last Fifty Years," rates Brontë as important but dated and marginalizes Charlotte's and Emily's works as relics of early Victorianism.[21] Oliphant's judgment ignores the novels' increasing sales and Thomas Wemyss Reid's then-recent 1877 biography of Charlotte and Emily. The decadent poet Algernon Swinburne, in response to denigrating remarks about Brontë in a review of Reid's biography, contributed the overheated tribute *A Note on Charlotte Brontë,* in which he declares Brontë the greatest of all women writers, even superior to George Eliot, and praises Brontë's "exceptional intellectual power."[22] The rationalist critic and biographer Leslie Stephen, retorting in turn to Swinburne, produced a cold appraisal faulting Brontë's ideological inconsistency in both questioning and affirming tradition. Because Brontë is emotionally but not intellectually compelling, Stephen argues, she cannot be described as a novelist "of the first rank."[23] The traditions of reading Brontë's works as autobiography and of judging her against Emily continued in Peter Bayne's 1881 essay "Two Great Englishwomen," which lauds all three sisters but places Emily above Charlotte in her quest for religious enlightenment.[24] The popular novelist Mary Augusta (Mrs. Humphrey) Ward, in her introductions to the seven-volume Haworth editions of the Brontës' works (published between 1899 and 1900), ended the century by investigating the sources of Brontë's works and the influence of her dual ancestral heritage—she was both an Irishwoman and a native of Yorkshire—on her writings. In spite of this major step forward in scholarship, however, Ward finds more to critique than to praise in Brontë's Celtic passion and promotes Emily at Charlotte's expense.[25]

By the 1880s, a full-blown Brontë cult had arisen, comparable in England only to the Browning Society. Haworth Parsonage, transformed into a museum and archive filled with manuscripts and memorabilia, became a pilgrimage site that drew visitors from all over the world. In 1883, the Brontë Society was formed to accommodate the public's desire to study and discuss the Brontës and their works. Since then, *Wuthering Heights* and *Jane Eyre* have remained continuously in print, and much of the time one or both have been included in the academic canon of great British literary works.

Late-nineteenth- and early-twentieth-century Brontë studies combined biography and criticism and continued to promote Emily's reputation at Charlotte's expense. "Until the mid-1950s," Miriam Allott notes, "critical studies of Charlotte are much fewer in number and generally less interesting, since, whatever her intensity of feeling, she has a less arrestingly original, and therefore less intellectually stimulating, quality of mind and vision."[26] The most notorious of these treatments is E. F. Benson's influential 1932 biography of Brontë. Benson, a distant relative of the Sidgwicks of Swarcliffe, a family for whom Brontë had worked as a governess, resented Gaskell's characterization of his family as exploitive and abusive.[27] Benson strived to write a corrective to Gaskell's laudatory 1857 *Life* and to expose Brontë as a "self-righteous, vengeful, and humorless, a hypocrite who could reject Branwell because of his infatuation for a married woman while undergoing herself a frustrated passion for a married man."[28] In a related biography, another Benson family member recalls that Brontë imposed hopelessly contradictory demands on the Sidgwicks, feeling persecuted if she were asked to attend church with the family and accusing them of ostracizing her if they neglected to invite her.[29] Yet the same biography acknowledges that one Sidgwick son, John, once threw a Bible at Miss Brontë, who at the time had been forbidden to complain about her treatment.[30]

Benson's hostile biography inaugurated a decline in Charlotte Brontë's literary reputation. Lord David Cecil's 1934 *Early Victorian Novelists: Essays in Revaluation* pronounces Emily superior to Charlotte, whose works he condemns as marred by structural weaknesses and melodramatic improbabilities and barely redeemed through verbal intensity. He calls Brontë "a very naïve writer" and alleges that "her faults have the naked crudeness of a child's faults," that "her imagination did not know the meaning of the word restraint." He continues: "Charlotte Brontë fails, and fails often, over the most important part of a novelist's work—over character." Cecil concludes that Brontë's works are "formless, improbable, humorless, exaggerated, uncertain in their handling of character" (p. 24).[31]

The Modern Biographies

The 1940s saw a nostalgic wartime resurgence in the Brontës and their work that was fueled initially by the film version of *Wuthering Heights* (1939), with Laurence Olivier and Merle Oberon, and then by the release of the successful and critically acclaimed film version of *Jane Eyre* (1944), with Orson Welles and Joan Fontaine. A long and inaccurate biographical film of the Brontës' lives—*Devotion*, starring Olivia de Haviland as Charlotte and Paul Henreid as an Arthur Bell Nicholls who spoke with a distinctly French accent—was also produced during the war. Clearly, an England in the grip of a life-and-death struggle for survival was willing to look back nostalgically on the rural and relatively simple world and problems that the Brontë myth embodied for the British psyche. At the same time, critical studies of the Brontës continued to appear; one, Phyllis Bentley's *Brontës* (1947), was a serious attempt to recuperate Charlotte's literary reputation in relation to that of each of her sisters.

In 1953, Margaret Lane, in *The Brontë Story: A Reconsideration of Mrs. Gaskell's Life of Charlotte Brontë,* made a somewhat amateur attempt to reconsider the new material that had come to light since Gaskell had published her biography. Lane alternates long passages from Gaskell's work and then attempts to explain where and how new material discovered since Gaskell has changed public perceptions of the major events in Brontë's life. Lane focuses largely on the Heger affair, offering a brief analysis of why Gaskell chose to suppress the letters she had been shown when visiting the Hegers in Brussels.

Modern scholarly biographies of Brontë, however, must be dated from the publication of Winifred Gérin's *Charlotte Brontë: The Evolution of Genius* (1967). Gérin, generally considered the major twentieth-century Brontë biographer, produced a work that is seemingly exhaustive, consisting of more than 600 pages of detailed Brontëana. Like earlier critics, however, Gérin does not distinguish clearly between Brontë's personal life and the lives of her heroines, although she was the first biographer to attempt to read the novelettes Brontë produced in her twenties as one of the major and overlooked keys to her life as a mature writer:

> The importance of Charlotte's childish writings as a key to her mature productions has long been realized; even more revealing, however, are the narratives of her early twenties, of which enough remain to indicate

the gradual mastery over self, over passion and temper that she achieved. The value of such tales as "Caroline Vernon," "Mina Laury," "Julia," "Henry Hastings" (left untitled by her) lies in the analyses of motive, of character, and in the precocious understanding of pieces to come. They also bear witness to their author's long struggle toward perfection; their heroines, unlike their later sisters in temptation, inevitably fall victim to their love for the all-pervading "Zamorna."[32]

Gérin's claim to authority as a biographer is based finally on her physical proximity to the locations where Brontë lived and worked. Having lived in Haworth and having covered the ground in Thornton, Cowan Bridge, Ireland, and Brussels, Gérin stresses her knowledge and feel for the physical realities of Brontë's life: "This familiarity with Charlotte Brontë's background, this wider study of unpublished works, has allowed, I hope, a closer, more continuous examination of her life than any since Mrs. Gaskell published the first biography."[33]

But Brontë is not a subject who has or, we suspect, ever will be definitively captured. She appeared different to the next generation of critics and biographers, who, viewing her from decidedly oblique angles, discovered a new, more feminist Brontë. In 1975, Margot Peters published *Unquiet Soul: A Biography of Charlotte Brontë,* a book we would now consider the first clearly new historicist and feminist view of Brontë. Peters's work, although firmly situated in the historical contexts of Victorian Britain, analyzes Brontë's life and works as separate entities. Peters's final judgments, however, reveal a certain condescension toward Brontë as evidenced in her conclusion that she was something of an artistic primitive:

> She is quite innocent of conventional manners so that her characters behave with refreshing originality. She did not know that a writer was supposed to sublimate and objectify his [*sic*] experience, so she filled her novels with the tensions of her own ambivalent desires. She was too naive to know when she was being "coarse" and as a result avoided both prudery and unreality. She did not know that a prose writer was supposed to stick to prose, so her fiction is colored by the language, rhythms, themes, and emotion of poetry.[34]

But to Peters, Brontë was the first female author to make her personal struggles as a woman the subject of her fiction:

> Her life was a frustrating yet productive struggle between living dutifully and yet, as a woman of genius, unconventionally. The tensions gen-

erated by this struggle electrify her fiction. They also give her novels
their realism, because for most intelligent and talented Victorian women
life could not be other than a battle between conformity and rebellion.
This is why Charlotte Brontë's novels still speak to us so persuasively of
what it was to suffer and triumph as a Victorian woman and—since the
issue of women's equality has still not been resolved—as a woman
today.[35]

Peters's work is generally credited with making possible the more
recent work of Tom Winnifrith, whose *The Brontës and Their Background*
(1978) focuses on the distinctions between Brontë biographies and
Brontë novels by examining the relationship between the novels and the
existing societal conditions in which they were produced. Winnifrith
concentrates on the role and importance of religion in the Brontës' lives
and works, claiming that

> Most writers have either given a false account of the Brontës' religion, by
> for example confusing a belief in eternal punishment with a belief in pre-
> destination, or have paid no attention to the religious element in the
> works of the Brontës. Yet not only did the Brontës have an obviously
> religious upbringing, but the country as a whole was vitally concerned
> with religion. Hell was an ever-present reality in Haworth. But the
> Brontës had the courage to break away from the almost universal belief
> that sinners merited eternal punishment.[36]

Winnifrith's book is also justly valued for presenting the first and
strongest condemnation of the "editorial" work of T. J. Wise:

> a detailed examination of some of the manuscript evidence shows Wise
> to have been both dishonest and inaccurate. Thus much of the biograph-
> ical evidence and juvenilia are unreliable sources for theories about the
> Brontës, but we need not, as some literary critics do, build theories on no
> evidence at all, as we can examine closely the text of the novels . . . and
> consider evidence on the background of the Brontës which has been
> insufficiently related to their writings.[37]

Winnifrith condemns the bulk of earlier Brontë biographers, calling
them "amateurs, making up in enthusiasm for what they lacked in scholarly training."[38] Rather, he advocates rigorous examination of texts that
have not been tampered with by the clumsy and greedy hands of Wise
and company, and he slightly disparages the growing trend to value the
juvenilia as a key to understanding the Brontës' mature writings:

The Brontës' juvenilia are larger in bulk than their adult writings, but this does not mean that we should devote more attention to the juvenilia than to the novels. Still less should we follow the example of Miss Fannie Ratchford who in between the writing of *The Brontës' Web of Childhood* and *Gondal's Queen* appears to pass from the view that Angria and Gondal are worth studying as means to an appreciation of the novels to the view that at any rate Gondal is worth studying as an end in itself.[39]

Whereas Winnifrith, writing in England during the 1970s, attempted to push Brontë studies away from the realm of speculation about the psychosexual dynamics of the sisters, other writers pursued different paths. Helene Moglen's *Charlotte Brontë: The Self Conceived* (1976), for example, is a fairly impressionistic work that explains the flowering of Brontë's adult work as the result of her condemnation of Branwell's conduct and her isolation from her father:

It is not inappropriate that this woman, whose masochistic dependence and passivity had evolved within the strictures of a patriarchal Victorian family, should find the sources of freedom in the moral and physical dis-integration of her brother and in the growing blindness of her father. Only thus could her ego survive at all. But freedom had also to be developed from within. A female child, a survivor, she had turned from the overwhelming terrors of reality to the imagined world of Angria. Rejecting those fantasies, she had reluctantly reached out to life. But the forces which shaped her fantasies made of her life a prison from which she could only escape—once partially freed—by returning again to art: an art which, as it became increasingly mature, became increasingly self-conscious and analytical. Here the haunting, regressive fantasies could be laid to rest.[40]

Moglen's psychoanalytical terminology suggests the impetus behind much of Brontë biography during the early feminist literary recuperation of Brontë's reputation. Much is made in the feminist criticism of Brontë's oppression as a dutiful daughter to an overbearing and absent father and a sister to a pampered and doomed brother.

Brontë's life was retold yet once more by Rebecca Fraser in *Charlotte Brontë* (1988), a work that justifies its publication by claiming that the discovery of new biographical material, such as the Seton-Gordon papers and Charlotte's marriage settlement, requires a new interpretation of Brontë's life. Fraser asserts that these newly discovered documents give us "a far fuller picture of the nature of Charlotte's husband, Mr. Nicholls, and their relationship; likewise that between Charlotte

and her publisher, George Smith."[41] Fraser's thesis, however, is that
Brontë was an iconoclast, a feminist rebel against the conventional standards of her day:

> Her assertive, passionate, realistic heroines were a threat to the concept
> of the "angel in the house," the unprecedented moral influence ascribed
> to women from around 1820 onwards. . . . Despite her lifelong battle
> with convention, she was enough a product of her society to be appalled
> by the reaction to her novels. Nevertheless, she continued defiantly to
> write as the spirit took her, calling boldly for sexlessness in authorship,
> regardless of what was considered proper or becoming for her gender,
> with a missionary commitment to the truth, unpalatable as it might be,
> that was the product of an upbringing by an Evangelical father.[42]

Fraser tries to place Brontë in her own milieus and considers the historical, social, political, and sexual pressures on her to conform: "At the
same time I wanted to show how the life of this complex, passionate
woman, so tragic in many ways, was also almost remarkable in its ordi-
nariness, its daily preoccupation with domestic duties, family and
friends."[43]

Charlotte's life forms one of the major focuses of the most recent and,
we might assume, the final statement on the family history: Juliet
Barker's *The Brontës* (1994). Written by the curator of the Brontë Parsonage Museum and close to 1,000 pages long, Barker's study includes
letters and documents never before published in an attempt to see anew
the complex relationship between personal and societal influences on
creativity and individual genius. Barker believes that Charlotte's life
cannot be written apart from the lives of her siblings and father, and
thus she produces a family biography that emphasizes the father as a
tireless campaigner for social reforms, a "man of liberal beliefs rather
than the rampant Tory he is so often labelled."[44] Barker states her intention in writing yet another biography:

> I sincerely hope that this biography will sweep away the many myths
> which have clung to the Brontës for so long. They are no longer necessary.
> Unlike their contemporaries, we can value their work without being out-
> raged or even surprised by the directness of the language and the brutality
> of the characters. It is surely time to take a fresh look at the Brontës' lives
> and recognize them for who and what they really were. When this is
> done, I believe, their achievements will shine brighter than ever before.
> For Patrick and Branwell, in particular, the time is long overdue.[45]

But who and what really were the Brontës? Surely trying to analyze the mystery and achievement of this family of creative artists brings up the entire issue of the human personality—the interlocking forces of nature and nurture—in its starkest terms. The riddle of how isolation, loss, and deprivation can lead to artistic production has intrigued biographers and literary critics for the past 150 years, and we suspect it will continue to compel future generations of biographers and critics.

It is certainly fair to claim that Charlotte Brontë has suffered more than any other literary artist from what Robert B. Martin has called "The Purple Heather School of Criticism and Biography." Further, Martin has complained about the Brontës that "their lives are so literally improbable as to tease one into considering the lives of the Brontës themselves as some wild metaphorical statement of the Romantic conception of the world."[46] But in the final analysis, perhaps all biography is a futile enterprise in its attempt to capture that ineffable combination of personality, temperament, experience, and actions that make up what we recognize as a human being. When Barker reminds us of Charlotte Brontë's words "This notice has been written, because I felt it a sacred duty to wipe the dust off their gravestones, and leave their dear names free from soil,"[47] we, like Barker, can think only with humility of Charlotte Brontë's struggle, her passion, her achievement against considerable odds. Like Brontë's many biographers, we find ourselves compelled to continue to brush her gravestone in respect.

Chapter Two
"The World Below": Charlotte Brontë's Juvenilia

It is a curious metaphysical fact that always in the evening when I am in the great dormitory alone, having no other company than a number of beds with white curtains, I always recur as fanatically as ever to the old ideas, the old faces, and the old scenes in the world below.[1]

Introduction

The works we call the juvenilia comprise Brontë's apprenticeship as writer between 1826 and 1839, from the age of about 10 to 23. Brontë's early writings, begun in collaboration with her three siblings, describe the byzantine political and social history of an imaginary West African empire called Angria and chart the fates of its dynastic rulers and the women they enslave emotionally. First the four children together, and later Branwell and Charlotte acting as partners, created an imaginary universe that absorbed and sustained their creative energies well into their twenties. These writings take the forms of miniature magazines, plays, short stories, fragments, diary entries, poems, and combinations of these genres. The saga reflects the influence of Byron and Scott, as well as the Brontë children's romantic conception of imperialism and war. The Brontë siblings found this imaginary world so absorbing that they created not only texts but their own system of "publication," maps, watercolors, and drawings, to describe Glass Town/ Angria and its protagonists. The tiny hand-bound volumes of minuscule print containing their first efforts were designed by the children at first to correspond in size to their wooden soldiers. Later, the small print helped them hide their works from the eyes of prying family members and gave the completed works the satisfying appearance of published manuscripts.

Throughout her childhood and young adulthood, Brontë wrote, revised, and expanded elements of the Angrian saga, steadily manipulating and developing a series of familiar characters and settings instead of moving on to new material. Despite the unifying force of common characters, however, it is misleading to impose a pattern of linear progress on the jumbled, recursive, and often achronologically composed juvenilia. Episodes are often elliptical, incomplete, or contradictory. The characters' multiple names make them hard to track: for example, Arthur Adrian Augustus Wellesley, Brontë's favorite male character, at various times also goes by the titles Marquis of Douro, Duke of Zamorna, and Adrian, King of Angria. Characters die and are resurrected at the will of their authors. They depart and return mysteriously from long periods of exile. They metamorphose dramatically to reflect their authors' changing needs and interests. In certain ways, the juvenilia anticipate Brontë's development into a mature artist, revealing the ways she works through and alters key themes and ideas. Yet the juvenilia's melodramatic, overblown nature contrasts markedly with the more restrained verisimilitude of Brontë's adult fictions. Many readers find the juvenilia melodramatic, derivative, and repetitive—adjectives not usually associated with Brontë's adult works.

Formal study of the juvenilia has been inhibited by the sheer volume of the manuscripts and by the unavailability until recently of reliable scholarly transcriptions and editions. The quantity alone of Brontë's complete juvenilia is intimidatingly large. Because she composed her juvenilia quickly and seldom edited, there are many volumes of prose and poetry as well as a host of fragments. Brontë's contemporary biographer, Elizabeth Gaskell, who was among the first outside readers to encounter the juvenilia in the form of "a curious packet confided to me," called it "an immense amount of manuscript in an inconceivably small space; tales, dramas, poems, romances, written principally by Charlotte, in a hand almost impossible to decipher without the aid of a magnifying glass."[2] Opposite this observation Gaskell reprints a facsimile of the first page of *The Secret* to give the reader a sense of its size. The "curious packet" nonetheless contained only a small portion of the juvenilia, for Gaskell elides discussion of the juvenile works written after 1833.

After Brontë's death, the juvenile manuscripts remained in the hands of her widower Arthur Bell Nicholls until 1894, when Clement Shorter, acting as an agent for T. J. Wise, purchased most of the extant juvenilia and letters from Nicholls. Shorter, however, was unimpressed by the contents of his purchase and, as is explained in the chapter in this work on Brontë's poetry, sold off the manuscripts he felt were least valuable. He also decided to omit the vast majority of the juvenilia from his early collections *Charlotte Brontë and Her Circle* and *The Brontës: Life and Letters*,

deriding the juvenilia as fatally flawed by Brontë's idolatrous "Wellington enthusiasm." Yet as an early scholar of the juvenilia points out,
Shorter probably failed to read the manuscripts thoroughly if at all and
consequently was seriously "mistaken in his judgment. . . . By Brontë's
fifteenth year the Duke of Wellington had given place to his elder son,
whom she fashioned as an unrestrained Byronic hero retaining few
Wellesley features. Mr. Shorter might with more accuracy have spoken
of Charlotte's Byron enthusiasm."[3] Within a few decades of Shorter's
dismissive gesture, in the 1930s, two volumes' worth of juvenilia were
transcribed and included in the *Miscellaneous Unpublished Writings* volumes of the *Shakespeare Head Brontë*. Fannie Ratchford, one of the first
scholars of the juvenilia, coedited some of the stories in *The Legends of
Angria* (1933) prior to her pioneering critical study *The Brontës' Web of
Childhood* (1941).

Not until the 1970s and the onset of the current renaissance in
Brontë studies did another major edition of the juvenilia appear, this
time a collection of five major stories edited and transcribed by Brontë's
biographer Winifred Gérin.[4] In the 1980s, Frances Beer's Penguin edition imposes a linear framework on the stories by selecting those that
focus on Angrian heroines and contrasting them with early stories by
Jane Austen.[5] As this book goes to press, Christine Alexander, author of
a comprehensive 1983 commentary on the juvenilia, is in the process of
transcribing a complete scholarly edition of Brontë's early manuscripts.
Alexander's enterprise has been complicated. The diminutive manuscripts must be transcribed from originals rather than from facsimiles
because the tiny print requires the use of magnifying glasses and occasionally even microscopes; every stray mark threatens to confuse the
transcriber. Brontë's frenzied composition style adds to the difficulty of
the transcriber's task. Gérin notes that "the impression made by any one
of these manuscripts is that it was written at a feverish speed which
nothing was allowed to impede, even to the detriment of sense. Para-
graphing is minimal, capitalisation is eccentric and haphazard (not even
new sentences necessarily call for the use of a capital), spelling aberra-
tions are frequent, the punctuation (where it exists) consists very largely
of dashes."[6] All of these conditions force transcribers to travel to examine the manuscripts, which are scattered throughout the world among
libraries, museums, and private collections. Moreover, since some of the
manuscripts have been lost or destroyed, a complete definitive edition of
the juvenilia will be difficult if not impossible to produce. To date, com-
paratively little critical work has been done on the juvenilia, partly

because critics have been restricted to a few editions of widely varying accuracy and quality.

At this point the reader might well ask, "Why go to the trouble of reading the juvenilia at all? What is distinctive about them?" This is a legitimate question; as Frances Beer notes, the juvenilia are plagued by many shortcomings, including "an absence of concern for such details as paragraphs and punctuation . . . [and] a baffling jumble of character and action—which make for what might tactfully be called uphill work on the part of the unsuspecting reader."[7] Yet the juvenilia offer us useful insights into the process of literary composition and into the intellectual and emotional development of a major artist.

The juvenilia began as a collaborative enterprise, the creation of a complete imaginary world created jointly by the four siblings. Significantly, the children began creating their imaginary worlds shortly after the deaths of their elder sisters Maria and Elizabeth, which resulted from the epidemic at Clergy Daughters School at Cowan Bridge. Collaboration provided each writer with an approving, supportive audience. The children guarded the juvenilia religiously from the eyes of friends and family, including their father. Collaboration also allowed the writers to develop on two levels: both independently, as they often deliberately defined themselves against one another, and as group of writers engaged in developing the same material. Branwell, for example, took on the parts of Napoleon and other French leaders in opposition to Charlotte's Duke of Wellington. Together they constructed a complete imaginary world, detailing its geography, climate, cities, characters, and situations, and responded to one another's ideas and innovations. Branwell and Charlotte's partnership also provided a stimulating source of intellectual and emotional conflict. Branwell took the early lead in initiating the saga, and his influence on Charlotte was strengthened in 1834 and 1835 by Emily and Anne's departure to found their own imaginary empire, Gondal. More often than not, however, Charlotte chafed against Branwell's obsession with violent battles and political machinations. Resentment led Charlotte to define her own interests more clearly, to experiment with new genres, and to refine her ability to write satirically in order to pillory her overbearing brother indirectly.

The juvenilia, including the letters and journal entries Brontë wrote during this period, also help us understand her unusual trancelike mode of composition. Her methodology "excluded all possibility of self-criticism and almost, one is tempted to think, suspended consciousness. She wrote with her eyes shut . . . the better to sharpen the inner vision and to shut out her bodily surroundings."[8] An aspiring visual artist, Brontë was extraordinarily capable of envisioning scenes as she wrote them. Her visualizing facility may also have developed in compensation for her nearsightedness. Christine Alexander notes that Brontë "had merely to shut her eyes to see those forms and features which . . . were so realistic that, like Pygmalion's statues, they appeared to have a life beyond that of their creator."[9] The chaotic organization and haphazard composition of the juvenilia resulted not from carelessness but as a consequence of the dreamlike state in which the fictions were composed. Gérin describes Brontë as functioning almost "like a medium through whom a spirit worked without control, and who could at the same time clearly register the sights and sounds, though not the significance, of what she saw."[10] Brontë's trance-writing intensified rather than abated as she grew older. Though she tried to shake off the impulse to retreat into "the old scenes in the world below," as late as 1843 she was recording the compulsion to use fiction writing to escape the humdrum routine of her work as governess and teacher.

Finally, the juvenilia reveal Brontë's early motives for writing. The earliest recorded fragment of her writing is a story written to amuse her youngest sister, Anne. Before reaching the age of 10, she was using her journal to discuss details of home life and to offer opinions about her readings in her father's library and political journals. The Brontë children's juvenilia cannot be dismissed as the product of eccentricity, loneliness, or emotional deprivation. Like most children, the Brontës found the stories an irresistible Aladdin's lamp that brightened their evenings and opened a new horizon to explore each day. The stories that began as an elaborate framework for play grew in scope and magnitude long after the wooden soldiers that inspired the story had been put aside. The children grew out of childhood and into sexual and emotional maturity in their imaginary worlds, transporting themselves into realms of experiences they would never enjoy as adults.

Sources of the Juvenilia

All four Brontë children were precocious, voracious readers, and everything they read, saw, and heard about was fodder for their burgeoning Angrian beast. By the age of seven, Charlotte was reading Milton and Bunyan and confidently declared the Bible "the best book in the world."[11] The children's father, whose approach to child rearing was unfairly maligned in Gaskell's biography of Charlotte Brontë, took a hands-on approach to his children's education, often making substantial financial sacrifices in order to obtain books or tuition for their schooling. In a typical gesture, he joined the Keighley Mechanics' Institute Library in 1825 to borrow books for the family, substantially increasing the reach of the children's reading. The Reverend Patrick Brontë also discussed contemporary political events with the children as though they were adults; these events turn up, slightly transfigured, throughout the juvenilia. Luddite industrial unrest in Yorkshire, for example, was transformed into a series of events known as "Rogue's rebellion" in the juvenilia. The children were also stimulated by visual art. The Angrian landscape is at least partly based on the engravings by John Martin that hung on the walls of the Brontë parsonage. The adolescent Brontë laboriously copied pictures and drew details of dress from popular fashion magazines in order to envision her heroines more completely.[12]

The children made creative use of nearly everything they read, and refused to honor distinctions between sacred and pagan, Eastern and Western, fictional and historical. Consequently, themes from the Bible, fairy tales told by the family servant Tabitha Aykroyd, *Arabian Nights,* Aesop's *Fables,* the apocryphal poetry of Ossian, the novels of Scott, and Byron's poetry are amalgamated willy-nilly in the juvenilia. The children identified simultaneously with the omnipotent geniuses, or genii, of *Arabian Nights* and with the vengeful Old Testament God who strikes down sinners with a single thunderbolt. In the early Angrian stories, the dynastic wanderings in exile of the chosen people of the Old Testament merge with the sadomasochistic, erotic structure of *Arabian Nights,* a series of tales framed by the threat of sexual violence. Glass Town is referred to as the Babylon of Africa; even the children's original explorers, the "Twelves," mirror the number and attributes of the apostles.[13] Yet Branwell's "pagan" classical studies, which included Virgil and Homer, also fed his obsession with military conquest, finances, the machinery of government, and the details of mercantile affairs, interests he developed in his sections of the Angrian saga between 1830 and 1837.

The children's favorite novels, poems, and religious and mythological texts merged easily with stories of imperialistic conquest they absorbed from contemporary nonfiction texts. *Blackwood's Edinburgh Magazine,* which was lent to the Brontës by the family doctor beginning in 1825, contained conservative political commentary and especially stories of imperialistic conquests of Africa. In addition to *Travels of Mungo Park,* which charted the contemporary exploration of the source of the Niger river and the conflict between British soldiers and the Ashanti tribe in West Africa, the children were galvanized by descriptions in *Blackwood's Edinburgh Magazine* of Major Denham's successive expeditions into northern and central Africa. The geography of the Glass Town Confederacy, the group of states comprised by Angria, was inspired by a map of the Gulf of Guinea published in *Blackwood's* in June 1826. Branwell promptly copied and relabeled the map with the names of the Glass Town Confederacy's four provinces.

The most important influences on the juvenilia, however, were the cultural heroes who embodied the imperialistic attitudes the children most admired. Branwell and Charlotte squared off against one another immediately by choosing the two great antagonists of the Peninsular Wars, Napoleon Bonaparte and the Duke of Wellington. Branwell's interest in Napoleon, who is called "Sneaky" in the tales, derived from his reading of Sir Walter Scott's sympathetic *Life of Napoleon* and was probably also fueled by Napoleon's death in 1827, just one year after the saga was begun. The Duke of Wellington, her Tory father's favorite, became Charlotte's cherished hero—the military genius whose successful campaign against Napoleon the children had followed in *Blackwood's* in the 1820s. As Fannie Ratchford has suggested, however, Brontë's interest in the dutiful, honorable Duke of Wellington gradually transmuted into a more Byronic heroic ideal. Brontë read most of Lord Byron's poetry in her early youth and followed it up with Thomas Moore's laudatory biography of Byron around 1830.[14] Consequently, Gérin asserts, "the impact of Byron's poetry was equal to that of the Napoleonic wars as a source of inspiration in developing the young Brontës' creative bent; Charlotte was acquainted with Byron's poetry by her tenth year and quoted from *Manfred* and *Cain* with glib familiarity in *The Islanders* (1829). In due course, it was inevitable that she would endow her hero with the demonic attributes proper to the Byronic male."[15] More than any single character, author, or work—and perhaps precisely because he represented a public persona, authorship, and a body of literary work—Byron became the chief influence on Brontë's early works.

Glass Town/Angria: An Overview

The Glass Town/Angria saga began in childhood play, as a series of games devised by the bright, isolated, imaginative Brontë children. As Charlotte records in her *History of the Year,* in June 1826 the children became fascinated with the wooden soldiers their father had given Branwell. Each selected a soldier and endowed him with the name, qualities, and glamour of a famous explorer or military hero. Anne chose Ross; Emily, Parry; Charlotte, Arthur Wellesley, the Duke of Wellington, and Branwell, Napoleon, or Sneaky. Though all four children presumably collaborated in inventing the early stories, Branwell's influence was dominant because he was both owner of the toy soldiers and the originator of the saga. Branwell and Charlotte struggled throughout their partnership for control of the narrative's focus, and the independent contributions of Emily and Anne are neither immediately discernible nor extant as discrete works.

In the works that follow, the children detail how 12 young adventurers, including the young Arthur Wellesley, later to the Duke of Wellington, make a difficult sea journey on the ship *Invincible* to the West Coast of Africa. (The West African locale was evidently suggested by an 1826 article in *Blackwood's* proposing this area as an ideal site for colonization.) During their journey and after their arrival, the explorers enjoy the magical assistance and protection of four "Chief Geniuses." These genii were the children themselves, who, like the God of the Old Testament, were able to strike down enemies and to bring dead heroes back to life when necessary. Once they arrive in West Africa, the explorers undertake to subdue the native inhabitants, the Ashantees, in a series of graphically violent battles. Victorious, they establish a new empire called the Glass Town Confederacy centered around the trading metropolis of Glass Town. The Glass Town Confederacy originally comprised four states named for the children's four favorite leaders: Parrysland, Rossesland, Sneakysland, and Wellingtonsland. With the assistance of the genii, the victorious Arthur Wellesley Sr. departs for England and returns 20 years later wealthy, famous, and bearing the title Duke of Wellington. He is then elected king of Glass Town.

As Branwell was developing this part of the saga, his three sisters, bored and frustrated by their brother's militaristic obsessions, generated their own collaborative fantasy narratives, which temporarily abandoned Glass Town and its heroes for new climes. *The Poetaster* is Charlotte's mocking, ironic send-up of her brother's literary aspirations. *The Islanders' Play* transplants the Glass Town heroes to an English island school. In this climate, the girls made liberal use of fairies and genii and focused their energies on fictionalizing such contemporary political events and issues as the Catholic question (the debate over whether Catholics and other dissenters should be allowed to vote and serve in the

House of Commons). From 1827 to 1828, Charlotte and Emily worked together on a series of secret, or "bed," plays, dramas presumably constructed in bed after lights out. Unfortunately these manuscripts have not survived. From 1827 to 1830, Charlotte also produced several fairy stories that allowed her to indulge her interest in the supernatural, an interest Branwell scorned.

By 1830, however, Brontë's narrative interest returned to the Glass Town series. Brontë's contributions to the saga continued to chronicle the exploits of the Duke of Wellington and his two sons, Charles Wellesley and Arthur Wellesley, Lord Douro. In *Albion and Marina,* her first love story, Brontë gives us the cynical narrator Charles Townshend, who recounts with ironic detachment the tender and tragic romantic relationship between Marina (whom she later transforms into Marian Hume) and Albion (whom she later transforms into Arthur, Marquis of Douro). Branwell meantime began developing Arthur's foil, Rogue, later Alexander Percy, a villain constantly in conflict with the conventionally virtuous Wellesley men.

From 1829 to 1831, Charlotte and Branwell worked so steadily together on the development of their saga that they sometimes signed their efforts "U.T." (us two) or "W.T." (we two). Their close partnership during this period was only partly inhibited by Charlotte's departure for Miss Wooler's School at Roe Head. There Charlotte relieved her homesickness by corresponding with Branwell as he established Glass Town's political structure and by returning to work on the saga when she returned from school at the holidays. The partnership between the two eldest siblings meanwhile chafed at their younger sisters, who sought a more realistic and local focus for their narratives. In December 1831, Emily and Anne announced their defection to write their own saga, Gondal, and Branwell and Charlotte were left to carry on the Glass Town stories alone.

After Brontë completed her education at Roe Head and returned to Haworth in 1832, her contributions to the saga shifted increasingly toward the duke's sons, Arthur and Charles Wellesley. As her focus on the two sons increased, her conception of the narratives became more Byronic than Wellingtonian. Arthur Adrian Augustus Wellesley, who received not only his father's first name but his father's title, Marquis of Douro, began life as a handsome, charming, gentle romantic figure, eager to please his father and others. Later, however, Brontë transmuted Douro into a figure of depravity and brutality as he gained political and social power and became first Duke of Zamorna and eventually King of

Angria. Throughout the juvenilia, Douro/Zamorna's most salient characteristic, besides his political ruthlessness, is his charismatic misogyny. Most of the stories focus on his succession of wives and mistresses, who masochistically submit themselves to his will, rendered powerless by his sexual magnetism. In contrast, Zamorna's brother—the more passive, introspective, and ironic Charles Townshend Wellesley—became Brontë's mouthpiece and her chief narrator. Brontë appeared to identify with Charles Townshend Wellesley to such an extent that she frequently used his name or initials as her pseudonym after 1830.

Brontë's story *The Bridal* revises the tale of *Marina and Albion* to describe the courtship and brief marriage of the Marquis of Douro to Marian Hume, a sweet, passive, ideally beautiful young woman who is possibly the prototype of Paulina Home de Bassompierre of *Villette*. Though the characters' courtship and early marriage are happy and though they eventually produce a son, their union cannot withstand Douro's infidelities with such women as the learned and beautiful Zenobia Ellrington. Douro's affair with Zenobia and her desperate attempts to bewitch him into abandoning his engagement to Marian had already been documented in *The Rivals*. But it is Douro's obsession with the daughter of his chief rival, Alexander Percy (formerly Branwell's character Rogue), that ultimately destroys his marriage and results in Marian's death from a broken heart.

Douro does not lose much time mourning Marian but promptly marries his latest love interest, Percy's daughter Mary. Before and during this second marriage, he continues to philander with many women, including his longtime mistress Mina Laury, who began her relationship with the Marquis at the tender age of 15. Nothing if not consistent, Douro abandons Mary after four years of marriage in order to express his rage at her father, Percy, over their political rivalries.

By 1833 Charlotte Brontë seemed to recognize the need for male foils for her antihero Douro. In *The Green Dwarf,* the valorous Ashantee tribesman Quashia Quamina, whom the Duke of Wellington raised as a foster son and foster brother to Charles and Arthur, leads a series of aboriginal insurrections against the Glass Town Confederacy. Though Quashia fails to overthrow Douro, he is persistent and his influence is difficult for Douro to eradicate.

During this period, Brontë also developed the character of Branwell's early cardboard villain Rogue into the more complex antihero Alexander Percy. Percy's vices—duplicity, atheism, amoral political expediency— mirror and complement Douro's chief vices of compulsive promiscuity and brutal treatment of women. As Brontë developed them, the two heroes grew more alike than different. Both were many times married, both had several mistresses, both lusted for political power and exerted control over Glass Town politics. Zamorna, once he becomes King of Angria, pairs his fortunes with Percy's by making Percy his prime minister. Percy, however, responds by inciting civil wars against his onetime ally. Throughout the Angria stories, Percy and Douro (or Zamorna, as he was later called) share a love-hate relationship that is constantly in flux. One way in which their relationship is articulated is through the appropriation of women: Douro/Zamorna marries Percy's daughter Mary, and Percy marries Douro's onetime mistress Zenobia.

Zamorna's longtime mistress Mina Laury is an orphan; like Jane Eyre and Lucy Snowe, her lack of parental protection enables her paradoxically to control her own destiny. Throughout the Angrian chronicles, Mina often displays verve, managerial skills, and physical courage. Yet she continues to view herself as "indisputably [Zamorna's] property as much as the Lodge of Rivaux or the stately woods of Hawkescliff."[16] Thus, in 1838's *Mina Laury,* when the aristocratic Lord Hartford proposes marriage to her, Mina's illicit connection to Zamorna leads her to refuse Hartford. Though the narrator describes Mina as "strong-minded beyond her sex—active, energetic & accomplished in all other points of view—here she was as weak as a child—she lost her identity—her very way of life was swallowed up in that of another."[17] Zamorna deliberately tortures Mina Laury by telling her that it was he who offered her to Hartford; only when she faints does he admit that he was simply testing her devotion and that he actually shot Hartford in a duel. Mina's fate, like Marian's and Mary Percy's, exemplifies the way the writer Brontë exploits and then abandons heroines just as Zamorna does, wringing them dry and then moving on to the next willing victim.

There is some progression in the emotional and psychological development of the heroines of the juvenilia. As Zamorna becomes increasingly sadistic and depraved, the heroines of the late juvenilia grow increasingly detached from his charms, though until Elizabeth Hastings none can be said to be immune to his charismatic pull. Elizabeth is the sister of the eponymous Henry Hastings (1839), and as Frances Beer notes, in her independence and self-discipline she anticipates both Jane Eyre and Lucy Snowe. Elizabeth deliberately repudiates her father over his ill treatment of her brother Henry; she resists seduction by the libertine Sir William Percy; and she demonstrates her devotion to the fugitive Henry by refusing to desert him and by facilitating his escape from authorities who are pursuing him. Though Elizabeth's life is thoroughly circumscribed by the wills and actions of patriarchs, her relative independence looks forward to the adult novels.

Though their plot lines (vastly oversimplified in the preceding paragraphs) are remarkably intricate and complex, the juvenilia are united by a few major themes and motifs. Foremost is the dominant metaphor of imperialistic conquest. The early opposition between Branwell's Napoleon/Sneaky and Charlotte's duke inaugurates a pattern that does not condemn imperialism itself but condemns imperialism perpetrated by one's enemies. Metaphors of empire and conquest govern all elements in the juvenilia: relationships between men and women, physical geography, monarchical rulers, political struggles in Glass Town/Angria. All human relationships are figured as political struggles for control of an inferior or weaker being or state. Individualism, no matter how crass or manipulative, always takes precedence over the welfare of a group. Heroes are entitled to use and are even admired for using (and using up) others, whom they view as instrumental rather than human.

There are obvious traces of these themes in the later novels. Yet their appearance in both *Jane Eyre* and *Villette,* in which the heroines travel to other locations to found modest "empires" of their own, reveal how the themes are transmuted. In the mature novels, it is often a female who makes an imperialistic conquest of new lands and men. Zamorna-like men (such as Rochester) who make imperialistic conquests (such as Bertha) are nearly destroyed by their amorality.

Like many works by children and young writers, the juvenilia are marked by an exaggerated late-romantic epistemological paradigm characterized by a rigid binary organization and by stable signifiers. Everything is organized according to extremes that always prove semiotically predictable. Inherited rank and physical beauty, for example, always signify greatness (for good or evil). Charles's description of Zenobia exemplifies this way of thinking: "What eyes! What raven hair! What an imposing contour of form and countenance! She is perfectly grand in her velvet robes, dark plume, and crownlike turban. The lady of Ellrington House, the wife of Northangerland, the prima donna of the Angrian Court, the most learned woman of her age, the modern Cleopatra, the Verdopolitan de Staël: in a word, Zenobia Percy!"[18] In the world of the juvenilia, a beautiful appearance reliably signifies a beautiful character; sensual reality obligingly reflects inner qualities and emotions. This pattern begins to blur only toward the end of the juve-

nilia, when the tales' narration becomes more ironic, reflecting Brontë's
increasing artistic maturity.

The juvenilia adopt a sadomasochistic erotic paradigm inspired by
Byronic romanticism—a paradigm that emphasizes the destructiveness
of overpowering emotions and casts love as a pleasant and inevitable
process of destruction. Male heterosexual desire within this paradigm is
characterized as serial and polygamous; homosocial bonds between men
are affirmed through exchanging women: Percy and Zamorna hand
Zenobia and Mary Percy back and forth between them. Women within
this paradigm are totally subjugated, as this excerpt from *Mina Laury*
suggests:

> Absorbed in this grateful task [of removing his helmet, Mina] hardly felt
> that his majesty's arm had encircled her waist; yet she did feel it, too, and
> would have thought herself presumptuous to shrink from his endear-
> ment. She took it as a slave ought to take the caress of a sultan, and
> obeying the gentle effort of his hand slowly sunk on to the sofa by her
> master's side.[19]

Heroines within this paradigm are characterized by their subjugation
to men. In Brontë's juvenilia, female power is limited to sexual power.
With the possible exception of Elizabeth Hastings, all heroines, whether
passive or assertive, are ultimately subdued by men (particularly
Zamorna), by their overpowering emotions, or by both. All enjoy being
subjugated. Some qualities of these subjugated heroines are carried over
into the adult works: Marian Hume has been posited as an early study
(based on traces in character and in name) for Paulina Home of *Villette*.
Flirts like Blanche Ingram, Ginevra Fanshawe, and others recall
Zamorna's various mistresses. These heroines, however, become transmuted in the adult works: instead of being presented as heroines, they
are represented as deeply flawed and are often rejected by Brontë's
heroes. Frances Beer argues that there is some evidence of an increasing
orientation toward independent women who reject the Byronic near the
end of Brontë's juvenilia, but she bases her case primarily on the character of Elizabeth Hastings, the single female character whom Beer is able
to characterize as "refreshingly immune to Arthur's quite jaded
charms."[20] Yet Elizabeth nonetheless devotes herself destructively to rescuing her dissolute brother Henry; her story is entirely taken up by her
unsatisfying relationships with men.

The "Farewell to Angria" and the Influence of the Juvenilia on Brontë's Later Works

In the late 1830s and early 1840s, Brontë, after maturing into an adult woman and in response to evaluations from respected writers that caused her to reevaluate her enterprise, very gradually began to move way from the fantasy world of the juvenilia and to shift her artistic focus toward the more reality-based world of her adult novels. This was an attenuated and difficult transition for Brontë, who continued to feel the pull of Angrian romance long after she had resolved to forswear its addictive charm. Though it occurred slowly, however, the shift between her early works and her adult fictions is striking. Brontë did more than simply abandon the world of Angria; she abandoned many of the key paradigms that governed it. These paradigms do not disappear completely from her adult writings, but they are considerably muted and complicated there.

The juvenilia are consumed by the magnetism of hypermasculine Byronic heroes characterized by overwhelming appetites for conquest, political power, and violence. Brontë's fascination with Byronic heroes persists into her adult works, though in a modified fashion. Of all of the heroes of the mature fiction, Edward Fairfax Rochester most closely resembles Zamorna: his numerous mistresses, the mad wife he has obtained through imperialistic conquest, his overpowering emotions, and his ruthless duplicity all mark him as an Angrian inheritor. As Brontë matures as a writer, the traces of Zamorna grow increasingly subtle and realistic; John Graham Bretton of *Villette*, for example, seems a watercolor version of the Rochester depicted in more vivid oils. St. John Rivers's physical beauty recalls Arthur's early character, and M. Paul Emanuel's irritability and overt misogyny recall Zamorna's degraded later days. The related themes of oedipal and internecine struggles between men—fathers fighting sons and brothers competing with brothers—also reemerges in the adult works in such competitive paradigms as the contest for Jane's heart between St. John Rivers and Rochester or the subtle but marked contrast of Lucy's two loves, M. Paul Emanuel and John Graham Bretton.

In the later works, the Byronic qualities of the Angrian heroes are unmistakably transfigured ideologically just as they are softened aesthetically. Instead of focusing on male subjectivity, Brontë's adult works explore the subjectivity of a female narrator or focalizer whose life is disrupted and perhaps even threatened by the Byronic male's importunings. The heroine, instead of enjoying victimization by these males, uses them to articulate her needs and desires through her relationships to twinned men who represent radically different life choices. She is fated not simply to suffer but to choose.

The process of separation began as early 1837, when Brontë asked Robert Southey, then poet laureate, to evaluate some of her work. He returned a famously discouraging and sexist response, admonishing her that "literature cannot be the business of a woman's life, and it ought not to be. The more she is engaged in her proper duties, the less leisure she will have for it, even as an accomplishment and a recreation." He concluded his letter by advising Brontë to "take care of over-excitement, and endeavour to keep a quiet mind." She responded by apparently agreeing to suppress her creative impulses:

> I carefully avoid any appearance of preoccupation and eccentricity which might lead those I live amongst to suspect the nature of my pursuits. Following my father's advice—who from my childhood has counselled me just in the wise and friendly tone of your letter—I have endeavoured not only attentively to fulfill, but to feel deeply interested in them. I don't always succeed, for sometimes when I'm teaching or sewing I would rather be reading or writing; but I try to deny myself, and my father's approbation amply rewards me for the privation.[21]

Though Brontë's later works reveal that she did not completely heed Southey's advice, her response suggests that his evaluation of her Angrian fictions had hit home. She did not resolve to stop writing fiction entirely but instead seems to have determined to write a different kind of fiction, one that more closely reflected the imperatives of her own life.

In 1840 Brontë again sought to have her work evaluated by a professional writer, the son of poet Samuel Taylor Coleridge. Brontë was emboldened to contact Hartley Coleridge because he had befriended Branwell while her brother was acting as tutor for a private family and had praised Branwell's translation of Horace's *Odes*. Brontë's letter to Coleridge is cautiously self-revealing, betraying her gender by pretending to disguise it, noting that the signature "C.T." might stand for "Charles Townshend or Charlotte Tompkins." Coleridge's response to Brontë has been lost, but from Brontë's reply Gérin guesses it was "cautious but kind" and probably helped mollify Southey's harsh rejection.[22] Nonetheless, around this time, in an undated document now known as the "Farewell to Angria," Brontë resolved to change her fictions: "I long to quit for awhile the burning clime where we have sojourned too long—its skies flame—the glow of sunset is always upon it—the mind would cease from excitement and turn now to a cooler region where the dawn breaks grey and sober, and the coming day for a time at least is subdued by clouds."[23]

Two years later, Brontë had an experience that further challenged her faith in the melodramatic, sadomasochistic paradigm of erotic love she had embraced in the juvenilia. From 1842 to 1844, Brontë lived in Brussels while first attending and then teaching English at the Pensionnat Heger, a girls' school owned and run by Madame and Monsieur Constantin Heger. The emotional, impressionable Charlotte fell in love with M. Heger, her intellectually rigorous teacher and a devoted family man who was in many ways the antithesis of the Byronic Zamorna. In transferring her affections, it is likely that Brontë began to embrace a new model of masculine attractiveness. Unfortunately, her love for M. Heger was unrequited and resulted in a humiliating dismissal from her teaching job. On her return to England she suffered a prolonged period of lovesick suffering during which she continued to send M. Heger impassioned letters and waited fruitlessly for a response from him. Yet in spite of this emotional disaster, Brontë responded less like her self-sacrificing Angrian heroines and more like the resourceful women she would later portray in *Jane Eyre, Shirley,* and *Villette:* she began to write a new kind of fiction, a story she had not yet told.

The transition was problematic and did not pay off immediately. Brontë's first full-length novel, *The Professor,* is widely regarded (as is the later novel *Villette*) as an attempt to work out her feelings about her experiences at the Pensionnat Heger. It was repeatedly rejected by publishers and printed only posthumously. Yet the novel, with its wooden, unconvincing male narrator William Crimsworth, reflects her aesthetic growing pains. Brontë's perseverance and growing confidence in her new style, however, were manifest in her completing *Jane Eyre* in spite of several publishers' discouraging rejections of *The Professor.* The preface to *The Professor* contains her new credo:

> I said to myself that my hero should work his way through life as I had seen real living men work theirs—that he should never get a shilling he had not earned—that no sudden turns of fortune should lift him in a moment to wealth and high station; that whatever small competency he might gain, should be won by the sweat of his brow; that, before he

could find so much as an arbour to sit down in, he should master at least half the ascent of the 'Hill of Difficulty,' that he should not even marry a beautiful girl or a lady of rank. As Adam's Son he should share Adam's doom, and drain throughout life a mixed and moderate cup of enjoyment.[24]

While working on *The Professor* in 1844 and 1845, Brontë struggled with the new demands of fictional verisimilitude. In the preface, Brontë reflects wryly, "A first attempt [*The Professor*] certainly was not, as the pen which wrote it had been previously worn a good deal in a practice of some years. I had not indeed published anything before I commenced *The Professor*, but in many a crude effort, destroyed almost as soon as composed, I had got over any such taste as I might once have had for ornamented and redundant composition, and come to prefer what was plain and homely."[25] Though Brontë overstated the case by claiming that she had completely "got over" her taste for "ornamented and redundant composition," her evaluation reveals her self-conscious effort to change her style. The influence of the juvenilia on the adult works is often very slight. One way to detect this slight influence is to compare early scenes with their later renditions. For example, in *Albion and Marina*, Albion sees an apparition of Marina on midsummer night that convinces him that Marina is his true love (Beer, *The Juvenilia*, 205). This scene is later recast in the proposal scene in *Jane Eyre*, when Rochester proposes marriage to Jane in the garden on midsummer eve. The first version of the scene is flattened by melodrama and supernatural interference; the later version makes full use of the subtle symbolism of the full-blown garden, Rochester's glowing cigar, and the sense of daylight at the meridian to suggest the zenith (and impending nadir) of Rochester and Jane's proposed union. The greater subtlety, the sensitivity to sensual detail and symbolism, and the verisimilitude of the later scenes mark how significantly Brontë's aesthetic sense and skill developed in less than a decade.

The emotional struggles Brontë underwent in the process of maturation forced her to abandon the romantic paradigms that had long sustained her. The difficulties of altering her aesthetic continued to be matched by unremitting emotional catastrophe. In 1848 and 1849, for example, she was unable to enjoy the success of *Jane Eyre*'s initially positive reception because of the deaths of her brother and sisters. Apparently, however, such tragic life experiences had a salutary effect on Brontë's fictions. The settings of her works changed utterly: instead of using the imaginary metropolises and "burning clime" of West Africa, the adult writer presents us with novels set in northern England or in Europe, landscapes she knew intimately. She abandoned her stories of monarchs and nobles in order to focus on characters whose class status mirrored her own: middle-class nonconformists struggling to adjust to a culture that would ostracize them. In Brontë's adult fictions, aristocrats are presented as weak and flawed. Even the teachers who people her adult fiction are figured unsentimentally: they are often bored, irritated, and burdened by a profession that is exploitive and often unrewarding.

Perhaps the most important change in Brontë's adult fiction was her decision to focus on female experience. And though she would continue to make and remake the same plots repeatedly—particularly that of the teacher searching for love and an appropriate vocation—her repetitions would gain the force of mythic reworkings. The adult novels reveal more than Brontë's unswerving acceptance of aesthetic challenges: they reveal her willingness to use fiction to work through a life that presented her with a relentless series of obstacles and disappointments.

Chapter Three

"Low at My Master's Knee I Bent": *The Professor*

After reading her posthumously published first novel, a contemporary critic was reminded of one of Johann Paul Friedrich Richter's favorite sayings: "God deals with poets as we do with nightingales, hanging a dark cloth round the cage until they sing the right tune" (Allott, *The Critical Heritage,* 345). Critics have consistently felt that Brontë's first novel, *The Professor,* was somehow just not quite in the right tune, although Brontë herself always defended the work, substantially revised it on at least three different occasions, and was never able to admit that she was not able to achieve the proper emotional distance from her subject matter to recast the material successfully. The first published reviews of *The Professor* appeared in conjunction with reviews of Gaskell's *Life of Charlotte Brontë*; one was an unsigned review in the *Athenaeum* (13 June 1857). This reviewer saw a number of positive similarities between *The Professor*'s prose style and that of the best in *Jane Eyre,* but went on to detect weaknesses not seen in the later works: "Unity and arrangement there is none. The sketches are carelessly left loose for the reader to connect or not, as he chooses. . . . The incidents of the story are few. . . . the quietness is unnatural, the level of fact too uniform, the restraint and the theory of life too plain" (p. 344).

In Mary Ward's introduction to the Haworth edition of *The Professor* (1899–1903), she praises the work's "pronounced manner," its "mature" composition, and its "power of analysis." She also admits, however, that it "lacks colour and movement," and that Crimsworth is not a particularly interesting hero: "His role is not particularly manly; and he does not appeal to our pity." Further, she says, there are "no vicissitudes in the plot," and the "reader's emotions are left unstirred." Ward recognizes that *The Professor* is "grey and featureless compared with any of Charlotte Brontë's other work," and she explains this inferiority by positing that Brontë was "working under restraint when writing it, and that her proper gifts were consciously denied full play."[1] In the 1940s, by contrast, Laura Hinkley claimed that in *The Professor*

Brontë "had begun to effect the union of realism and dream in the Eng-lish novel."[2] The transition between denigration and critical recupera-tion evidenced in these statements demonstrates in miniature *The Profes-sor*'s literary history.

The Professor and Brontë's Literary Career

In her Roe Head diary late in 1839, Brontë composed her well-known prose essay "A Farewell to Angria," a confessional leave-taking of the imaginary childhood landscape she had shared with her siblings since that fateful day in June 1826 when their father brought home the toy soldiers and unleashed four unrestrained imaginations. During the next six years she continued writing, skirting perilously close to immersion once again in the seductive landscape of Angria. But by June 1846 she had completed the manuscript of her first full-length adult novel, and her mature writing career began—ironically—with a book never pub-lished during her lifetime. *The Professor* did not appear until 1857, two full years after Brontë's death, yet as the first completed novel of her adult writing career, the work stands at the beginning of any attempt to assess the themes and patterns in those works that constitute her mature oeuvre. Brontë herself always believed in her first novel, although nine publishers rejected it in her lifetime, and she finally—regretfully—con-signed the manuscript to a bottom drawer in 1851 after writing a new preface for it.

In 1849, after the success of *Jane Eyre* and *Shirley,* Brontë was optimistic enough to think that her publishers would then be happy to publish *The Professor*. In the new preface she composed for her first work she confesses to her reader that the novel was written after many years of juvenile apprenticeship: "In many a crude effort destroyed almost as soon as com-posed, I had got over any such taste as I might once have had for orna-mented and redundant composition, and come to prefer what was plain and homely." *The Professor,* in other words, is the attempt by a romantic to be a realist; it fails largely because Brontë could not successfully bury her romantic tendencies, which emerge symbolically throughout the text—as in the scene at the end of the book in which Crimsworth shoots the dog Yorke. Brontë also staunchly defends the quality of her writing in this book, asserting that its middle and latter portions contained "more pith, more substance, more reality than much of *Jane Eyre*" (*SHB LFC* II: 161).

April 1846 is the earliest known date of any communication about this novel from Brontë to Messrs. Aylott and Jones, the same publishers who published the slim book of poems written in collaboration with her sisters. The novels written by Emily (*Wuthering Heights*) and Anne (*Agnes Grey*) were accepted, but Charlotte's *Professor* could find no taker. As Brontë would later recall about her rejections, "Currer Bell's book found acceptance nowhere, nor any acknowledgement of merit, so that something like the chill of despair began to invade his heart" (Gaskell, *The Life of Charlotte Brontë*, 305). Although she was 30 years old when she wrote *The Professor,* Brontë had not yet found her true subject matter or her own unique voice, and the work suffered as a result. Two famous stories about the novel's frustrated publication history bear repeating. The first reveals Brontë's naiveté, or perhaps her obstinacy. She told Gaskell that when the novel came back from one publisher rejected, she simply wrote the next publisher's name and address over the old mailing wrapper and sent it out again immediately. The second story concerns one of the novel's rejections, which occurred August 25, 1846, the very day that Brontë's father was to undergo an operation on his cataracts in Manchester. That night, in the small rented rooms she shared with Rev. Brontë as his nurse and ambivalently devoted daughter, she began the novel that would find a publisher quite quickly— *Jane Eyre.*

The publication of *Jane Eyre,* and later *Shirley,* made Brontë a luminary in Victorian literary circles, and she rightly felt that her publishers, Mr. Smith and Mr. Williams, should bring out her long-ignored first effort. They rather diplomatically persuaded her that the publication of *The Professor* would not further her reputation and suggested that she revise the material, particularly the Brussels setting in a girls' pensionnat, into a new work. From this suggestion Brontë crafted the infinitely superior book *Villette,* her final completed novel and generally considered her most mature and complex work. It is significant that Brontë began and ended her writing career meditating on her Brussels experience, clearly the most painful and imaginatively powerful experience of her life, and for that reason *The Professor* deserves more attention than it has generally received in critical studies of her career.

So how did *The Professor* finally see the light of day? Only after the publication of Elizabeth Gaskell's *Life* did the public interest stir enough to demand that anything written by Brontë become available. Gaskell herself had examined *The Professor* in manuscript as she was writing her biography and had pronounced the work "very interesting." After a fairly ruthless editing by Brontë's husband, who was still grieving and concerned that his wife's good name and reputation would be sullied by some of the language she used in the first version of the novel, it was prepared for publication and brought out in 1857.

Masculine Ventriloquism

In writing *The Professor* Brontë attempted to create a realistic bildungsroman from a male point of view. But shortly after the novel was published a strain of criticism emerged that did not simply attack the occasionally crude language or the lack of action in the novel but critiqued the characters themselves. Numerous reviewers specifically complained about the characters' gender ambivalence. For instance, an anonymous reviewer for the *North British Review* wrote,

> It is quite obvious to any reader who attends to the sketch of the character of the Professor, that the Professor is a woman in disguise, . . . for she is quite properly stripped of her male costume. . . . There is a shyness, a sulky tenderness, and a disposition to coquet manifest in the Professor's relations with his friend . . . which betrays to us at once that the picture is drawn from a lady's experience of her friendship with the other sex.[3]

This particular criticism—of Crimsworth's "womanishness"—has continued throughout the novel's history and has ironically led to the work's recent reappraisal and appreciation by contemporary feminist critics.

The portrait of a "feminine" Crimsworth emerges in the first six chapters of the novel, which are set in England and present the early life and education of William Crimsworth, the novel's hero, described retrospectively by the narrator in a letter sent to a school friend who never figures again in the novel. The novel's clumsy beginning was intended to align the work with the epistolary tradition of Samuel Richardson, who was a major literary influence on all the young Brontës. Brontë's unsuccessful attempt to use a letter, which she revised over and over again, suggests that she had not as yet found her own narrative voice and was trying instead to write in a safe style that would be recognizable to her reading audience.

Crimsworth, the young hero of her first novel, is, like most of Brontë's later heroines, an orphan. Born to a young woman who defied her aristocratic family to marry beneath her, William is seen by his older brother Edward as the cause of their mother's death in childbirth. Edward, 10 years old at the time of William's disastrous birth, is destined to become William's lifelong adversary and familial rival. It might be said that Edward is masculinity personified, or even caricatured—he is violent, hot tempered, and an abuser of his wife and employees. William, on the other hand, is a decidedly "feminine" man—he is sensitive, proud, and desperately needy for love and family. Unlike his brother, William is educated rather grudgingly by his maternal uncles, the Seacombes, upper-class snobs who agree to educate him if he will enter the church after his graduation. After leaving Eton, however, William defies them by opting instead to work as a low-level clerk and translator for his brother's manufacturing business at Bigben Close. Edward Crimsworth's dislike of his younger brother, whom he considers spoiled and pampered, intensifies. In the rivalry of the two male siblings and in their physical confrontation, which culminates in a fist-and-whip fight (chap. 5), we can see the residue of the feuds between the Percy brothers of Angria that rages so incessantly throughout Charlotte's adolescent literary efforts with Branwell.

The strange emotional and psychological relationship between the two Crimsworth brothers repeats a theme that occupies Brontë's early juvenilia and that surfaces throughout all of her mature fiction: the master/slave dichotomy. The need to find and then rebel against a stronger and tyrannous male figure is a strong element in Brontë's fiction and, indeed, in her life. Virtually all of Brontë's heroes and heroines exhibit a strong streak of persecutory fantasy that merges with the need to be abused, as well as a decided sadomasochistic tendency. William Crimsworth is no exception. He apprentices himself to his brother with the full knowledge of his brother's flaws. In comparing their physical features, William cannot fail to note his own inadequacies:

> In face I resembled him, though I was not so handsome—my features were less regular—I had a darker eye and a broader brow—in form I was greatly inferior—thinner, slighter, not so tall. As an animal, Edward excelled me far—should he prove as paramount in mind as in person I must be his slave—for I must expect from him no lion-like generosity to one weaker than himself; his cold, avaricious eye, his stern, forbidding manner told me he would not spare. Had I then force of mind to cope with him? I did not know—I had never been tried.[4]

The struggle here—one person's Nietzschean will to power over another —is repeated in all of William's relationships, and the effort obviously began in the struggle to form a family unit with his overbearingly masculine and jealous brother.

Whereas a typical Angrian saga like *The Spell: An Extravaganza in Eight Chapters* (21 June–21 July 1834) concerns the feud between the brothers Edward and William Percy exclusively, *The Professor* drops the active and intensely masculine Edward after only six chapters. *The Professor* focuses completely on the growth and maturation of the more feminine William, clearly the more passive and contemplative of the two brothers, and on some level focuses on an autobiographical portrait of the female author herself. William Crimsworth, that is, does not present a convincingly masculine character but instead, as many critics have noted, Brontë's self-portrait in masculine ventriloquism.

If Crimsworth is unconvincing as a male character, Yorke Hunsden is even more eccentric as a realistically drawn male character. Chapters 7 through 13 depict Crimsworth escaping his brother's tyranny, largely through the intercession of their meddlesome neighbor Hunsden, who suggests that Crimsworth relocate to Brussels as an English teacher (chap. 6, p. 47). One finds it hard to imagine a man like Hunsden, who makes it his business to consistently meddle in all of Crimsworth's personal and professional affairs. At a birthday party for his brother, William compares himself to an androgynous wallflower that "look[s] weary, solitary, kept-down—like some desolate tutor or governess" (chap. 3, p. 19). In this state of depression, William does not know whether he should think of himself as a paid male or a paid female servant. Hunsden then appears and proceeds to read William's destiny in his face and bearing, pronouncing, " 'It is you, William, who are the aristocrat of your family and you are not as fine a fellow as your plebeian brother by a long chalk' " (chap. 3, p. 22). Note that it is Hunsden who shores up William's sagging ego by seeing virtues and superiority that William cannot see in himself. This sort of character—a projection, or a living wish fulfillment, of the protagonist—functions throughout Brontë's later novels, most notably as Miss Temple (*Jane Eyre*) and as M. Paul Emanuel (*Villette*).

Charles Burkhart has noted that the only way to understand why Brontë created both Crimsworth and Hunsden is to probe beneath the surface of the text to uncover her unconscious motivations. Burkhart claims that "Charlotte had strong masculine components in her personality" that would have explained why she could project her experiences onto a man. Burkhart, however, like many earlier critics, points out Crimsworth's inadequacies as a convincing man: "It takes an odd man, too, to know quite as much about bonnet trimmings and fancy needlework as William does."[5] Burkhart also believes that the profanity in which Crimsworth indulges in the earliest versions of the text, later censored by the Reverend Arthur Nicholls, is probably drawn from Brontë's memories of listening to Branwell curse the world, and that her attempts at "male humour are usually clumsy and sound like dated schoolboy slang." Like many other critics, Burkhart finds Hunsden "the most interesting character in the book and the most unsuccessful." Frequently seen as an avatar of the Byronic hero or as a precursor to Rochester, Hunsden is criticized by Burkhart for having "no function" in the novel. Such a charge is unfair, however, because it is Hunsden who addresses Crimsworth as "Wilhelmina Crimsworth" and who generally functions throughout the novel as Crimsworth's alter ego, acting rebelliously where Crimsworth will not allow himself to.[6]

Burkhart considers the curious wrestling match that Hunsden and Crimsworth have on a Brussels street to be "the strangest moment" in the novel,[7] a sentiment that a number of recent critics of the novel share. This odd scene can now be read as a homosocial interlude (chap. 24, p. 224). After meeting and being favorably impressed by Frances, Hunsden accosts Crimsworth about the folly of marrying beneath his status, jealous that he has nonetheless managed to find an intelligent and attractive woman:

he swayed me to and fro; so I grappled him round the waist; it was dark; the street lonely and lampless; we had then a tug for it, and after we had both rolled on the pavement and with difficulty picked ourselves up, we agreed to walk on more soberly. (chap. 24, p. 224)

This strange scene in the dark streets of Brussels reads like the dead end of masculine ventriloquism in this narrative. Unable to continue to present these two male characters realistically in opposition, Brontë simply has them resort to physical violence to resolve their differences about Frances Henri, the ostensible object of both their affections. But as Eve Sedgwick has noted, the body of the woman is always a screen or a blank space on which men write out their repressed desires for each other. Sedgwick's theories enable us to claim that on some level Brontë is exploring her society's basic homosocial arrangement, whereby women function either as exchange commodities or fetishized objects of sexuality and femininity, or are used as transfer points between men engaged in conscious or unconscious scenarios of homoerotic desire.

The Professor as Autobiography

Crimsworth's life experience begins with a journey to Brussels to work as an English teacher at a boys' school. The similarities to Brontë's own life are clear, and in creating Crimsworth's adventures she relives her own trip and two-year stay in Brussels as both pupil and employee of M. and Mme. Heger. Shortly after his arrival in Brussels and with Hunsden's letter of support, Crimsworth finds himself teaching at a boys' school presided over by the sexually sophisticated M. Pelet (chap. 7, p. 58). This rather amoral Frenchman, a thinly veiled portrait of M. Heger, Brontë's love interest while she lived and taught in Brussels, arranges for Crimsworth to augment his earnings by also offering English lessons at the neighboring girls' school run by Mlle. Zoraide Reuter, another thinly disguised portrait, this time of Mme. Heger, M. Heger's scheming wife and Brontë's rival and nemesis. In these early chapters Crimsworth drifts in a European culture that he finds both alien and inexplicable, just as Brontë herself did. Crimsworth is so sexually insecure, for instance, that he imagines M. Pelet's mother is trying to seduce him when she invites him for a visit (chap. 8, p. 64). He can respond only with contempt and the usual Brontëan streak of anti-Catholicism to his young female students (chap. 10, p. 76). Rather suddenly, however, he forms an intense infatuation for Mlle. Reuter, whom he describes in blatantly maternal terms and whose cheek is as lovely as a "bloom on a good apple" (chap. 12, p. 96; chap. 9, p. 71). Reuter is for Crimsworth's sexually repressed imagination the apple of temptation in the garden of femininity she has constructed in her school.

The central crisis of the text occurs when Crimsworth comes face-to-face with the oedipal and hopeless nature of his attraction to both M. Pelet and Reuter, his substitute parent figures. Although chapters 14 through 20 ostensibly center on the relationship and eventual marriage of Crimsworth and Frances Evans Henri, the real action in these chapters is Crimsworth's fall from his naive life in a self-deluded Eden presided over by his idealized parent figures, M. Pelet and Reuter, to a more experienced reality of nonoedipal passion.

This disillusionment and fall into sexual awareness occurs one evening when Crimsworth spies his two employers walking together in the enclosed garden that lies between the two schools. Crimsworth has acted as voyeur on this very garden on a number of occasions, even though he has been warned by M. Pelet not to peek through the opening in the window of his apartment down onto *l'allée défendue,* the gardenlike domain of the girls' school. This evening Crimsworth is confronted with a painful secret and an even more painful fall into sexual knowledge. He not only sees but hears M. Pelet and Reuter declare their matrimonial intentions and laugh at his folly and infatuation for Reuter (chap. 12, p. 101). Crimsworth's wound is intense, suggesting that this scene comes close to replaying Brontë's own disillusionment with both the Hegers, whom she perhaps felt had betrayed her love, devotion, and trust on some level.

Shortly after his awakening and disillusionment, Crimsworth meets—again, like a wish fulfillment—the love of his life, Frances Henri, a Protestant and half-Swiss, half-English teacher of lace mending at the girls' school (chap. 14, pp. 111–12). The class and religious implications of Frances's precarious position are significant, as is her orphaned and socially vulnerable status. Frances and Zoraide are contrasted as types of women in a style that Brontë would develop over and over again in her novels (chap. 15, p. 117). The passive and demure Frances reminds the reader of Jane Eyre, whereas the more experienced and duplicitous Zoraide recalls both Bertha and Blanche Ingram. This polarization of women is mirrored in the polarization of the male characters, suggesting that Brontë was compelled to repeat in her mature works the narrative styles and techniques she first developed in the radically dichotomous universe of Angria.

Crimsworth begins his academically inspired courtship of Frances as her English master, a plot device that recalls Brontë's own tutoring in rhetoric by M. Heger and her attempt to teach him English. This theme of courtship in Brontë's novels is developed much more fully in the bookish courtship of *Villette*'s M. Paul Emanuel and Lucy Snowe. Frances reveals her idealistic, Protestant, and nationalistic character when she composes her devoir on the nature of British monarchy and the character of the king (chap. 16, pp. 122–25). The attempt to read the personality through one's writings, art works, and written compositions is a standard device in all of Brontë's works. As one means of deciphering the mystery of personality, the attempt to read one's creations was surpassed as an analytical tool only by her belief in the accuracy of phrenology, the reading of the bumps on the head, the shape of the forehead, and the cut and color of the eyes. All of Brontë's novels are concerned with this issue, the challenge and dangers inherent in one human being trying to read another the way one reads a text. One senses in this scene, as well as in so many later ones, the frustration of an extremely bookish imagination steeped in the knowledge gained through reading but stymied when it came to reading real human beings of flesh and blood.

As quickly as Zoraide realizes Crimsworth's interest in Frances, Frances disappears from the school, seemingly with no trace (chap. 18, p. 139). Crimsworth tries to locate her, with no success and with no cooperation from Zoraide, who jealously wants to keep Crimsworth's attentions to herself. Finally, after weeks of frustration, Crimsworth almost literally stumbles upon Frances in the Protestant cemetery (chap. 19, p.155), where she has gone to keep watch at the grave of her last relative, an aunt who has recently died.

Reuniting in a cemetery is a particularly potent, erotic image in Brontë's novel and reminds the reader of the significance of Helen Burns's tombstone, erected by the adult Jane Eyre. Surviving trauma and living to tell the tale are repeated images in Brontë's novels, as we will witness again in the tales of survival told throughout *Villette*. Chapters 21 through the conclusion of the novel, chapter 25, recount the marriage and idyllic life of Crimsworth and Frances, who return to England and conclude their days in a country estate that adjoins their old friend Hunsden's property. The reunion of the two Protestants allows Crimsworth to break completely and decisively with the corrupt and exploitative Pelets and begin his search for a new position that will remove him from the scene of Zoraide and M. Pelet's recent marriage (chap. 20, p. 174). A melodramatic touch, the rescue from drowning of a young pupil, provides Crimsworth with the credentials he needs to secure a new teaching position, and almost simultaneously Hunsden arrives in Brussels with the portrait of Crimsworth's mother that he purchased from Edward, now financially ruined and destitute (chap. 22, p. 192), a fitting punishment for his fraternal abuse of the deserving and righteous Crimsworth.

The traces of the master/slave dichotomy, so central to the issues of both masculinity and autobiography in this novel, resurface again in the next chapter, which presents the curious poem "Jane," an incipient trace of Brontë's next novel, *Jane Eyre* (chap. 23, pp. 202–5). The many references to Crimsworth as Frances's "master" also are reminiscent of the streak of female passivity and masochism that emerge in all of the relationships throughout Brontë's canon. Before Crimsworth and Frances can marry, however, there are a series of quasiconfrontations with Hunsden, who initially thinks Frances inferior to Crimsworth and not suitable as his spouse (chap. 24, p. 215). Frances proves her worth to Hunsden in a series of fireside chats, which are reminiscent of the verbal sparring

and dueling in which Jane Eyre and Rochester engage. One recalls the
stories of the tongue-tied Brontë trying unsuccessfully to make small
talk with Victorian literary luminaries, including her erstwhile mentor
Thackeray. The heroine who can triumph in quick verbal sparring is
clearly not a realistic portrait in Brontë's autobiography but yet another
of the pathologically shy author's wish fulfillments.

In Brontë's depiction of her hero and heroine running their own
school so successfully that they threaten the prominence of Pelet-
Reuter's establishment, we can detect yet another clear strain of
Brontë's wish fulfillment. Her sense of powerlessness and frustration at
the hands of the Hegers, her need to try to compete with them as an
instructress and mistress of a successful school, must have been intense.
Chapter 25, the final long chapter, concludes the novel by spanning the
following 10 years. The chapter begins with the simple wedding of
Crimsworth and Frances, followed by their success as schoolteachers and
masters running their own very popular school in Brussels.

After 10 years of immense success in Brussels, the Crimsworths are
financially able to retire to England to a country estate named Daisy
Lane, a bucolic fantasy, where they spend the rest of their days in idle
rambles with their son Victor and with Hunsden, their constant companion and Crimsworth's alter ego. The novel ends with the curious
shooting of Victor's rabid dog, Yorke, given to him as a present by
Hunsden. This melodramatic scene, symbolically incongruous in a novel
that has claimed to be "realistic," suggests that Brontë was beginning to
explore and acknowledge the themes of passion and romanticism that
she had tried so unsuccessfully to bury in this text.

The Psychology of William Crimsworth

Brontë's preface to *The Professor*—written sometime between late 1849
and early 1850—is the earliest critical assessment we have of the novel;
the next is the supportive opinion of her sympathetic biographer Elizabeth Gaskell a few years later. Brontë's preface is interesting for its tone
of apologia and its attempt to lay out the novel's claims to the tenets of
realism. Brontë claims that her early writing was "ornamented and
redundant," and as such she had come to reject it in favor of "what was
plain and homely." Her first attempt to develop this new style can be
found in her choices of hero and heroine: "I said to myself that my hero
should work his way through life as I had seen real living men work
theirs—that he should never get a shilling he had not earned. . . . As

Adam's Son he should share Adam's doom—Labour throughout life and a mixed and moderate cup of enjoyment."[8]

But for all of Brontë's noble intentions, Crimsworth is lavished with gifts, most notably his mother's valuable portrait, and he is rewarded with a teaching position for saving the life of a wealthy student, another melodramatic and unrealistic touch in a novel that purportedly eschews both modes. Finally, Crimsworth does not earn only a "moderate cup of enjoyment." He ends his days in a bucolic retreat, blissfully surrounded by an adoring family and friends. The only blight on his days would appear to be that strange dog, hardly an adequate symbol of Adam's cursed fall. Brontë goes on optimistically in her preface, sharing with her readers her struggle to revise the text to meet her publishers' demands for "the wild wonderful and thrilling—the strange, startling and harrowing" and presenting the text as something so small and innocuous that it will not offend anyone: "He that is low need fear no fall."[9]

As we have noted, despite Brontë's hopes that her publishers would bring out *The Professor* after the immense success of *Jane Eyre* and the more subdued appreciation of *Shirley,* the book did not appear until two years after her death, largely because Elizabeth Gaskell championed its "genius," "felicity of expression," and "deep insight."

In a series of letters to George Smith and to Emily Shaen, Gaskell outlined her reactions to the novel.[10] She was initially most concerned that the novel would irritate the Hegers, who had agreed not to publish Brontë's letters to M. Heger but might be persuaded to change their minds if they thought another novelistic attack was directed their way. Gaskell was particularly charmed by the portrait of Frances Henri ("the most charming *woman* she ever drew, and a glimpse of that woman as a mother—very lovely") and by the scenes of idyllic married life that conclude the novel. She was alarmed by what she considered to be the occasional "coarseness,—& profanity" in the male characters, and she decided after examining the text to add a defense of Brontë's essential purity of thought and mind to her biography, then in process (Allott, *The Critical Heritage,* 319).

Gaskell set the stage, however, for the critical attitude toward *The Professor* that would continue: that it was an important novel. For Gaskell, the novel was "a very curious link in her literary history, as showing the *promise* of much that was afterwards realized." Although Gaskell wished that Nicholls had "altered more!," she still praised the novel as yet another example of Brontë's uniqueness and literary originality:

I suppose biographers always grow to fancy everything about their subject of importance, but I *really* think that such is the case about her; that
leaving all authorship on one side, her character as a woman was unusual
to the point of being unique. I never heard or read of anyone who was for
an instant, or in any respect, to be compared to her. And everything she
did, and every word she said & wrote bore the impress of this remarkable
character. I as my own reader should not be satisfied after reading the
Memoir . . . if I did not read her first work, looking upon it as a phsy-
cholgical [*sic*] curiosity. (Allott, *The Critical Heritage,* 320)

The "psychologically curious" aspects of *The Professor* have only recently
been plumbed, but Gaskell pinpointed the early direction of at least
some of the attempts to understand this work in an addendum to the
biography.

As their titles suggest, the early critical works about the novel con-
sisted of attempts to analyze some limited imagery pattern or the
vagaries of the revision process and the corruption of the manuscript at
the hands of Brontë's husband.[11] *The Professor* also received lukewarm
analyses in most of the early full-length studies of Brontë's career: those,
for instance, written by Charles Burkhart, Margaret Blom, and W. A.
Craik. In a critical discussion typical of the 1960s, Craik praises the
novel's "originality" but faults its slightness and Brontë's often uneven
attempts to capture masculine psychology.[12]

For all of the novel's weaknesses, Blom asserts that its strengths lie in
its "ability to use plot, setting and metaphor to plumb the depths of the
psyche. . . . Charlotte's ability to depict emotions with great power
enabled her to infuse a complex truth into her story of a fallen soul who
is filled with pride and who struggles to avoid the temptations of the
flesh and to achieve a love which combines passion with charity."[13] Typical of the early psychological readings of the novel, Blom sees this novel,
as well as Brontë's others, as a sort of psychomachia:

William, Jane Eyre, and Lucy Snowe closely resemble one another: each
has a sense of being at once superior and inferior to others; an awareness
of being a predestined victim; a willingness to escape from torment by
tormenting others; a thorny coldness, priggishness, and pride which
increase alienation; and a capacity for passion which wars with the dic-
tates of conscience.[14]

In a similar vein, Burkhart explains the weaknesses in all the major
characters in the novel as originating in the fact that "these characters

are all based on Charlotte herself"; "They are all Charlotte, though incomplete, unrealised, and also they are all one another."[15]

Other early critical studies of Brontë's work do not treat the text sympathetically. Typical of the prefeminist attacks on the novel are those by Earl Knies, Robert Bernard Martin, and Fannie Ratchford. Knies sees the novel as a "transitional piece" and a component of Brontë's literary apprenticeship. He goes on to state that Brontë lacked both the imagination and the experience to "create a male exclusively through his own words." Furthermore, Crimsworth reveals "the constant discrepancy between real masculinity and Charlotte's interpretation of it." For Knies, "Crimsworth's character does not achieve the same intensity as that of the heroines because as a man he has more mobility in nineteenth-century society; his fate, we feel, is more his to do with as he will than is Jane's or Lucy's."[16] Martin asserts that the novel illustrates "the doctrine of self-reliance, but he goes on to argue, "*The Professor* is, in part, a repudiation of its preface, for Miss Brontë was unable to avoid showing the necessity of the emotions." Another early assessment, by Fannie Ratchford, examines the Angrian roots of the feud between the Crimsworth brothers and Yorke Hunsden.[17]

From its early days, *The Professor* has suffered a variety of rejections. However, Annette Tromley believes that the main problem critics have with the novel is that they have seen it as characterized by both artistic immaturity, which marks it as a beginner's work, and an incomplete detachment of the author from the book and its characters. Both narrative weaknesses conspire to reveal rather too baldly Brontë's personal opinions.[18] Another area of criticism has focused on the character of Frances Henri, who has traditionally been seen as an idealized self-portrait of Brontë herself.

Although the novel begins awkwardly with the letter to Charles, this device makes clear that the dominating narrative voice heard throughout the novel is Crimsworth's. According to Tromley, his presence as narrator is constantly reiterated by the way he reacts to events. He has a tendency to overreact to the insignificant and to underplay the important. This manipulation of the truth functions as a warning to the reader to be wary of his claims because they are based on a self-serving attitude that overevaluates their significance. Further, images of enclosure characterize Crimsworth as defensively self-protective. For example, when he feels uncomfortable, as in his dealings with his brother and his students, he retreats to enclosed places to maintain a tenuous psychological balance. This need to self-enclose forces Crimsworth to perceive the world as a hall of mirrors composed of distorted pictures. Thus he misrepresents their subject matter and often focuses on physical characteristics to the detriment of the inner person, a problem exemplified in his reduction of his female students to works of art. Even Crimsworth's past is enclosed as framed works of art; for instance, the portrait of his dead mother is valued as a distancing mechanism, an attempt to establish a distance from the pain of his past losses. Through these pictures, Crimsworth tries to make sense of a life in which he lives in self-imposed innocence or as a martyr who is trying to avoid pure self-analysis.

Crimsworth presents others, such as Frances, Hunsden, and Reuter, through this distorted vision, but he fails to obliterate completely their true selves. For example, as Tromley points out, Hunsden illuminates Crimsworth as someone with the same background and characteristics but not the same emotional deficiencies. Hunsden functions as something of a savior and a foe, and the savior part is unsavory to Crimsworth, who appears, at least unconsciously, to realize that Hunsden represents what he could be. Frances and Reuter also represent female opposites to Crimsworth, and the novel itself illustrates their similarities as school directresses. In fact, neither woman is what he thinks she is, especially Frances, who wishes to continue teaching and accepts his marriage proposal in part as an avenue by which to keep her career.

Crimsworth's apparently displaced attack of hypochondria serves to qualify his creation of himself as a hero. His admission of sensuality contradicts his earlier self-perception, and his marriage to Frances further alters his mistaken sense of himself as being somehow above sexual desires. The meeting with Hunsden suggests a Frances different from the one Crimsworth sees, just as scenes with Victor imply that she feels different about the child as well. Crimsworth is unaware of the complexities associated with Hunsden, as his complacent observation of the relationships between Frances and Hunsden and between Victor and Hunsden reveals.

In the conclusion to the novel, Crimsworth paints his own self-serving picture of his life in a type of Eden. He possesses a nice home and family that largely function as embellishments to his starved ego. By placing Frances in this Eden, Crimsworth not only rescues her from a lonely, poverty-stricken life but also puts her in an enclosure. For Crimsworth, the imposition of physical enclosure only serves to emphasize his mental enclosure or insensitivity, and he thus deludes himself into believing he has achieved worldly success. Crimsworth finds art more real than life, which is nothing more than another self-delusion created by his self-imposed mental enclosures.[19]

Analyzing the curious psychology of William Crimsworth—and its relation to the psychology of the author herself—has been the major focus of a number of studies of the novel. One particular style of depth psychology—Jungian in nature—is practiced by Bettina Knapp in her study of the Brontës' novels (1991). Her reading of *The Professor* is predicated on Jungian models; for instance, she sees "brother hatred" as representative of the "Operative Shadow," and the dual women as the two faces of the anima. Knapp interprets William Crimsworth as "oblivious to the fact that the 'evils' he condemns in his brother are the very ones he detests and seeks to annihilate in himself." She goes further to suggest that "both Edward and William are split-offs of *one* person—the shadow side of each juxtaposed to the positive aspects of the other. Since Edward is the more emotional of the two, and affects usually emerge when adaptation is weakest, his uncontrollable behavioral patterns disclose an inability to cope with his sense of inferiority." After William's departure for Brussels, brought about by the intercessions of the "fire principle," Hunsden, William succumbs first to the "illusion-creating anima figure," Mlle. Zoraide Reuter, a "negative feminine principle" who can deliver only danger and suffering to the gullible William. Zoraide is supplanted in William's soul, however, by Frances Evans Henri, the half-Swiss, half-British lace mender teaching in Zoraide's pensionnat. It is Frances who will "play the role of beloved" as well as a "nourishing and kindly mother figure." Knapp's Jungian reading concludes that the novel succeeds "in cutting open the bruised soul of her protagonist—a manifestation of her own—but she did not know how to express the workings of the masculine psyche." All of which brings us back to one of the very earliest critical responses to the novel: blame the masculine ventriloquism.[20]

In another psychological reading of the novel, Helene Moglen (1976) suggests that William Crimsworth is a "transitional hero" who bridges Brontë's "identification with a male persona" and her "commitment to a female voice" in her later works. His weakness as a character is caused by Brontë's reexamination of "her deepest assumptions" about literature and by her recognition of the need for a new kind of literary heroine. Claiming that Brontë never "encountered a 'heroine' in her personal, cultural, or political experience or, for that matter, in literature," Moglen suggests the characteristics that the Brontë heroine would need to possess: outspokenness, self-respect, self-actualization, and self-love. Out of her "novelistic inexperience," however, Brontë simply "accepted automatically the male point of view as the 'official perspective,' but did not understand her protagonist"; therefore, "never conscious of his own experience on any but the most immediate level, [Crimsworth] is unable to bring to the events he describes a vital complexity of vision."[21]

Dianne Sadoff's discussion of the novel (1982) employs Lacanian psychology to explore Brontë's narrative strategies, specifically the way she repeatedly employs "the dialectic of mastery and submission" in her works. In summarizing Lacanian theory, Sadoff observes that "language inscribes desire by virtue of its role in constituting the subject." The unconscious is constructed on the traces or residues of what operates to create the subject, that is, language. Traces, signifiers, or representations become available to consciousness only by entering the language of the subject's "therapeutic discourse." The unconscious works like language and structures on tropes that we can recognize as condensation, displacement, metonymy, and metaphor. For Sadoff, "Brontë identifies with both male and female desire and so partakes of the pleasures of both libidinal economies. The language of desires takes as its metaphors for such gender difference, for crossing the bar between the sexes, the woman's voice, the man's gaze."[22] When Sadoff applies this paradigm to *The Professor* she produces some new and interesting angles for reading William Crimsworth's purported masculinity:

> When she bids "farewell to Angria," however, quitting the "burning clime" for the "study of real life," Brontë's masculine narrator enters a libidinal economy of gender-based dominance and submission. As speaker-narrator, William Crimsworth purposively defines his identity by mastery of linguistic structures and of human intersubjectivity. For only by dominating a succession of women can Crimsworth become the master, patriarch, and father he imagines himself.[23]

Sadoff's analysis of the novel is much more sophisticated and subtle than any of the earlier attempts to get at the psychology of Crimsworth, and her use of Lacanian and Kristevan psychoanalytic paradigms allows her to open new territory: castration theory, voyeurism, and the theory of the gaze. She remarks, "the gaze serves as metaphor for this masterful and dominating male sexuality by virtue of the third term in Lacan's (and Freud's) intersubjective structure of masculine desire: castration. . . . The male gaze substitutes for castration and thereby achieves the potency, mastery, and dominance which castration threatens. Voyeurism becomes specifically male and exhibitionism female; the man spectates, the woman is spectacle." For Sadoff, the repetitions in Brontë's canon, the tellings over and over of essentially the same story, reveal her attempts to "master desire" and to demystify her status as a victim of "daughterly desire."[24]

Clearly there is no consensus on the psychology of either Crimsworth or his creator. In writing the book Brontë demonstrated her need to recast the Brussels experience from the point of view of a man who finds a superior true love whom "he" rescues from a fate worse than death—spinsterhood. Reliving this traumatic episode in her life—an experience that she could have understood only as yet another rejection and loss of powerful, attractive, and loving parent figures—allowed her to refigure herself as the victor rather than the vanquished. The son of Frances and William, aptly named Victor, clearly figures Brontë's own imagined victory over her pain. In creating William and Frances, the literary traces and avatars of her own experience, Brontë relives the experience as lover, beloved, and product of love, a particularly potent erotic rearrangement of psychic energy.

The Feminist Reclamation of *The Professor*

Recent feminist reinterpretations of *The Professor* have emphasized not simply the masculine mimicry of William Crimsworth but the importance of reading Frances Henri as a protofeminist heroine. Other feminist emphases in the new approaches to the novel concern the gender ambivalence that suffuses the narrative, its undercutting of its own ostensible concerns, and its problematic psychology. Recent feminist reappraisals of *The Professor* began in earnest with the chapter on the novel—"A Secret Inward Wound"—in Sandra Gilbert and Susan Gubar's *The Madwoman in the Attic* (1979). According to Gilbert and Gubar, *The Professor* develops several crucial elements in the basic female enclosure-escape story. These enclosure-escape stories are resolved through what they call Brontë's "trance-like," or obsessive, focus on gender issues, which has several interesting implications for the suppression of women and women authors in a stiflingly patriarchal nineteenth-century British society.[25] The use of a male narrator indicates that Brontë wished to separate herself from the story, yet her trancelike writing (she repeatedly tells the same compulsive narrative of love lost and found over and over again) helps to disperse the anxieties of female authorship and instead allows her to assess herself as a man would. In other words, by writing as a man she gains an element of male power.

For Gilbert and Gubar as well as for most recent feminist critics, *The Professor* examines the plight of the disinherited female through the medium of a male narrator, which thereby transforms the author into a professor type, or one who has gained a measure of power or at least the semblance of narrative authority. By adopting the Richardsonian epistolary strategy in the novel's beginning, Brontë deconstructs the ideology of woman as domestic angel by contrasting this construction with Angrian-type men, such as Crimsworth's uncles and brother. Compared to the many passive women and overassertive men in the novel, Crimsworth is remarkably androgynous. Although he desires women, he also lacks male ambition and possesses the qualities of one disinherited and orphaned, much as Brontë felt herself to be in a male-dominated society.

For Gilbert and Gubar, *The Professor* is both a statement of the major themes that would have importance throughout Brontë's career and an exploration of the variety of paths to wholeness. Crimsworth and Frances are drawn together because they are both misfits; they possess difficulties similar to Brontë's own and they both struggle to be themselves, to find a home and wholeness. The pensionnat where Crimsworth lives and teaches suggests restraint, as well as mystery or sexual secrets. His invitation to teach there suggests that the mystery of femininity will be revealed to him. His voyeurism from the window represents a form of narrative espionage from a male point of view; he is revealed a series of characters and provided a picture of women preparing for a series of hypocritical female roles. For example, Mlle. Reuter at first appears to be a traditional woman but is later revealed to possess a crafty duplicity (Brontë later developed both traits at much greater length in her portrait of Madame Beck in *Villette*).

Also crucial to the recent feminist reevaluation of *The Professor* is the awareness that in spite of the male narrator, the novel reveals as much about Frances Henri as it does about Crimsworth. For instance, their two careers are almost parallel and mirror each other in a blatantly unrealistic manner. Frances's mourning for her dead aunt actually makes Crimsworth's transformation possible, for he too evolves from orphan/outcast to master. Frances is a physical clone of Brontë in appearance and position and is also a misfit because she is an artist surrounded by the forces of injustice, personified by Mlle. Reuter. Crimsworth, on the other hand, profits from Frances's sense of displacement to become her master and teach her the ways of the world, literary tradition, and her mother tongue. Frances is deprived of her imagination, the pain of which is depicted in the poem "Jane" and characterized by the ambiguity of women's conflicting ambition—her teaching career, and the continuing wound—the lure of heterosexual romance and marriage.

William and Frances's son Victor, according to Gilbert and Gubar, is the crux and symbol of their relationship. To Crimsworth he represents all that Crimsworth is not. He is a small version of Hunsden, who acts as an image of Brontë's anger toward the enclosure she feels. Hunsden is the voice of rebellion, a plot manipulator, a narrator in disguise, and a commentator on events. Victor, the literal result of the ambiguities of Frances and Crimsworth's marriage, is the only possible product of such a marriage. To Crimsworth he, like Hunsden, represents the rebellion that Crimsworth symbolically destroys when he shoots Victor's dog.[26]

Another feminist critic whose position is representative of much of the current thinking about the novel, Rebecca Rodolff, claims that *The Professor* needs to be read as a necessary stage in Brontë's development, for in writing the ending Brontë encountered the idea of a feminine point of view that was to appear later in *Jane Eyre*.[27] Whereas *The Professor* follows the pattern of a prologue followed by a love story in two main parts, like the other Brontë novels, it differs from them in that it continues in depth after the proposal scene, introducing and developing new material. In fact, the basic two-part story actually occurs twice. Brontë concludes Crimsworth's story with the proposal scene and then shifts her focus to the heroine and repeats the same pattern. In the latter section on Frances Henri, Brontë creates an intermediate character who exists between Crimsworth and Jane Eyre and embodies in embryonic form many elements that would appear shortly thereafter in the character of Jane Eyre. Similarities between *The Professor* and *Jane Eyre* rely on the narrators' experience with oppression, and the differences rely on the reactions and defenses available to each sex. Crimsworth, due to his position as a man, is able to overcome his oppression more easily than Jane Eyre does. Frances serves only to emphasize his success; she functions as the human embodiment of his complacent morality. As a result of this masculine dominance, Frances and Crimsworth's relationship cannot develop further in the first part of the novel, so the focus shifts to Frances. Her heartfelt expression in the poem "Jane" indicates the need for a female narrator who more nearly represents Brontë's own qualities and actions, who represents a woman's awakening.

Rodolff argues that Frances's attempt to achieve masculine dominance is a delusion, since Frances, like Jane Eyre, turns out to be anything but a complacent, yielding observer. Note that Frances refuses to yield completely to Crimsworth's argument for her unemployment and instead accepts it as a temporary situation only. Frances's assertion of her desires makes her more of a peer to Crimsworth. Eventually, though, Crimsworth's reluctance to fully accept this equality requires that his friend Yorke Hunsden assume it, and Hunsden in turn reaffirms Frances's attractiveness, which emphasizes her individuality and causes complications in her relationship with Crimsworth. This admiration by two male characters of one female foreshadows similar relationships in *Jane Eyre;* as Rochester is interested in Jane, so does Hunsden find himself drawn to Frances's refreshing unconventionality, a quality Crimsworth cannot fully appreciate. Critics have often complained about the lack of a love relationship between Frances and Hunsden, which leaves the possibilities of Frances's unconventionality void of conflict. Whereas in *Jane Eyre* Brontë skillfully uses character conflict to further the story, in *The Professor* conflict merely illustrates fairly static character types and unimaginative situations.

A close reading of the last chapter of the novel reveals, according to Rodolff, a Frances more developed and important than the narrator. In exploring the woman's point of view, Brontë distances the narrator through Frances's adoption of hypochondria, a problem formerly associated with Crimsworth and through Frances's dissatisfaction with her lower income. Crimsworth responds to both concerns with inconsequential attempts at appeasement and eventually becomes an instrument of oppression, illustrated by Frances's daily change from the school director to lace maker or from an attitude of determination to one of submission. This duality of personality appears again in Jane Eyre's relationships with Rochester and with St. John. Whereas the last two chapters of *The Professor* are unnecessary to the story of our hero, they are necessary in order to show a Victorian woman's attempt to overcome oppression. Brontë would later elaborate on this attempt to portray oppression in *Jane Eyre,* in which the woman gains a measure of equality that the man is finally able to accept. In other words, the ending of *The Professor* acts as a catalyst to the themes and concerns of *Jane Eyre*.[28]

Another recent feminist approach to the novel can be found in the work of Judith Williams, which attempts to read the novel in terms of Brontë's continuing immersion in the world of the juvenilia. William Crimsworth's life has the appearance of a quest, although he does not grow or obtain wisdom with age, since he maintains only tenuous control over his situation throughout the novel. This control makes him unimaginative and reflects Brontë's attempts to gain control over the imaginative excesses found in the Angrian stories. To maintain control

Crimsworth avoids the necessary connection between the inward and outward worlds and the joining of male and female sexuality that so often characterizes true perception in Brontë's novels.[29]

Emphasizing gender dichotomies and the psychological ambiguities implicit in such oppositions, Williams analyzes Crimsworth's attempts to avoid psychological conflict by seeing his difficulties as purely practical: he controls his enemies by keeping them apart from himself. Even in unfamiliar situations, like in Brussels, he attempts to control the complexities rather than understand them, as is illustrated by his mistaking foreignness for sexual license. In fact, Crimsworth uses M. Pelet and Reuter as displacements for his own sensuality and for the baser sexual feelings he denies in himself. Whereas M. Pelet and Reuter are controllable substitutes for these feelings, however, Yorke Hunsden represents the uncontrollable evils in Crimsworth's life. As Crimsworth's opposite, Hunsden is a presence who causes a change in gender roles that places Frances in the role of heroine, or central female figure. She is to her classmates what Hunsden is to Crimsworth: an intelligent antithesis. Her central female role is emphasized by the first passage she reads as Crimsworth's student, which indicates her need for reconciliation with the action-dominated male world.

As Williams argues, Crimsworth's relationships with both Frances and Hunsden suggest a dissolution of the traditional boundaries between male and female. Crimsworth treats Frances much like Hunsden treats Crimsworth, and together Frances and Hunsden compose the novel's true protagonist. Hunsden possesses the stereotypically "masculine" dark qualities of humanity, whereas Frances possesses such "feminine" virtues as love and forbearance. Because Hunsden treats Crimsworth like Crimsworth treats Frances, both Hunsden and Frances represent male and female power developed further than in Brontë's subsequent novels. Crimsworth and Frances's apparently ideal married life is undermined by their lack of relationship with their son Victor, who becomes a type of miniature Hunsden. Crimsworth's shooting of Victor's dog Yorke, a gift from Hunsden, represents Crimsworth's desire to rid Victor of Hunsden-like evils. Victor is representative of the entire novel—a controlled facade punctuated by a spontaneous and unpredictable side. In fact, the novel's abrupt ending implies that Crimsworth, in an attempt to maintain control over his environment, wants to avoid examining and knowing Victor further. The final scene also suggests and predicts the coming *Jane Eyre,* a novel that begins with the complexities of a child's perceptions of an inexplicable universe.[30]

In the final analysis we must admit that *The Professor* has enjoyed something of a literary renaissance in feminist critical practice largely because there has been so little work on the text, and the tendency has been to see the novel as unjustly neglected. There seems to be little hope, however, that the work will ever be widely read or taught. Despite the best efforts by numerous contemporary feminist critics, *The Professor* will most likely remain the stepchild of the Brontë canon.

Chapter Four

"I Know No Medium": *Jane Eyre*

Publication and Early Reception

Though discouraged by publishers' repeated rejections of *The Professor,* Charlotte Brontë continued to tinker with ideas for another novel. Several manuscript fragments suggest that Brontë began sketching ideas for *Jane Eyre* as early as 1844, fashioning her memories and impressions of people and places into vignettes that would later be incorporated into the longer work.[1] During a trip to Manchester in the summer of 1846, where she supervised her 69-year-old father's convalescence from cataract surgery, Brontë began putting together a new novel, one that would conclude with the blinding and the magical restoration of a flawed patriarch's sight. Depressed, troubled by chronic toothache, and impatient with her demanding father, Brontë was sustained only by her creative drive and by a crumb of encouragement she had received from an unlikely source: the seventh publisher to refuse *The Professor.* Though William Smith Williams of the then-obscure publishing firm Smith, Elder & Company had rejected Brontë's first novel, his tactful and constructive response, according to Brontë, "cheered the author better than a vulgarly expressed acceptance would have done. It was added that a work in three volumes would meet with careful attention."[2] Thus when Brontë completed the manuscript of *Jane Eyre* in August 1847, nearly a year to the day after beginning it, she sent it to Williams. Smith, Elder quickly accepted the work—one that would enrich the firm's partners and establish its reputation among publishers. Just six weeks later, on 16 October 1847, the first edition of *Jane Eyre* was rushed into print. The intense, introverted Brontë, though she had attempted to insulate herself with the pseudonym Currer Bell, was catapulted to fame and notoriety.

Jane Eyre's early readers reacted enthusiastically. Brontë's favorite novelist, William Makepeace Thackeray, to whom Williams had sent the manuscript, responded,

> I wish you had not sent me *Jane Eyre*. It interested me so much that I have lost (or won if you like) a whole day in reading it at the busiest

period with the printers I know waiting for copy. Who the author can be I can't guess, if a woman she knows her language better than most ladies do, or has had a "classical" education. It is a fine book, though, the man and the woman capital, the style very generous and upright so to speak. . . . The plot of the story is one with wh[ich] I am familiar. Some of the love passages made me cry, to the astonishment of John, who came in with the coals. St. John the Missionary is a failure I think, but a good failure, there are parts excellent. I don't know why I tell you this but that I have been exceedingly moved and pleased by *Jane Eyre*. It is a woman's writing, but whose? Give my respects and thanks to the author, whose novel is the first English one (and the French are only romances now) that I've been able to read for many a day.[3]

Thackeray's comments epitomized the early positive responses to *Jane Eyre*. Until Brontë's identity was publicly revealed, the question of authorship was foremost in readers' minds: the identity of the putative editor Currer Bell was a tantalizing mystery that demanded resolution. The sexual ambiguity of the name Currer Bell and the novel's focus on the experience of a rebellious heroine led readers correctly to suspect that the novel was the work of a woman writer whose pseudonym was designed to deflect critical reprisal.

Readers were equally electrified by the novel's vigorous style and by its handling of the familiar romance plot, which in 1847 Thackeray himself was reworking, with quite different effect, in *Vanity Fair*. From the very first notice, which appeared in the *Atlas,* Currer Bell was credited with transforming the conventional romance:

This is not merely a work of great promise, it is one of absolute perfor-mance. It is one of the most powerful domestic romances which has been published for many years. It has little or nothing of the old conventional stamp upon it; none of the jaded, exhausted attributes of a worn-out vein of imagination . . . but it is full of youthful vigour, of freshness and origi-nality.[4]

In *Fraser's,* the progressive critic and novelist George Henry Lewes affirmed Currer Bell's "perception of character, and power of delineating it; picturesqueness; passion; and knowledge of life. The story is not only of singular interest, naturally evolved, unflagging to the last, but it fas-tens itself upon your attention, and will not leave you."[5] When such other influential periodicals as the *Westminster Review* and the London *Times* followed suit, sales skyrocketed. By December 1848, *Jane Eyre* had been reprinted four times. It has been continuously in print ever since, translated into dozens of languages, transformed into plays and screen-plays, and many times filmed.[6]

The question of Currer Bell's identity was resolved in 1848, shortly after Emily and Anne's unscrupulous publisher, Thomas Newby, attempted to capitalize on *Jane Eyre*'s success by claiming that Ellis, Currer, and Acton Bell were one and the same "man." At the request of George Smith, Charlotte and Anne traveled to London, where they revealed their identities and were treated to five days of exhausting hos-pitality. The wisdom of using pseudonyms, however, was affirmed when *Jane Eyre* was later condemned in a series of blistering responses—from family and friends as well as from professional critics—that attacked the novel's revolutionary tone and nonconformist politics.[7]

The most famous of these condemnations came in December 1848, in a review of *Jane Eyre* and *Vanity Fair* that conjoined the two best-selling governess stories with a critique that Victorians' exploitation of governesses betrayed the double standard by which male and female writers were judged. The review thus inaugurated a new critical tradi-tion for *Jane Eyre* that focused on the book's politics.[8] The *Quarterly Review*'s anonymous reviewer, later revealed to be Elizabeth Rigby, argued that governesses suffered from unjust treatment in Victorian households since they were subject to overwork and underpayment and deprived of the pensions enjoyed by other household servants, such as housekeepers and butlers. Connecting this analysis with two popular novels about governesses, Rigby praised Thackeray's satiric account of a governess who learns "how to succeed on nothing a year" by bilking powerful men out of their money. *Vanity Fair,* Rigby argued, was a amus-ing and insightful, despite the fact that Thackeray's antiheroine, Becky Sharp, was a liar, a swindler, and probably a murderer.

In contrast, Rigby derided nearly every aspect of *Jane Eyre*. Although she had a few words of praise for the novel's "fine writing," Rigby rejected other readers' praise of the novel's originality by saying that "in these days of extravagant adoration of all that bears the stamp of nov-elty and originality, sheer rudeness and vulgarity have come in for a most mistaken worship." Brontë's governess novel, in Rigby's view, was irrevocably "stamped with a coarseness of language and laxity of tone." Rigby saw *Jane Eyre* as evidence of a destructive cultural trend: "The popularity of 'Jane Eyre' is a proof of how deeply the love for illegiti-mate romance is implanted in our nature." Rochester, "a man who deliberately and secretly seeks to violate the laws both of God and

man," was little more than "coarse and brutal." But if Rochester was
bad, Jane was worse: Rigby saw her as a "personification of an unregen-
erate and undisciplined spirit" who sinned by persistently questioning
rather than resigning herself to the persecutions and deprivations she
encountered:

> Altogether the auto-biography of 'Jane Eyre' is preeminently an anti-
> Christian composition. There is throughout it a murmuring against the
> comforts of the rich and against the privations of the poor, which, as far
> as each individual is concerned, is a murmuring against God's appoint-
> ment—there is a proud and perpetual assertion of the rights of man, for
> which we find no authority either in God's word or in God's provi-
> dence. . . . We do not hesitate to say that the tone of mind and thought
> which has overthrown authority and violated every code human and
> divine abroad, and fostered Chartism and rebellion at home, is the same
> which has also written 'Jane Eyre.'

Addressing the rumors that Currer Bell might be a woman writer,
Rigby concluded by impugning Brontë's femininity:

> Without entering into the question whether the power of the writing be
> above her, or the vulgarity below her, there are, we believe, minutiae of
> circumstantial evidence which at once acquit the feminine hand. No
> woman . . . makes mistakes in her own *métier*. . . . If we ascribe this book
> to a woman at all, we have no alternative but to ascribe it to one who
> has, for some sufficient reason, long forfeited the society of her own sex.[9]

Though Rigby's vituperative review seems overreactive and harsh
even to modern readers, it masks an awed respect for Brontë's power.
Rigby is honest enough to hint that she identifies not with Jane but
with the novel's hypocrites and oppressors—the Reeds, the Brockle-
hursts, the Ingrams:

> One feels provoked as Jane Eyre stands there before us—for in the won-
> derful reality of her thoughts and descriptions, she seems accountable for
> all done in her name—with principles you must approve in the main,
> and yet with language and manners that offend you in every particular.

Early in the novel Jane confides that "had I been a sanguine, brilliant,
careless, exacting, handsome, romping child—though equally dependent and friendless—Mrs. Reed would have endured my presence more
complacently; her children would have entertained for me more of the

cordiality of fellow-feeling; the servants would have been less prone to make me the scapegoat of the nursery" (chap. 2, pp. 12–13). Elizabeth Rigby, like the character Sarah Reed, had a divided response to Jane, finding her refusal to act "more attractive and sprightly . . . lighter, franker, more natural" both understandable and unforgivable (chap. 1, p. 5). *Jane Eyre's* first-person narrative forced readers like Rigby to participate directly in the experience of oppression and thereby to become viscerally conscious of injustice, temptation, and evil as they emerge in ordinary bourgeois life. Because Brontë's novel critiques such familiar social structures as marriage and family, education, Christianity, and the idea of vocation, it is not surprising that some readers denigrated her as a dangerous revolutionary—just as the Reed household regards Jane as "a sort of infantine Guy Fawkes" (chap. 3, p. 21). Rigby's outraged response, like others of its kind, reads in retrospect as a backhanded tribute to Brontë's success. Rigby's review also marks the beginning of a long tradition of debate about the psychological, sociological, and political issues raised *Jane Eyre.*

Formalist Readings

The most densely plotted of Brontë's adult works, *Jane Eyre* is structured around a teleological journey that takes Jane to five symbolically named houses or institutions: Gateshead, Lowood, Thornfield, Marsh End/ Moor House, and Ferndean. Each place metonymically signifies both a particular social institution and a discrete step toward greater spiritual growth and self-determination for Jane. The plot of *Jane Eyre* has been faulted for depending too heavily on coincidences, such as Jane's sudden discovery of both her inheritance and her blood ties to the Rivers family. Brontë also relies on improbable supernatural voices to direct Jane's action during times of crisis, such as when a fairy voice tells her to "advertise" for a new position (chap. 10, p. 75) or when Rochester's disembodied voice persuades her to refuse marriage to St. John. To readers expecting a realistic fiction, in which events must be plausible and empirically verifiable, *Jane Eyre's* plot may seem contrived. Yet the novel is more than a realist bildungsroman; it partakes of the conventions of a variety of genres, including the novel of spiritual awakening, the gothic novel, and the courtship romance. The plot summary that follows reveals the extent to which two of these genres, the bildungsroman and the narrative of spiritual awakening, are unified by the composing metaphor of the journey.

Gateshead Hall, where the narrative opens, signifies the beginning of a journey inaugurated by Jane's first decisive act of self-assertion. At Gateshead, the orphan Jane perceives herself as existentially isolated: "I was a discord in Gateshead Hall; I was like nobody there; I had nothing in harmony with Mrs. Reed or her children, or her chosen vassalage" (chap. 2, p. 12). Though Jane recognizes that ostracism and exile are inevitable punishment for being "a heterogeneous thing" (chap. 2, p. 12), she embraces her impending martyrdom because it promises escape and confers moral superiority. In the opening scene, Jane is physically and verbally assaulted by her cousin John Reed, who ferrets her out of a window seat where she has been reading quietly. John seizes her book and exults in his patriarchal privilege, affirming her subordinate status as an impoverished, unconnected female:

> "You have no business to take our books; you are a dependent, mamma says; you have no money; your father left you none; you ought to beg, and not live here with gentlemen's children like us, and eat the same meals we do, and wear clothes at our mamma's expense. Now, I'll teach you to rummage my book-shelves; for they *are* mine; all the house belongs to me, or will do in a few years." (chap. 1, p. 8)

The deeply symbolic gesture of a male bully wresting a book away from a small girl inaugurates Brontë's critique of patriarchal privilege in *Jane Eyre*. When John then hurls the book at Jane, bloodying her head, Jane retaliates violently for the first time in her life, noting that "he had closed with a desperate thing. I really saw in him a tyrant: a murderer" (chap. 1, p. 9). She shouts and strikes back at John, but when the servants arrive it is Jane who is blamed and punished. Locked in the "Red Room," a little-used and reputedly haunted chamber that Jane identifies with her late uncle, the only supporter she can remember, Jane broods over her fate until she sees a flash of light she fears may be her uncle's ghost. Yet her terrified pleas for release are ignored until she experiences "a species of fit" and loses consciousness (chap. 2, p. 15).

Though her verbal entreaties carry little weight, Jane's bodily distress secures her release from the Red Room. While convalescing, Jane confides her version of events to the sympathetic apothecary, Mr. Lloyd, who privately advises Mrs. Reed that Jane be sent to school. After recovering Jane finds that her rebellion and martyrdom have endowed her with new emotional detachment. When Mrs. Reed invites the charity-school director Brocklehurst to reprimand and catechize Jane, Jane ignores Brocklehurst instead of trying to refute his accusations. After he leaves, Jane coolly confronts her benefactress with some uncomfortable truths: "I am not deceitful: if I were, I should say I loved *you,* but I declare I do not love you: I dislike you the worst of anybody in the world except John Reed: and this book about the liar, you may give to your girl, Georgiana, for it is she who tells lies, and not I" (chap. 4, pp. 30–31). At Gateshead Jane has learned not to suffer in silence but to confront oppression calmly and openly. Having mastered rebellion, though dreading the unknown conditions that await her at school, Jane departs tearlessly from Gateshead Hall (chap. 5, p. 35).

Lowood School, modeled on the Clergy Daughters School at Cowan Bridge where Brontë's elder sisters Maria and Elizabeth had perished in the typhoid (or "low fever") epidemic of 1825, is a paradoxical scene of privation and enlightenment for Jane. While at Gateshead, Jane remarked that "poverty for me was synonymous with degradation," adding, "I was not heroic enough to purchase liberty at the price of caste" (chap. 3, p. 20). Lowood School confirms her worst fears, as Jane undergoes severe physical trials: the pupils' food, heat, and clothing are woefully inadequate, the students are persecuted by mean-spirited teachers, and an epidemic of typhoid fever carries off many, including Jane's friend Helen Burns. Yet at Lowood Jane learns that patriarchal power can be subverted, as when, following the epidemic, Brocklehurst is deposed and Miss Temple is given charge of the school. At Lowood Jane is finally trusted. Though Brocklehurst attempts to scapegoat Jane by publicly denouncing her as a liar, her fellow students wordlessly affirm their confidence in her innocence. She exults: "How the new feeling bore me up! It was as if a martyr, a hero, had passed a slave or victim, and imparted strength in the transit" (chap. 7, p. 58). Eventually Mr. Lloyd confirms the reliability of her narrative, and Jane is publicly cleared of Brocklehurst's charges (chap. 8, p. 64). Gradually Jane's academic achievements and close friendships begin to compensate for the school's wretched conditions; eventually Jane writes, "I would not have exchanged Lowood with all its privations, for Gateshead and its daily luxuries" (chap. 8, p. 65). Jane rises to the head of her class and eventually is promoted to teacher. Only Helen Burns's death from typhoid fever and Miss Temple's departure for marriage spur Jane to seek new challenges, which she finds by advertising her services and securing a position as governess at Thornfield Hall.

Thornfield Hall's name encodes its dangers for the pilgrim, who can expect martyrdom along with ecstasy. Thornfield presents Jane with a series of semiotic puzzles: as Mrs. Fairfax warns, "It is an old saying that 'All is not gold that glitters.' . . . There will be something found to be different to what either you or I expect" (chap. 24, p. 233). At Thornfield Jane keeps making startling discoveries. Mrs. Fairfax turns out to be not Thornfield's mistress but its housekeeper; Grace Poole is not an eccentric but a prison warden; Adèle Varens is not Rochester's daughter but his ward; Blanche Ingram is not Rochester's beloved but a hated fortune hunter. Most important, the mysterious laughter Jane hears periodically comes not from Grace Poole but from a madwoman imprisoned in the attic. The master himself, Edward Fairfax Rochester, is absent until Jane, in a gesture that embodies Thornfield's confused hierarchies, inadvertently unhorses him on the road to Millcote. There Rochester also stumbles in decoding Jane's appearance:

> "You are not a servant at the hall, of course. You are—" He stopped, ran his eye over my dress, which, as usual, was quite simple: a black merino cloak, a black beaver bonnet: neither of them half fine enough for a lady's maid. He seemed puzzled to decide what I was: I helped him.
> "I am the governess." (chap. 12, p. 100)

Although throughout Jane's tenure at Thornfield Blanche Ingram and others remind her of her inferiority, "the governess" nearly usurps the manor. Jane's plain dress and sober countenance conceal a raging heart. She gradually makes herself emotionally indispensable to Rochester by helping allay several mysterious disasters (a fire, a stabbing, a midnight visit of a "vampyre" who silently rends Jane's wedding veil and then glares at her menacingly, chap. 25, p. 249–50). Intuitively, however, Jane recognizes that Rochester's existing commitments preclude their union. When she informs him that "You are a married man—or as good as a married man, and wed to one inferior to you—to one with whom you have no sympathy—whom I do not believe you truly love; for I have seen and heard you sneer at her" (chap. 23, p. 222), she refers to Blanche Ingram but unwittingly describes Bertha Mason Rochester. To win Jane, however, Rochester enlists a series of ruses, including charades designed to stimulate her jealousy, a stint as a gypsy designed to help Rochester gauge Jane's attachment to him, and a midsummer-night marriage proposal. The last ruse is the most serious, since it signals Rochester's intent to commit bigamy. Only at the altar, on the objection of a witness, does Jane learn that "an insuperable impediment" to the marriage exists (chap. 26, p. 254), in Rochester's insane wife,

Bertha, the source of Thornfield's mysterious laughter and midnight violence. Confronted with the feral Bertha, Jane recognizes that "My hopes were all dead—struck with a subtle doom, such as in one night, fell on all the first-born in the land of Egypt" (chap. 27, p. 260). Jane's metaphor invokes the Old Testament flight of the Israelites, an archetypal religious pilgrimage from slavery to freedom. She resolves to leave Thornfield and sets out blindly without plan or destination, noting only that "I could not turn, nor retrace one step. God must have led me on. As to my own will or conscience, impassioned grief had trampled one and stifled the other" (chap. 27, p. 283).

Paralleling the Israelites' wanderings in the wilderness, Jane's flight from Thornfield releases her from the problematic domestic enclosures that have protected and imprisoned her all her life. Goaded by the recognition that she has placed too much faith in worldly relationships, she learns to survive by surrendering to divine guidance. Set down by the coach driver at a crossroads, lacking money, possessions, and connections to family and friends, Jane vacillates between a comforting sense of divine protection and the growing imperative of "Want" (chap. 38, p. 285), constituted by hunger, thirst, and the need for shelter and work. Too bourgeois-looking to work in a shop or factory yet lacking the money and family connections that would guarantee shelter, Jane is rebuffed as suspicious-looking by the locals. Eventually she is reduced to begging for food. Finally, in desperation, she seeks asylum at the house of the local cleric. When an elderly servant rebuffs her, Jane is able only to sink down on the doorstep, saying "I can but die . . . and I believe in God. Let me try to wait His will in silence" (chap. 28, p. 295).

The threshold of Moor House proves to be providential, however. Here Jane finds not only "mooring" but the end of her "march," as encoded in the house's other name, Marsh End. After she satisfies her hosts' curiosity by providing a guarded narrative of her origins, renaming herself Jane Elliott, Jane is restored to emotional and physical health by St. John Rivers and his sisters Mary and Diana. St. John finds her a teaching position at a one-room girls' school at Morton, where she flourishes. A series of unlikely coincidences reveals that Jane is related to the Riverses and that she has inherited £20,000 from an uncle whose bequest was subverted by the vindictive Mrs. Reed. Expressing generosity and gratitude, Jane "Heir" divides the legacy equally with her newfound cousins, thus rescuing Diana and Mary from careers as governesses and underwriting St. John's imminent mission to India.

Though all seems well, however, a threat to Jane's integrity has developed. St. John Rivers has mistaken Jane for his wifely ideal: a "sufferer, a labourer, a female apostle . . . a missionary's wife" (chap. 32, p. 329). Despotic and manipulative, St. John demands that Jane marry him. She rejects his proposal, however, refusing to accept a loveless marriage to a man who views her as little more than a "useful tool" (chap. 35, p. 366) and for whom she feels "only a comrade's constancy; a fellow-soldier's frankness, fidelity, fraternity" (chap. 34, p. 359). St. John, however, refuses Jane's alternative plan to accompany him as an "assistant" or "curate" (chap. 35, pp. 363–64). For several weeks, St. John inexorably reiterates his demands. Just as Jane is about to yield, she hears Rochester's voice and rebuffs St. John, saying that if God wills it, she will marry him.

Prayer, however, convinces Jane to pursue to a different "mission." Her next journey is not to India but to find Rochester. The "vocation" (literally, "calling") she hears issues from Rochester and convinces her to refuse St. John categorically. Jane undertakes the long trip to Thornfield, confident that there she will find that "my journey is closed" (chap. 36, p. 372). Instead she finds a "blackened ruin" (chap. 36, p. 373), the shell of the burned-down Thornfield. The innkeeper at the Rochester Arms explains that when Bertha set fire to Thornfield, Rochester was mutilated and blinded in a vain attempt to rescue her; "now quite broken down," Rochester lives quietly at Ferndean, 30 miles distant (chap. 36, p. 378). Arriving there posthaste, Jane finds Rochester unkempt and humbled, nearly blind and missing his right hand. Jane, however, sets about restoring him to health. All obstacles and inequalities having been removed from their relationship, she concludes, "Reader, I married him" (chap. 38, p. 395). Their marriage is an ecstatic partnership that produces a son, and their extended family prospers.

Each of Jane's five homes presents a new challenge to her self-determination and sense of ethics. At each destination she is forced to resist a coercive patriarch's attempt to possess and subdue her by assigning her a degrading identity as his dependent. (Because Brontë is indicting patriarchy in general, such female characters as Mrs. Reed, Miss Temple, Blanche Ingram, and Mrs. Fairfax participate to varying degrees in victimizing Jane.) John Reed labels Jane a "bad animal" and treats her as chattel; Brocklehurst slanders her publicly. Rochester attempts to engage her in bigamy and then adultery, and St. John Rivers seeks to prune her into a suffering amanuensis. Jane's resistance of these dependent roles is framed by two forces: her recognition of want, the material imperative of daily existence that motivates her to earn her keep, and her acceptance of the will of a protean God too complex to be contained by organized Christianity. Her experiences as a wandering beggar after leaving Thornfield and before arriving at Moor House bring a spiritual awakening that affirms Jane's apparently paradoxical commitment to God and to her own self-determination.

In *Jane Eyre,* the plots of the religious pilgrimage and of the educating journey overlap with two archetypal plots that address the vagaries of adult female sexual experience: the romance plot and the gothic plot.[10] The romance plot, epitomized by the cross-culturally universal folktale "Cinderella," focuses on the travails of a child, oppressed by her female guardians, whose intrinsic worthiness must be discovered by a man capable of marrying and thus rescuing her.[11] Though the hero's rescue of the heroine is beset with difficulties, the story closes with their marriage and the punishment of their detractors. Those gothic narratives that focus on courtship and marriage present men as exploitive and violent and marriage as an institution that threatens women's independence and even their lives, enlisting the paradigm of the less-well-known folktale "Bluebeard" as their archetype.[12]

The romance plot shapes the first half of *Jane Eyre.* Jane, like Cinderella, is unfairly victimized by her stepfamily and by Brocklehurst and is scorned by such haughty beauties as Blanche Ingram. Jane is finally recognized as worthy and is brought close to rescue from the ignominy of governessing by Rochester's marriage proposal. Jane acknowledges the parallel when she answers Rochester's marriage proposal by saying that "to imagine such a lot befalling me is a fairy-tale" (chap. 24, p. 227). But Brontë alters "Cinderella" early. Throughout her stay at Thornfield, Jane is troubled by sounds of "a demoniac laugh—low, suppressed, and deep—uttered, as it seemed, at the very key-hole of my chamber-door" (chap. 15, p. 130). This laugh, the reader later discovers, signals the existence of a woman who serves as a cautionary tale for Jane, since her madness and imprisonment confirm Rochester's potential for duplicity and for violence against women. At the altar this threat is confirmed when Rochester's attempted bigamy and shameful secret are publicly revealed. In the middle of the novel, the "handsome prince" has been revealed as fraudulent. Though Jane will eventually return to Rochester to claim him as her husband, she must first undergo a series of trials and courtship by another suitor while Rochester is symbolically punished.

In *Jane Eyre,* the gothic traces of "Bluebeard" coexist with the romantic traces of "Cinderella": Thornfield Hall is both Jane's home and her prison, both the promise of her deliverance from poverty and ignominy and a palpable threat to her well-being. Certainly, however, the inhuman Bertha Mason Rochester and her attic cell are redolent of the death chamber discovered by Bluebeard's nameless wife. Like Bluebeard, Rochester has sexually consumed and discarded not only his wife, Bertha, but three European mistresses. When, after the aborted wedding, Rochester proposes that Jane join his series of mistresses, Jane flees Thornfield like a prisoner evading capture.

Though Rochester, unlike Bluebeard, is not destroyed for his sins, Bertha, the emblem of his ill treatment of women, manages indirectly to avenge herself when he is maimed trying to rescue her in the Thornfield fire. Jane's later courtship by St. John Rivers echoes several of the "Bluebeard" elements of her relationship with Rochester, as when the emotionless St. John casually abandons his first love, Rosamond Oliver, in order to transform Jane into his missionary helpmate. The subtle violence of St. John's attempt to coerce Jane to accept his marriage proposal is arrested only by a magical rescue, when Jane hears Rochester's disembodied voice calling her. At this point, the endings of "Cinderella" and "Bluebeard" are combined and transformed by an alternative closure in which Jane is the agent rather than the object of rescue.

Jane Eyre's merging of the romance and gothic plots mitigates the import of both, allowing Brontë to provide a complex and ambiguous portrait of the rewards and dangers of marriage. In Brontë's hands, as Robert Heilman points out, the two plots become almost a "new gothic," a vehicle for exploring such forbidden emotions as Jane's childhood anger at her abusers or her sexual desire for Rochester, emotions that are elided or minimized in the folktale originals and many of their derivatives.[13] This achievement is enhanced by Brontë's parallel (and simultaneous) transformation of bildungsroman and pilgrimage-narrative conventions. *Jane Eyre*'s converging plots create a female coming-of-age parable that offers multiple interpretative options and implies that female experience is far too complex and varied to be contained within the limitations of the traditional courtship plot.

Jane Eyre's imagery was the focus of much early criticism of the novel. Several critics explore its imagery of fire and ice, two elements embodied in the novel's characters. Jane's emotional intensity and her need to control her emotions are persistently represented in metaphors of cleansing and destroying fire:

A ridge of lighted heath, alive, glancing, devouring, would have been a meet emblem of my mind when I accused and menaced Mrs. Reed: the same ridge, black and blasted after the flames are dead, would have represented as meetly my subsequent condition, when half an hour's silence and reflection had shown me the madness of my conduct, and the dreariness of my hatred and hating position. (chap. 4, p. 32)

The tension between the purifying and destructive potential of fire is repeated in the consumption of Helen "Burns" by fever; in Bertha Mason Rochester's persistent attempts to destroy her faithless husband by burning him alive; and, with a positive resolution, in Jane's incremental mastering of her overwhelming emotions. As the novel progresses and Jane's "fire" thaws and melts such ice figures as St. John Rivers, the "fire" of her nature is likewise affected: it is cooled, subdued, and purified. These metaphors argue implicitly that "fiery" individuals may be destroyed by the intensity of their emotions, whereas colder individuals, like the quiescent St. John Rivers, may freeze from their own lack of feeling—or be melted by Jane's intensity or by the "broiling" climate of India.[14]

Political Readings

Since its publication in 1847 on the cusp of political agitation and revolution in Europe, *Jane Eyre* has been read as an indictment of inequities of gender, social class, and race. Politically oriented critiques have flourished since the late 1960s, as materialist, feminist, and postcolonialist criticism and cultural studies have gradually emerged as mainstream critical modes.[15] The ideologies of Brontë's novel are notoriously difficult to isolate: where one critic reads subversive rebellion against political oppression, another accuses Brontë of reproducing or endorsing precisely the oppressive paradigms Jane seems to resist. Many political analyses of *Jane Eyre* overlap significantly and cannot be subsumed under a single rubric.

From Rigby to the present, *Jane Eyre*'s presentation of gender inequities has attracted much analysis. In 1925, Virginia Woolf deemed *Jane Eyre*'s emotional intensity characteristic of "poetry" but not of "philosophy," implying that Brontë's art was framed more by unconscious emotion than by conscious craft.[16] Woolf's focus on "passion"—a term that signifies rage, lust, and intense love—inaugurates a key issue in feminist interpretations of *Jane Eyre* because women historically have been heavily penalized for expressing passionate feelings. In keeping with traditional social control, Woolf censures Brontë for presenting passionate characters and condemns her as excessively "self-centred" and "self-limited," incapable of profiting from reading others' works, a "country parson's daughter" whose art is limited by its emotional excess. Certainly Jane, whom the Reeds label a "mad cat" and a "picture of passion" and who admits feeling like a "rebel slave" resolved to "go all lengths" against oppression (chap. 2, pp. 5, 9), is clearly "passionate," as are such other central characters as Rochester, Bertha, and St. John Rivers.

Female "passion," whether it takes the form of rage, lust, or love, affirms the existence of unsatisfied desire and thus threatens women's subservient position by flooding the boundaries of acceptable conduct and appearing to co-opt the male privileges of resistance and self-expression. The most straightforwardly "political" of the novel's passions may be Jane's objections to the limitations placed on women's lives. These objections are not limited to the ignominy of Jane's class status as an unmonied and thus declassed female member of the middle class; they apply to women of all social positions, whether factory workers or affluent bourgeois wives. On the threshold of adulthood, the narrator Jane provides a detailed analysis of the "smooth career" that apparently awaits her as a governess. She unsentimentally dismisses both Mrs. Fairfax and Adèle as pleasant but unexceptional, admitting that her judgment "will be thought cool language . . . but I am not writing to flatter . . . egotism, to echo cant, or prop up humbug; I am merely telling the truth" (chap. 12, p. 95). Indirectly having affirmed her overqualification for domestic responsibilities, she ruefully anticipates censure: "Anybody may blame me who likes. . . . Who blames me? Many, no doubt" (chap. 12, pp. 95). Jane's "discontent" and "restlessness" are relieved only by trips to Thornfield's third story, where she experiences imaginative visions "quickened with all of the incident, life, fire, feeling, that I desired and had not in my actual existence" and, as if in response, hears the "low, slow, ha! ha!" she attributes to Grace Poole (chap. 12, pp. 95–96). From these musings arises a protofeminist credo:

> It is vain to say human beings ought to be satisfied with tranquillity; they must have action; and they will make it if they cannot find it. Millions are condemned to a stiller doom than mine, and millions are in silent revolt against their lot. Nobody knows how many rebellions besides political rebellions ferment in the masses of life which people earth. Women feel just as men feel; they need exercise for their faculties

and a field for their efforts as much as their brothers do; they suffer from too rigid a restraint, too absolute a stagnation, precisely as men would suffer; and it is narrow-minded in their more privileged fellow creatures to say that they ought to confine themselves to making puddings and knitting stockings, to playing on the piano and embroidering bags. It is thoughtless to condemn them, or laugh at them, if they seek to do more or learn more than custom has pronounced necessary for their sex. (chap. 12, p. 96)

This brief diatribe against Victorian women's imposed position of passive inferiority was not extraordinary for its time; in the United States, for example, participants in the 1848 Seneca Falls convention revised the 1776 Declaration of Independence to state that "all men and women are created equal." There is little evidence, however, that Charlotte Brontë supported such political movements as women's suffrage, or that she read the works of eighteenth- and nineteenth-century feminist theorists like Mary Wollstonecraft and Margaret Fuller. *Jane Eyre* nonetheless reveals the influence of the arguments of Wollstonecraft's 1792 *A Vindication of the Rights of Woman* and anticipates the arguments of John Stuart Mill's 1861 *On the Subjection of Women*.[17] These traces led Rigby to object to *Jane Eyre*'s revolutionary "tone of . . . mind and thought which has overthrown authority and violated every code human and divine abroad, and fostered Chartism and rebellion at home." In Rigby's view, this novel had the capacity to inspire readers to participate in the kinds of political and social revolutions that were sweeping England and Europe at mid-century.

The narrative intrusion in chapter 12, however, is uniquely overt and polemical. Jane Eyre's "feminism" is often complex, covert, and overlaid with other political implications; as many critics have suggested, Brontë's apparent feminism is undercut by conservative ideological messages. The renaissance in Brontë studies that began in the late 1960s was stimulated in large part by the work of feminist critics exhilarated by *Jane Eyre*'s depiction of a woman's resistance to patriarchal oppression. A key example of such criticism is the poet Adrienne Rich's 1973 essay "Jane Eyre: The Temptations of a Motherless Woman," which takes as its epigraph Phyllis Chesler's observation that all "women are motherless children in patriarchal society" (p. 91).[18] Rejecting earlier writers' assertions that *Jane Eyre* lacks range and depth (the elements Woolf called "philosophy"), Rich suggests that *Jane Eyre* offers "a depiction of alternatives—to convention and traditional piety . . . [and] to social and cultural reflexes internalized within the female psyche"

(p. 106).[19] Rich concludes that *Jane Eyre* should not be measured against the traditional bildungsroman, which focuses on a male protagonist, because a novel detailing the emotional and intellectual education of a young woman is essentially a different genre. Rather than criticize Brontë for failing to imitate the male tradition epitomized by Tolstoy and Flaubert, Rich praises her for creating of a new kind of heroine, imaginative and resourceful, whose "inner clarity helps her to distinguish between intense feelings which can lead to greater fulfillment, and those which can only lead to self-destructiveness" (p. 96). In a society that punishes female independence, Rich argues, Jane overcomes obstacles individualistically, negotiating her own fate rather than completely rejecting or accepting what her world has designed for her. Bertha Mason Rochester, the novel's gothic paradigm of unspeakable female passion, has long haunted readers who seek to explain her presence and function in the text.[20]

In discussing the Thornfield section of *Jane Eyre,* Rich remarks that although Bertha Mason Rochester repeatedly tries to kill her husband, "she does not, interestingly enough, attack Jane" (p. 99). This fact has inspired a critical tradition that handles Bertha not as Jane's enemy but as her double. With Helen Burns, Bertha functions as a key aspect of Jane's identity, an emblem and articulator of a potential self whose extreme passion she has rejected. If Helen functions as Jane's Freudian superego, her controlling intellectual and spiritual consciousness, Bertha serves as Jane's id, the source of insatiable desires or drives that precede language. Brontë's aesthetic paradigm anticipates Freud's psychoanalytical paradigm: these doubles, or alter egos, must be controlled, even destroyed, so that Jane may mature into the paradigm of the ego, integrating spirit, intellect, and body.[21]

Saintly Helen Burns, who submits herself to the will of "the invisible world and the kingdom of spirits . . . [who] see our tortures [and] recognize our innocence" (chap. 8, p. 60), has attracted less critical attention than has Bertha, possibly because Helen's self-abnegation threatens Jane's Enlightenment individualism. Helen helps temporarily assuage Jane's fury at patriarchal injustice and with Miss Temple infuses Jane with "more harmonious thoughts" to the extent that Jane admits that "what seemed better-regulated feelings had become the inmates of my mind. I had given in allegiance to duty and order; I was quiet; I believed I was content; to the eyes of others, usually even to my own, I believed I was content" (chap. 10, p. 73). But the repeated subjunctive "I believed" and the metaphors of surveillance and imprisonment betray

Jane's discomfort. These newly adopted attitudes mark eight years of proper behavior at Lowood—eight years of eventlessness elided from Jane's text. The "rebel slave" gradually reemerges once Miss Temple and Helen Burns have disappeared and Jane is left in her "natural element, and beginning to feel the stirring of old emotions" (chap. 10, p. 73). She confesses,

> I felt that it was not enough: I tired of the routine of eight years in one afternoon. I desired liberty; for liberty I gasped, for liberty I uttered a prayer; it seemed scattered on the wind then faintly blowing. I abandoned it and framed a humbler supplication; for change, stimulus: that petition, too, seemed swept off into vague space. "Then," I cried, half desperate, "grant me at least a new servitude!" (chap. 10, p. 74)

The "rebel slave" has not disappeared entirely but has become self-regulating. Here Jane promptly modifies her "gasp" of desire for liberty into a "humbler supplication" for "a new servitude." Employment as a governess promises such a "new servitude," but soon it too begins to chafe, leading Jane to identify with the "millions [who] are in silent revolt against their lot" (chap. 12, p. 96).

Bertha, though she never speaks, silently articulates the lust, rage, and defiance Jane has learned to repress. As Sandra Gilbert and Susan Gubar have famously argued, the tension between conformity and rebellion is articulated in the twinned figures of Jane and Bertha.[22] Rather than threatening Jane, Bertha acts as her "truest and darkest double" (p. 360), expressing emotions, such as lust and anger, that Jane is forbidden to articulate. Consequently Bertha erupts into the text—as her laughter or the effects of her violence are perceived by the other characters—at precisely those moments when Jane has most destructively repressed emotion. For example, Bertha comes downstairs to warn Jane of Rochester's duplicitous designs; similarly, just before the wedding, Bertha enters Jane's bedroom in the middle of the night and symbolically rends Jane's wedding veil, a pantomime that evokes the destruction of both marriages and echoes the earlier splitting of the chestnut tree.

Gilbert and Gubar argue that Jane's forbidden emotions and behaviors are magically "exorcised" through "the literal and symbolic death of Bertha" (p. 362). Yet Gilbert and Gubar seem unsatisfied with *Jane Eyre*'s essentially conservative closure. Bertha's destruction facilitates Jane and Rochester's withdrawal into the isolated utopia of Ferndean.

At Ferndean Jane loses every trace of her earlier rage, and metamorphoses into a loving wife and devoted producer of a son who bears his father's eyes and name. Furthermore, the signs of Bertha's vengeful anger—Rochester's wounds—are gradually effaced by connubial bliss. Many small details, such as Jane's continued use of the formal title "Sir" to address the husband who refers to her simply as "Jane," undermine the apparent egalitarianism of their new, improved relationship. Jane has not actually resolved the dilemma of handling her "forbidden emotions"; instead, another female character has been scapegoated and destroyed in order to redeem her. The paradigm of self-sacrifice forms the basis of the Christian gospels and frames the life of the evangelizing St. John Rivers, whom Jane salutes extravagantly in the closing paragraphs of her narrative (chap. 38, p. 398). Yet such feminist critics as Gilbert and Gubar are uneasy about the implications of this paradigm, particularly since European novelists from Richardson through Tolstoy have persistently endorsed the destruction of excessively passionate heroines. Gilbert and Gubar conclude their chapter by pointing the reader forward to Brontë's final work, *Villette,* which offers a more compromised conclusion about women whose passions exceed cultural norms.

Political critiques of *Jane Eyre* have persistently focused on the margins of the text: themes of alienation and exclusion, minor or extremely disruptive characters, moments at which the text seems to repress or elide information. These apparently marginal themes or moments provide clues literary detectives read in order to get a deeper sense of the text's complexities, internal contradictions, and multiple meanings. The critical tradition does not so much alter as shift focus; Elizabeth Rigby's attack on *Jane Eyre*'s rebellious tone is mollified into Virginia Woolf's probing of Brontë's raw emotionality. The burgeoning of Brontë criticism in the last half of the twentieth century has extended analysis into the corners of the text, where critics have illuminated its margins not only by probing *Jane Eyre*'s formal elements but also by using tools drawn from other disciplines, such as history, politics, economics, psychology, and sociology.

A theme that has provoked readers since Rigby, who devoted part of her review of *Jane Eyre* and *Vanity Fair* to the topic, is the position of the governess in Victorian culture. As we have noted, Rigby caps her analysis of the two "governess fictions" with an indictment of the peculiar status of governesses, who were neither master nor servant in the Victorian household, neither wife nor nanny, but something indeterminate. Their employment provided neither the security of family life and social position accorded to a Victorian wife nor the promise of lifetime employment and pensioning accorded to other servants. M. Jeanne Peterson picks up this thread in her influential essay on the incongruent status of the Victorian governess, demonstrating that well-educated middle-class women gravitated toward employment as governesses largely because their legitimate employment options were severely limited.[23] The presence of a governess, like the presence of an orphan, as Jane Eyre's career suggests, could be severely disruptive because it posed such a strong challenge to the hierarchy of Victorian class and gender arrangements.[24] The word *governess* itself encodes the instability of the role. Though the word originated as the feminine cognate of *governor,* a term that in British English still signifies "boss," *governess* quickly became debased in practice to signify "one who governs children." The governance of another family's children presented authority problems to the governess, as the Ingrams' accounts of torturing their family governesses confirm (chap. 17, pp. 155–56). The governess had extensive responsibility but little authority and could be replaced whenever she failed to meet the complicated and sometimes contradictory requirements of her job.

Though at Thornfield Jane experiences no difficulty handling her sole charge, Adèle Varens, she is still excluded from full participation in any of the spheres of Thornfield Hall. The servants, including Mrs. Fairfax, refuse to enlighten Jane about the presence of Bertha Mason Rochester, a fact that is crucial to her self-preservation. When Jane overhears Leah and the charwoman discussing Grace Poole, they clam up instantly, and she notes, "All I had gathered . . . amounts to this: that there was a mystery at Thornfield, and that from participation in that mystery I was purposely excluded" (chap. 17, p. 144). Even when Jane helps nurse the injured Mr. Mason, she is forbidden to talk with him and only later discovers the cause of his injuries. Likewise, she is excluded from full participation in the gay house party Rochester assembles at Thornfield. She quickly becomes depressed by the disdain of the wealthy guests and her apparently unrequited passion for her employer (chap. 17, p. 142, 158–59). Rochester, dressed as a gypsy fortune-teller, must reiterate his request for an audience with Jane because she does not consider herself one of the "young, single ladies" of the party (chap. 18, p. 171). Though Rochester lifts her momentarily from ignominy to apparent equality by proposing marriage, Jane recognizes that his gesture actually threatens to subordinate her further. She accuses him of seeking to make her one of his "seraglio," or harem, refuses to accept his gifts of elegant, expensive clothing and jewelry (chap. 24, pp. 227, 236), and leaves behind the few gifts he has given her when she leaves Thornfield (chap. 27, p. 281). When Jane leaves Thornfield, her indeterminate social status nearly proves her undoing; she finds herself unable to secure employment because she looks too affluent to work in a factory or shop. After Jane has completely exhausted herself by wandering and begging, Hannah, the Riverses' housekeeper, turns her away from the parsonage on a rainy night, chiding, "You are not what you ought to be or you wouldn't make such a noise" (chap. 28, p. 295).

The Victorian governess became a source of cultural anxiety because she was a constant reminder of the predicament of middle-class women who did not marry and who were unable to find legitimate work.[25] The governess embodied the fact that not all women could be "contained" in middle-class marriages and that some needed to work in order to supplement family income. Charlotte Brontë understood these imperatives only too well: she, Anne, and Branwell all found it necessary to work as governesses or tutors to support themselves as adults, and all three fared miserably in such positions. The necessity of the governess—a woman responsible for teaching and nurturing children—also emphasized the status of child care as labor, a job too onerous for a middle-class wife to manage without help. This disturbing recognition might well be compounded by the sexual threat, implicit or explicit, represented by the governess, whose presence in the household challenged the wife's monogamous sexual claim on her husband. Numerous writers since Brontë have depicted the governess as a figure whose educative role does not mitigate her disruptive effect on the family. Often, as in Henry James's 1898 short story "The Turn of the Screw," the nameless first-person governess's excessive emotions—that is, her sexual hunger and rage at having to settle for half a life—cause her literally to disrupt the household in a style reminiscent of Bertha Mason Rochester.[26]

Though Brontë unsparingly depicts the humiliations and privations Jane undergoes as governess at Thornfield, she softens the implicit critique in two ways. First, at Marsh End, Brontë provides Jane with a teaching position that gives her a substantive authority and allows her to redress the inequities of her own experience as a student. Second, by endowing Jane with an inheritance, she reprieves not only Jane but also Diana and Mary Rivers from their duties as governesses. Jane is saved less through her own efforts than through the essentially conservative means of inheriting wealth, a tradition as old as Britain's feudal past. In Victorian England, earning as opposed to inheriting wealth was beginning to become socially acceptable for members of the middle class.

Jane's inheritance and her marriage to Rochester endow her with the class status of a Victorian wife, just as her adoption of Adèle Varens supplants Rochester's indifferent guardianship with a concerned, loving family. Jane also discovers a new branch of her own family—a definite improvement over the Reeds—inadvertently, literally by stumbling upon the Riverses. Social change in *Jane Eyre* can thus be said to come about as the result of nearly magical interventions that redress nonconformity with the comfort of traditional solutions.

Jane's inheritance of £20,000 comes from the British crown colony of Madeira, where her uncle John Eyre, like Bertha Mason Rochester's brother Richard, has made his fortune as a wine merchant. In the nineteenth century, Great Britain was expanding and consolidating a colonial empire so vast that it was no exaggeration to assert that "the sun never sets on the British empire."[27] Thus it is not surprising to find traces of imperialist thinking throughout *Jane Eyre.* The search for a home and a livelihood can be construed as an individual's attempt to "colonize" other people and places by discovering and absorbing them. Jane's geographical movements between the five major loci of her text (Gateshead, Lowood, Thornfield, Marsh End, Ferndean) assume the pattern of discovery, mastery, and annexation. Though Brontë accomplishes this subtly, unmistakable clues in the text suggest that Jane "conquers" the "inmates" of these locales and bends them to her will. Jane's self-conscious aura of self-effacement should not blind readers to the trail of deposed or destroyed enemies she leaves in her wake. John Reed and Mrs. Reed both meet with unhappy premature deaths; Brocklehurst is deposed from his position at Lowood when the epidemic is publicized; Eliza Reed consigns herself to "burial alive" in a convent and the blowsy Georgiana Reed is married to an exhausted nobleman; Blanche Ingram is jilted by Rochester; Bertha leaps to her death from Thornfield's third story; Rochester is permanently mutilated; and St. John Rivers "broils" to death in India, as his sisters predicted. Even friendly characters tend to die or to be frustrated in some manner connected with their relation to Jane: Helen Burns dies in the epidemic; Uncle Reed is dead before the novel begins and Uncle John dies of fever in Madeira; the lovely, virtuous and privileged Rosamond Oliver is spurned by St. John in favor of Jane.

The deaths and punishments visited upon those who interfere with her progress allow Jane to accomplish several things. First, the deaths or oustings of father figures help ensure Jane's physical survival, as in the cases of Uncle Reed and Uncle John Eyre, who provide her with money and a place to stay, and Brocklehurst, whose mother founded and endowed Lowood School. Second, the destruction of women, such as Bertha, Blanche, and Rosamond (as well as Rochester's former mistresses Clara, Céline, and Giacinta), clears the way for Jane's sexual conquests of Rochester and St. John Rivers. Third, the deaths or jiltings of Jane's female peers, such as Helen Burns, Eliza and Georgiana Reed, Blanche Ingram, and Bertha Mason Rochester, represent the elimination of unwanted options from Jane's life and implicitly confirm the correctness of her chosen path. Finally, the deaths and dismemberments of male peers, such as John Reed, St. John Rivers, and Edward Rochester, act as punishments for patriarchal tyranny. Each death or ousting represents the easing of an obstacle and opens a new territory ripe for Jane's exploration and assumption. (For example, when Jane returns to Gateshead to attend Mrs. Reed on her deathbed, she supplants Georgiana and Eliza as a manager of crisis and as the virtuous forgiver of her aunt's concentrated, obsessive hatred, which itself constitutes a profound kind of attention.) The pattern of Jane's assumption of eminent domain is subtle but striking. Even when she seems weakest, as when she is punished for striking John Reed, or unhorses Rochester on Hay Lane, or begs for succor at Marsh End, Jane's entry into a scene always presages a later conquest. Typically she does not triumph on her first attempt but through perseverance reveals that she has made a conquest by becoming "first girl of the first class" (chap. 10, p. 73) or mistress or benefactress of every place to which she travels. Thus the "governess" gradually rises to the position of "governor"; by the end of the novel, Jane has produced both a narrative and a son, has handsomely rewarded her friends, observed the punishment of her foes, and miraculously restored the eyesight of a damaged patriarch. The pattern casts a disturbing light on Jane's triumphant march. Though she does not deliberately seek to destroy her enemies, her ascension mirrors Great Britain's march of empire—the annexation of foreign lands, the establishment of colonies, the imposition of governments, and the assumption of resources in every part of the world.

The allusions to the expansion of empire are not restricted to the level of personal conquest. *Jane Eyre* abounds with references to England's colonies and the problematic riches plundered by their conquerors.[28] John Eyre, the mysterious uncle who endows Jane with his fortune, may have been named for the British colonial officer John Eyre (1815–1901), governor of New Zealand at the time Brontë wrote *Jane Eyre* and an extreme advocate of colonialist expansion. In the 1860s, some 15 years after the publication of *Jane Eyre,* the severity of Eyre's methods for quashing workers' rebellions in the Caribbean led British intellectuals to accuse him of murder. By naming Jane's benefactor John Eyre and by possibly naming Jane herself for this political figure ("Jane" is the feminine of "John"), Brontë seems to telegraph unequivocal approval of imperialism, a theme that is certainly familiar from Branwell's and her Glass Town saga.

But *Jane Eyre* also communicates the anxieties Britons felt about the dubious boons extracted from the colonies. Bertha's embodiment of unspeakable passions emblematizes these anxieties. Because she is unable to tell her own story, the reader must settle for Rochester's version of events while keeping in mind that he has often been duplicitous in his dealings with Jane. (Jean Rhys's novella *Wide Sargasso Sea* attempts to redress Brontë's silencing of Bertha by presenting Bertha's story from her own viewpoint.)[29] Rochester explains that his father and brother conspired to trick him into marriage. As a younger son, Rochester initially stood to inherit little from his family, and Bertha was both sexually alluring and wealthy, with a dowry of £30,000. After the wedding, however, Rochester tells Jane, he quickly recognized Bertha's combination of a "pygmy intellect" and "giant propensities," the passionate appetites conservative Britons felt marked all colonial subjects as inferior, "savage," "animal." "Intemperate and unchaste," Bertha disgraced him publicly throughout their early married life in the West Indies, until a vision of freedom inspired him to have "the maniac" transported to England and immured in the attic of Thornfield. Rochester, meanwhile, traveled to the Continent and indulged himself with a series of European mistresses (chap. 27, pp. 273–75).

Although Rochester gratefully accepted Bertha's dowry (which ironically became superfluous when he inherited the family estate on his brother's untimely death), Rochester was unable to live with Bertha either in the West Indies or in England. The "boon" of his conquest could not compensate him for the "uprising of the natives" that Bertha's behavior seemed to signify. Yet Bertha horrified Rochester less because of her foreignness than because she reminded him of his own "giant propensities;" he was every bit as lustful, appetitive, duplicitous, and passionate as she. Throughout *Jane Eyre,* evil female characters, such as Bertha, Blanche, and even Mrs. Reed, possess the dark skin, voluptuous flesh, passionate emotion, and material acquisitiveness Britons felt marked colonial subjects as inferior. Yet the novel's central characters— Rochester and Jane—share these characteristics. Though Jane is "pale and little," she is nonetheless repeatedly described as a heathen who badly needs conversion, a racial outsider: a "Turk," a "rebel slave resolved to go all lengths," an "interloper not of [the Reeds'] own race" (chap. 1, p. 9; chap. 2, p. 13), a member of the loathsome "tribe," the "anathematized race" of governesses (chap. 17, p. 155).

The colonialism theme coalesces three central elements in *Jane Eyre*: the novel's problematizing of gender, of outsiderness, and of excessive passion. The chief "native" that is busy uprising in *Jane Eyre* is of course Jane herself, the Caliban-like "bad animal" of the opening chapters who feels "just as men feel" and struggles to find a place in a culture that discriminates freely on the basis of gender, citizenship, and social class. The difference between Jane and Bertha is that Jane throughout the novel allows others, even those like Mrs. Reed, whose values she repudiates, to "uproot her bad propensities" (chap. 3, p. 16). Jane is thus vulnerable to the influence of Helen Burns, who is arguably Brocklehurst's star pupil at self-abnegation, and after Helen's death spends her adolescence at Lowood learning to "master" herself until she is able to think "more harmonious thoughts: what seemed better-regulated feelings had become the inmates of my mind. I had given in allegiance to duty and order; I was quiet; I believed I was content: to the eyes of others, usually even to my own, I appeared a disciplined and subdued character" (chap. 10, p. 73). Such terms or phrases as "inmates," "given in allegiance to duty and order," and "disciplined and subdued" conjure the image of an enforced, military self-mastery that is undermined by the subjunctive "I believed" and "I appeared." Jane's self-mastery is illusory; she has repressed rather than eliminated the passions and appetites that will later trouble both her and Rochester. Rather than reject the machinations of a sadomasochistic "civilization" that abuses orphans and sells young people into marriage, these two central characters project their passionate outrage onto one who has no words to defend herself: the colonial subject.

Colonized subjects, as represented by characters as diverse as Jane and Bertha, are not totally victimized in *Jane Eyre*. As Bertha's repeated attempts to burn down Thornfield suggest, their retaliatory destructive power is considerable. St. John Rivers, like Edward Rochester, finds his fate in the colonies, but unlike Rochester, whose mission is to extract money from the colonies, St. John seeks to impose "civilization" on them: "My vocation? My great work? My foundation laid on earth for a mansion in heaven? My hopes of being numbered in the band who have merged all ambitions in the glorious one of bettering their race—of carrying knowledge into the realms of ignorance—of substituting peace for war—freedom for bondage—religion for superstition—the hope of heaven for the fear of hell?" (chap. 32, p. 329). St. John begins his imperialistic journey by "colonizing" Jane when first he convinces her to shift from studying German to studying Hindustani, the better to assist him in his missionary work (chap. 34, p. 349). Later, however, he is unsuccessful in manipulating her into accepting his proposal of marriage by threatening her with eternal damnation if she refuses (chap. 35, p. 364). This failure is followed by his destruction in India, which Jane anticipates in the closing paragraphs of her narrative. The binary oppositions of his creed, which attributes knowledge, peace, freedom, religion, and the hope of heaven to his own (British, Christian) ideology and ignorance, bondage, war, superstition, and the fear of eternal damnation to the Indian colonials, are belied in the metaphors of St. John's daily life, which ironically are rife with images of battle, violence, hellfire, and enslavement. Like Jane and Rochester, St. John has not rid himself of unruly emotions but simply projected them onto imaginary colonials; his lifework is shaped and ultimately thwarted by this denial.

Of all the novel's colonizers and colonized natives, Jane alone escapes destruction or mutilation, though her trials at the hands of those who are trying to colonize her (from the Reeds to St. John Rivers) are severe. Jane voices her creed in terms that can be described only as imperialistic when she tells Rochester of her plans for him: she says, "I am preparing myself to go out as a missionary to preach liberty to them that are enslaved—your harem inmates amongst the rest. I'll get admitted there, and I'll stir up mutiny, and you . . . shall find yourself fettered amongst our hands; nor will I . . . consent to cut your bonds till you have signed a charter, the most liberal that despot ever yet conferred" (chap. 24, p. 237). The duality of Brontë's presentation of imperialism—particularly her depiction of female characters as both colonizing and colonized—underscores the other ambiguities and tensions that emerge without being resolved throughout the text.

Psychoanalytical Interpretations

The phenomena of projection and denial that are the dominant tropes of imperialistic objectification are drawn not from politics but from psychoanalysis, a set of practices used to access the unconscious elements of a mind or a text. The first psychoanalytical critiques of *Jane Eyre* enlisted the tenets of the founder and first major practitioner of psychoanalysis, Sigmund Freud. Freud viewed all mental events, even such accidental and seemingly insignificant ones as dreams and slips of the tongue, as deliberately expressive and redolent with meaning. He theorized that each person had an unconscious mind directed by instinctual drives, which were often repressed (pushed back into the unconscious by the conscious mind) because they were not socially acceptable. Beginning in early childhood, the human personality develops in response to the imperative to sublimate such instinctive impulses through the process of learning. Freud's sketchy handling of female sexuality and psychology is often cited as one of his severest limitations as a theorist. It may be useful to think of him as much a describer of Victorian sexual arrangements as a theorist of human universals. Since a great deal of criticism of *Jane Eyre* has focused on Brontë's presentation of the difficulty of managing unacceptable desires and emotions, Freudian paradigms have helped explain the novel's tension between expression and suppression. Freud's division of consciousness into three spheres—the id, the ego, and the superego—has encouraged readers to view Brontë's bildungsroman as a novel of psychic as well as emotional and intellectual education. The novel presents Jane as gradually developing an ability to mediate between the superego and the id—what she calls "the extremes of absolute submission and determined revolt" (chap. 34, p. 352). As we have seen, certain characters, such as Helen Burns and Bertha Mason Rochester, serve to embody the fragmentation Jane experiences when she is forced to suppress and repress strong emotion.

Mid-twentieth-century critics, notably Richard Chase, have used Freudian frameworks to critique the novel's feminism, depicting Brontë as a young woman struggling to master the overpowering sexuality of older men and going so far as to castrate Rochester symbolically (when he is injured in the Thornfield fire) in order to tame him. In Chase's view, Jane's preservation of her integrity is achieved at the cost of Rochester's, which Chase essentializes as sexual potency.[30]

Freud's onetime colleague Carl Jung focused less on the influence of sexuality than on the primacy of myth and its influence on the individual's unconscious. *Jane Eyre*'s complex vacillation between paganism and Christianity (or Christianities) seems to express Jane's psychological state, which is so dynamic that it resists classification under a single rubric. The metaphors of blood, mother, and moon alone (with their complex religious as well as physiological resonances) have offered Jungian critics an opportunity to read *Jane Eyre* as a mythic story, a melding of pantheistic and monotheistic religious motifs that is challenging in its complexity. Some, pointing to Jane's miraculous redemption by supernatural voices emerging in consonance with the moon, have found in *Jane Eyre* an affirmation of maternal religions, with Diana and Mary Rivers serving as symbols of the pagan and Christian "great mothers" (the Greek goddess Diana and the Virgin Mary), whose wisdom directs Jane's path—she is attracted to Moor House when she sees them through the window; they advise her against marrying St. John; they are among the few characters in the novel who are permitted uncomplicated happiness and prosperity at closure. Another possibility is to consider *Jane Eyre* in light of the myth of Demeter and Kore, in which Jane is viewed as a kidnapped child separated from her mother who is abducted into an underworld where her integrity is repeatedly violated and where she is kept against her will. Only when she is released from this pattern of servitude with the assistance of her "mother" can the earth flourish and nature return to its rightful state. Equally convincing are readings that analyze Jane's development as a scapegoat, a figure equally prophetic and despised who bears the negativity of a larger group and is sacrificed to relieve the group's collective guilt. Jane's development from a scapegoat in the novel's early scenes (as a child at Gateshead and at Lowood, and as a governess at Thornfield) is marked by a sudden transformation: after leaving Thornfield, she manages to avoid further blame for others' transgressions; one could argue that at this point, Bertha and other characters assume the role in her place.

The French psychoanalyst Jacques Lacan sought to revise Freud's theories by theorizing the relationship between language and psyche.[31] His famous assertion that "the unconscious is structured like a language" owes much to Freud's theory of oedipal development: the prelinguistic child, Lacan argues, dwells in an "Imaginary" in which the child believes itself to be one with its mother and perceives no separation between itself and the world. In the Imaginary, there is no difference and no absence, only identity and presence. The child's eventual oedipal crisis precipitates the subject into the world of the Symbolic Order—a world characterized by such figurative systems as language and law, in which the child perceives another competitive being as a threat.

Jane Eyre, whose narrative teems with metaphors of limitation and threat, seems to have been precipitated abruptly into the Symbolic Order, like Carroll's Alice after she falls into the rabbit hole. Note that in the opening scene and throughout the narrative, Jane looks at and draws pictures rather than reading and writing, which reveals her status as being on the cusp of transformation from the Imaginary to the Symbolic Order. Throughout the narrative, she defines herself in opposition to various inadequate mother figures such as Mrs. Reed, Miss Temple, and Mrs. Fairfax, who affect her development but are powerless because of their position in patriarchy to forestall the sense of fragmentation Lacan argues is inevitable. In addition, several direct challenges by malevolent patriarchs shake her sense of existence right down to the ground. This process begins when John Reed tells Jane, "You have no business to take our books; you are a dependent, mamma says; you have no money; your father left you none; you ought to beg, and not live here with gentlemen's children like us. . . . Now, I'll teach you to rummage my bookshelves: for they are mine; all the house belongs to me, or will do in a few years" (chap. 2, p. 8). When John then throws the book at Jane, cutting her forehead, she responds both verbally, by quoting historical example, comparing him to the sadistic Roman emperors Nero and Caligula, and nonverbally, in a way that cannot even be revealed in the text: "I don't know very well what I did with my hands, but he called me 'Rat! rat!' and bellowed out loud" (chap. 2, p. 9). Since Lacan refers to the phallus as the "transcendental signifier" of masculine privilege, the possibility that Jane is engaging literally in below-the-belt pugilistics is provocative. Jane's confusion in this scene, and in subsequent scenes when language is deployed to deceive or subdue her, reveals her difficulty in negotiating the symbolic order that clearly does not serve her best interests.

Though she gains a brief reprieve when Mr. Lloyd, the apothecary, pays her the great psychic boon of soliciting and believing her story (chap. 3), she learns that women of all stripes are generally silent: Miss Temple and Helen accept even unjust criticism without protest, and Mrs. Fairfax and Bertha Mason Rochester, who exhibit two extremes of female behavior, are incapable of telling Jane the stories Rochester reveals only after his hand has been forced. Jane's development can be traced, if anywhere, in her gradual assumption of control over the truth value of narratives of her life. Jane's assumption of control eventually culminates in the accurate narrative of her life delivered by an unknowing servant as she stands before the burned shell of Thornfield (chap. 36, pp. 374–78), which reveals how far the little girl, who was unable to make people believe her version of events, has come in enforcing others' acceptance and iteration of her role and viewpoint. This episode also links Jane implicitly to Homer's epic hero Odysseus, whose return to Ithaca after 10 years' absence follows a similar pattern. Later she shows her complete control of language and of the circumstances it shapes by making Rochester the object of her statement "Reader, I married him" (chap. 38, p. 395).

Though by choosing to write fiction Brontë seems to have eschewed political analysis, and though the novel's politics are not necessarily coherent, her novel nonetheless has been viewed since its publication as a critique of its culture. The novel's richness continues to lie in its multivalence—its simultaneously radical and conservative energies, its melding of apparently incompatible elements, the way it transforms familiar elements and genres. In *Villette* Charlotte Brontë would take the same story and retell it in a radically different way. The years spanning the gap between *Jane Eyre* and *Villette* were filled with personal tragedy for Brontë, who witnessed the deaths of her three remaining siblings and found her consequent loneliness almost impossible to bear. Her waning confidence in fairy-tale solutions is reflected in *Villette*'s uncompromising depiction of the lonely vigil of a woman who regards all social attachments with justifiable suspicion.

Chapter Five

"How to Endure without a Sob": *Shirley*

Introduction

In writing her third novel, *Shirley,* published in 1849, Brontë imaginatively revisited the scene of her father's involvement with the angry Luddite risings in the Yorkshire woolen district during the 1820s. The only novel not to originate directly out of her own life experiences, *Shirley* was not the successful follow-up to *Jane Eyre* that either Brontë or her publishers hoped it would be. Written during and after the deaths of her three surviving siblings and during a period of great social unrest in England and in Europe, *Shirley* was criticized before and after it was published for lacking unity. Her publishers futilely attempted to shape the novel during its composition along the lines of *Jane Eyre,* but the novel was not well reviewed after its publication. In fact, one of the earliest published reviews, written by George Henry Lewes, injured Brontë so badly that she burst out, "I can be on guard against my enemies, but God deliver me from my friends!" (*SHB LFC* iii, 67). In a letter to her publisher W. S. Williams (January 1850) she went further: "[The review] is very brutal and savage. I am not angry with Lewes, but I wish in future he would leave me alone, and not write what makes me feel so cold and sick" (p. 66). Lewes's "brutal and savage" attack reads in part:

> Again we say that *Shirley* cannot be received as a work of art. It is not a picture; but a portfolio of random sketches for one or more pictures. The authoress never seems distinctly to have made up her mind as to what she was to do; whether to describe the habits and manners of Yorkshire and its social aspects in the days of King Lud, or to paint a character, or to tell a love story. All are by turns attempted and abandoned; and the book consequently moves slowly, and by starts—leaving behind it no distinct or satisfactory impression. (Allott, *The Critical Heritage,* 165)

This criticism—that the novel is confused and ineffectively torn between the public and the private—determined the tone for much of the critical discussion for the next hundred years.

But set against Lewes's complaints is the early assessment published by Eugene Forcade, a Frenchman who detected what he saw as the novel's feminist concern:

> The cause of women is defended throughout the book with a conviction and skill characteristic of those who are pleading their own cause. As a picture of society the novel could have been called *Shirley, or the condition of women in the English middle class.* (Allott, *The Critical Heritage,* 143)

For Forcade, the novel displayed the combined qualities of what he called "rational" feminism, "a morality inspired by a powerful and exuberant individualism" and based on the writings of Mary Wollstonecraft, coupled with what he called "romantic" feminism, "a spirit of insubordination" and an endorsement of "the absolute legitimacy of desire" (p. 146).

This mixed feminist sympathy appears in the novel in the very different characters of Shirley Keeldar, an aristocratic, gifted, and proud woman, the heiress of Fieldhead Hall, and Caroline Helstone, a meek and dispossessed orphan living with her widowed, unsympathetic uncle. Although the two women appear to be vastly different temperamentally and intellectually, they end up married to two brothers, essentially functioning as mirrored doubles of each other. We might observe that when Shirley constructs her alternate visions of Eve/nature/woman (chap. 18, pp. 320–21), she is expressing romantic and protofeminist visions of women that would appear to be repudiated by the conventional marriages that both Shirley and her double Caroline make by the novel's conclusion. The split in the text between its quasifeminist aspirations and its seeming endorsement of middle-class realities for women has formed the central contested issue in the recent feminist reappraisals of the novel's value and stature.

There is finally a good deal of pain—both social and personal—in *Shirley,* and for that reason alone the novel can fruitfully be examined as another example of Brontë's attempt to rewrite and reshape her personal pains and frustrations in her fiction. In the story of a young woman who magically recovers her long-missing mother, we can see all too clearly how desperately Brontë continued to feel the wound of her own mother's death, which she experienced as a form of desertion that she could transform endlessly in her fiction, this time as a literal return. And in her castigation in the novel of corrupt curates and a complaisant, established church, we can see Brontë's own frustration with her father's religious status as curate of a sleepy and isolated parish that failed to appreciate his talents. Finally, the double wedding that concludes the novel—which matches idealized doubled heroines, who remarkably resemble both Anne and Emily Brontë, with two brothers who themselves remarkably resemble the Crimsworth brothers—is evidence of Brontë's fantasy wish fulfillment. Resurrecting and revising her dead sisters, making them strong and desirable, and then marrying them off to idealized brothers—keeping all her siblings, real and imagined, within a fictitiously extended family—was a desperate, imaginative act of recovery. When Brontë confessed to W. S. Williams (17 September 1849) that she had consulted no one in writing *Shirley* and that its composition had come completely out of the "silent workshop of [her] own brain" (*SHB LFC* iii, 21), she revealed the very personal sources for a novel that aspires to a large and sweeping religious, social, and political agenda. The personal, however, is never far below the surface.

Realism and Romance

The conflict between the impulse toward realism and the resurgence of romance is a standard critical issue in Brontë criticism, and the text of *Shirley* is perhaps one of the most explicit examples of that conflict. Brontë begins the novel in a tone of angry satire that is more pronounced than it had been in her two earlier novels. Describing a "shower of curates" who have fallen on the British countryside like so much snow, rain, or sleet, she effectively begins her work in a tone of social and religious criticism, which she consistently uses throughout the novel when describing the failure of the established Anglican church to mediate or reform the social ills that led directly to the mill riots during the 1820s.

The novel's very next paragraph, its second, appears to mock Brontë's readers' literary expectations by warning them not to expect the sort of emotional fireworks that were delivered by the same author in *Jane Eyre:*

> If you think, from this prelude, that anything like a romance is preparing
> for you, reader, you never were more mistaken. Do you anticipate senti-

ment, and poetry, and reverie? Do you expect passion, and stimulus, and melodrama? Calm your expectations; reduce them to a lowly standard. Something real, cool, and solid, lies before you; something unromantic as Monday morning, when all who have work wake with the consciousness that they must rise and betake themselves thereto.[1]

Brontë forces her reader, then, to focus on the oppositional meanings of *realism* and *romance* right from the beginning of the novel, a dichotomy that allows her to question the validity and institutionalization of the patriarchal values we define as "realism" and "reality."[2] The public, or "real," aspects of *Shirley* can be found largely in the novel's focus on Robert Moore, a half-British, half-Belgian mill owner who attempts to maximize his profits by replacing his workers, mostly children, with machinery. The struggle by the working classes to hold on to their precarious livelihoods in the midst of rapid economic transformation is just one of the major public issues Brontë attempts to explore in this work, a novel she researched largely through reading newspaper accounts of the mill riots in *Leed's Mercury* from 1811 through 1814.

In addition to warning the new class of British industrialists—like Moore—that they would destroy the fabric of their society through rapid and inhumane technological application, Brontë also issues warnings to the clergy, largely the established Anglican church, that it faces real threats to its power from the dissenting denominations— Methodists, Baptists, and Antinomians—unless it makes its worship more inclusive and less class bound. The fact that a mad Antinomian weaver eventually shoots and almost kills Robert Moore brings together the two public strands—the economic and the religious—of this novel in a starkly threatening and violent manner.

Set against the economic and religious concerns are the love stories of the novel's two heroines—Shirley Keeldar and Caroline Helstone—who both undergo protracted and painful hunger strikes in their quests to marry the men of their choice. Caroline is in love with her cousin Robert Moore, and Shirley loves his brother Louis, also her former French tutor, who is currently in the employ of her wealthy and snobbish uncle. Louis Moore is in many ways a masculinized governess figure; he is treated like a dispossessed servant and generally is despised by Shirley's wealthy family, the Sympsons.

Intermingled with the love story of the women and the Moore brothers is the strangely wish-fulfilling story of Caroline's rediscovery of her long-lost mother, who abandoned Caroline as a small girl because she was a beauty who appeared to physically resemble her evil, alcoholic father. Brontë's own extreme prejudice against female beauty, her virtually pathological suspicion of physically attractive women, is evidenced in this irrational and extremely unconvincing explanation. Mrs. Pryor, Caroline's mother, who has spent her life as a governess and is now a companion to Shirley, reappears and identifies herself just as Caroline is sinking into death, which has been induced by her futile and initially unrequited passion for Robert Moore.

The novel oscillates continually between realism and romance, public and private issues, in a way that has frustrated readers and caused the work to be considered Brontë's least successful published novel. For instance, when Shirley arrives on the scene it would seem that we have been introduced to a figure who can mediate between the female/private world and the male/public world. Although Shirley and Caroline hold intimate private conversations with a variety of male characters and attempt to be a part of the male/public world, largely they encounter a variety of frustrations in these attempts, for instance during the Whitsuntide march or during their observation of the attack on Moore's mill. The latter event causes Shirley to advise Caroline that men simply will not tolerate women meddling in their business or observing their mishaps. In other words, women can be passive observers of the public realm but not equal participants in its activities.

Conflicts between public and private life are also illustrated by Robert Moore's near-fatal shooting. This event occurs as Robert appears to be working toward some form of humanitarian reform in his mill and thus suggests that he may never be able to achieve the changes he envisions. The wound, however, also places him in a position of solitary isolation, analogous to Caroline's experience with her hunger and fever, from which he, like Caroline, learns to recognize emotional inadequacies in himself in a way he has never had to before. Robert succumbed earlier in the novel to the lure of having power over his workers and thus deceived himself into believing that the welfare of his employees was unimportant, that Shirley loved him, and that marriage to her would be prudent for him because it would be economically profitable.

However, Robert's purely economic vision of reality is questioned throughout the text by an alternate feminist reality embodied in the allusions to fairies, Sleeping Beauty, and Rapunzel. After the shooting Robert is described as being a sort of male Sleeping Beauty imprisoned in Yorke's mansion and held captive by Mrs. Horsfall, a nurse who subjects him to the same isolation and deprivation Caroline felt earlier in the novel. These fairy-tale aspects conclude with an almost magical transformation: Martin Yorke sneaks Caroline into the Yorke household disguised as a "wood nymph" (chap. 32), and she helps Robert regain his sense of himself as a man rather than a machine. In committing this act of heroism, Caroline causes Robert to arrive at a new understanding of her and the values she represents. The feminist reality of fairy-tale motifs and devices suggests that the marriages of Louis and Shirley and Robert and Caroline represent man's education into a new-world feminist reality. Brontë would appear, therefore, to have reversed or at least complicated the dichotomy between romance and reality in this novel.

The "Woman Question"

G. H. Lewes, the notorious early reviewer of *Shirley,* saved his most painful thrust for the end of his review, when he quoted Schiller's reaction after reading Madame de Stael's *Corinne* (1807): "This person wants every thing that is graceful in a woman; and, nevertheless, the faults of her book are altogether womanly faults. She steps out of her sex—without elevating herself above it" (Allott, *The Critical Heritage,* 169). Lewes applied this condescending evaluation to *Shirley,* and to add insult to injury he claimed,

> Currer Bell: for she, too, has genius enough to create a great name for herself; and if we seem to have insisted too gravely on her faults, it is only because we are ourselves sufficiently her admirers to be more desirous to see her remove these blemishes from her writings, and take the rank within her reach. She has extraordinary power—but let her remember that *"on tombe du côte ou l'on penche!"* [*one falls from one's perch*]. (pp. 169–70)

This review was one of the first to definitively identify Currer Bell as a woman and to begin the process by which her writing was judged according to established "womanly" standards. Brontë herself chafed under this standard, defiantly asking why her writing could not be accepted without the constant querying into her sex. Her personal frustration over this issue is evidenced throughout *Shirley*'s text in the various limited and limiting options that all the women in the novel— Shirley, Caroline, the Yorke women, Mary Cave, Mrs. Pryor, the "old maids"—have to confront and finally negotiate. In the final analysis, however, *Shirley* seems to endorse a romantic feminism embodied in Shirley's visions of Eve and of Mother Nature, although these high-flown metaphysics are, as we have noted, undercut by the novel's ambivalent conclusion.

Romantic feminism and its affirmation of the individualism of liberal England are illustrated in the fates of the doubled heroines Caroline and Shirley. In part their destinies are written according to the theories of Rousseau; Caroline is the less tolerant of romantic, or Rousseauist, characteristics and values and chooses practicality, whereas Shirley stands as the English version of a Rousseauist woman of genius who voices her dreams in her vision of Eve as earth mother. Mrs. Pryor's "masculine" act of abandoning her child out of moral revulsion for the father becomes a protofeminist act of conscience, and Caroline's search for friendships with the two "old maids," Miss Mann and Miss Ainley, as well as her earned respect from the girls she teaches, reveal her to possess incipient feminist sympathies.[3]

In *Shirley* the role of women as educators is emphasized in order to actively criticize the clergy who are concerned with little but their own consumption of food at a variety of superficial social gatherings. As a result some curates, like Malone and Donne, must be punished in the text, whereas others, such as Hall and Helstone, are a study in contrasts or are representations of what the clergy should and should not be. Rev. Hall shows proper concern and nurturing for the members of his parish, regardless of class or sex, whereas Rev. Helstone possesses a more distant and ineffective relationship with his parish.

The central focus of *Shirley,* then, is the "woman question" posed through a nationalist—social, political, economic—context. The novel uses two important literary conventions in order to structure feminist themes: the role reversal that places Shirley in the position of squire of Briarfield and the revision of the tradition of paired heroines, one representing sense and the other sensibility. The good squire figure first appeared in Richardson's *Sir Charles Grandison,* a major source for *Shirley;* in Richardson's book the hero adopts virtues normally ascribed to a heroine and illustrates the true gentleman's duty to secure women their rightful societal place. Brontë goes a step further by reversing the roles and giving Shirley the power to secure Louis's proper place in society. *Sir Charles Grandison* also provides an influential English version of the motif of the paired heroines that eventually became an important device for nineteenth-century women writers as a result of its use by Madame de Stael in *Corinne.* The scheme of paired heroines, which appears in realist works before *Corinne* and after *Sir Charles Grandison,* examines the head/heart question when the sensible heroine mentors the heroine of sensibility. In the case of *Shirley,* the emphasis is on the more decidedly romantic heroine, Shirley.[4]

Another issue involved in the "woman question" concerns the limited options that women have in a society that offers them little scope for their activities beyond marriage. Brontë had already addressed this topic directly in *Jane Eyre;* in *Shirley* she examines the question in relation to Caroline Helstone's dearth of meaningful possibilities. In *Shirley* Brontë explores the idea that the status of women in bourgeois society can be found only in their labor and in the products of that labor.[5] For Caroline, who has no skills and therefore creates no work of her own, labor is an absent signifier; she tries to pursue purposeful work through her teaching or her sewing, but even she realizes the limited nature of both actions. Caroline initially sees labor as a "release from mental anguish," or a way to keep her from thinking about Robert Moore. Caroline proposes to Shirley and Mrs. Pryor that she could become a governess in order to find some purpose, some meaning to her life besides her futile unrequited longing for Robert:

> And what am I—standing here in shadow, shrinking into concealment, my mind darker than my hiding-place? I am one of this world, no spirit—a poor, doomed mortal, who asks, in ignorance and hopelessness, wherefore she was born, to what end she lives; whose mind for ever runs on the questions, how she shall at last encounter, and by whom, be sustained through death? (chap. 13, p. 235)

One of the central questions in the text is posed by Shirley to Caroline: " 'Can labour alone make a human being happy?' " (chap. 12, p. 229); Caroline responds, " 'No, but it can give varieties of pain' " (chap. 12, p. 229). And sadly, seeking "varieties of pain" would appear to be the best option for a woman with Caroline's limited choices. Her work toward self-actualization is negative: it alternates between the work of distraction and the work of construction. She imagines her release to come not from within herself but through death. Caroline places all her psychic and emotional energy into her relationship with Robert Moore, and when he rejects her she sees herself as rejected goods, his inferior. Her dependence on Robert for her very existence not only leaves her unable to find identity outside of that relationship but also forces her to internalize that rejection by self-consciously adopting the style and mannerisms of an old maid—almost in parodic form—in order to fill the time until her death.

Caroline questions the value of "resignation of self" (chap. 10, p. 174) when she realizes that she may be facing the fate of being an "old maid." She says to herself in desperation, " 'I have to live, perhaps, till seventy years. As far as I know, I have good health: half a century of existence may lie before me. How am I to occupy it? What am I to do to fill the interval of time which spreads between me and the grave?' " (chap. 10, p. 173). And although she attempts to resolve the ambiguities of her status as an unmarried woman, she would appear to be aided by friends who help her develop her character. Her friendship with Shirley allows Caroline the freedom of self-expression seen in the liberation that Caroline finds in their walks. These walks produce a friendship that allows Caroline to think momentarily that there can be life apart from Robert Moore. For Caroline, Shirley exemplifies a nearly self-defined single woman because of her economic independence, ancestral roots (unlike Caroline, she at least knows who her parents are), and class. These factors provide a security for Shirley that is impossible for Caroline, and their companionship provides Caroline with a means to independence of action and thought.

One of the high points of female-identified sympathy occurs when Shirley presents her alternative visions of nature and Eve to the theologically unsophisticated Caroline. Following Shirley's example, Caroline refuses to enter the church at Whitsuntide, and Shirley offers instead an alternative to the Christian concepts of women: first a portrait of nature, then of Eve, then of a female Titan. In her description of nature, Shirley worships an ancient female fertility source:

> Nature is now at her evening prayers: she is kneeling before those red hills. I see her prostrate on the great steps of her altar, praying for a fair night for mariners at sea, for travellers in deserts, for lambs on moors, and unfledged birds in woods. Caroline, I see her! and I will tell you what she is like: she is like what Eve was when she and Adam stood alone on earth. (chap. 18, p. 319)

Shirley makes it clear to Caroline that she is not describing Milton's Eve, who was basically no more than his cook, but a more powerful and primitive force, the source of all life:

> I would beg to remind [Milton] that the first men of the earth were Titans, and that Eve was their mother: from her sprang Saturn, Hyper-

ion, Oceanus; she bore Prometheus. . . . I say, there were giants on earth
in those days: giants that strove to scale heaven. The first woman's breast
that heaved with life on this world yielded the daring which could con-
tend with Omnipotence: the strength which could bear a thousand years
of bondage,—the vitality which could feed that vulture death through
uncounted ages,—the unexhausted life and uncorrupted excellence, sisters to immortality, which, after millenniums of crimes, struggles, and
woes, could conceive and bring forth a Messiah. The first woman was
heaven-born: vast was the heart whence gushed the well-spring of the
blood of nations; and grand the undegenerate head where rested the
consort-crown of creation. (chap. 18, p. 320)

This grand and gigantic female force becomes the feminine deity, the
source of all life and growth, that Shirley encourages Caroline to
embrace rather than the weak and pale shadow of a woman proffered by
traditional and conventional Christianity. In her strongest visionary
statement, Shirley describes this female force as a Titan:

I saw—I now see—a woman-Titan: her robe of blue air spreads to the
outskirts of the hearth, where yonder flock is grazing; a veil white as an
avalanche sweeps from her head to her feet, and arabesques of lightning
flame of its borders. Under her breast I see her zone, purple like that
horizon: through its blush shines the star of evening. Her steady eyes I
cannot picture; they are clear—they are deep as lakes—they are lifted
and full of worship—they tremble with the softness of love and the lustre
of prayer. Her forehead has the expanse of a cloud, and is paler than the
early moon, risen long before dark gathers: she reclines her bosom on the
ridge of Stilbro' Moor; her mighty hands are joined beneath it. So kneel-
ing, face to face she speaks with God. That Eve is Jehovah's daughter, as
Adam was his son. (chap. 18, p. 321)

In spite of these rhetorical dramatics, however, Caroline and Shirley
cannot entirely escape the influence of Christian dogma. Shortly after
these declamations and their escape from the church, they are confronted with the antediluvian attitudes of Joe Scott, amateur theologian,
who tells the two that women, like children, should be seen and not
heard in church. Caroline responds to Joe's extremist reading of I Timo-
thy 2:11 with an equally extremist reading based on historical context
and mistranslation, and she suggests that the passage says the opposite
of Joe's interpretation:

[St. Paul] wrote that chapter for a particular congregation of Christians, under peculiar circumstances; and besides, I dare say, if I could read the original Greek, I should find that many of the words have been wrongly translated, perhaps misapprehended altogether. It would be possible, I doubt not, with a little ingenuity, to give the passage quite a contrary turn; to make it say, "Let the woman speak out whenever she sees fit to make an objection,"—"it is permitted to a woman to teach and to exercise authority as much as may be. Man, meantime, cannot do better than hold his peace," and so on. (chap. 18, pp. 329–30)

Shirley castigates Joe's religious views as a form of "primogeniture." Later she is more explicit in her condemnation of Joe's opinions: " 'You might as well say, men are to take the opinions of their priests without examination. Of what value would a religion so adopted be? It would be mere blind, besotted superstition" (chap. 18, p. 329). Clearly Brontë is attempting to unify her emphasis on social issues—in this case, religion—with the personal effects they have produced on individual women's lives.[6]

Political and Religious Criticism

Critics have consistently argued that *Shirley* lacks unity or a clear and consistent relationship between public and private themes. One early review in the *Westminster Review* (January 1850) compared *Shirley* to *Mary Barton,* claiming that both are "laid in the manufacturing districts, and the wrongs and rights of mill-owners and their operatives form the subsidiary parts of the story. In treating of these questions, a discriminating and a kindly spirit is evinced, with a manifold desire to heal the antagonism of classes; and we are glad to notice generally this great improvement in modern works of fiction" (Allott, *The Critical Heritage,* 159). But many other readers were not pleased with the social and religious criticism that Brontë proffered in *Shirley,* and those who wanted her to write another emotional and personally focused novel like *Jane Eyre* were severely disappointed by her foray into realpolitik.

Brontë points to English national selfishness as the corrupter of patriotism and honor in favor of material profit and confronts those so unconcerned with humanity, namely businessmen, that they have adopted methods of mechanized production at their workers' expense. The tie between society and human beings is severed when there is a conflict between business and labor, Whig and Tory, care for profit and care for human feeling, or the maintenance of artificial class barriers. In mid-nineteenth-century England, each person, whether businessman or worker, was concerned solely with his or her own interests and viewed everyone else as an instrument or machine to be used for profit.[7] Like the businessman's use of the worker as machine, the upper class used the lower class as though they were not human. This argument is made explicitly by Lady Sympson, who insists that the maintenance of upper-class purity depends on those within its ranks to keep a distance from the hired help—whether governess or tutor.

But Brontë also develops the idea that political affiliation has failed to produce an effective form of human sensitivity that in turn can foster social concerns. Neither Caroline's Tory uncle, who believes in women's inferiority, nor the "liberal" Hiram Yorke, who espouses nonthreatening equality, possesses sympathy for those in less fortunate positions, namely women and exploited workers. Both men are proud and self-righteous toward others, largely because of their class privileges. Utilitarianism—or what is simply called "selfishness" in the novel—ultimately defines everything from marriage to political and religious beliefs in this society. As William Farren, the displaced worker, tells Caroline and Shirley, "Human natur'. . . is nought but selfishness. It is but excessive few; it is but just an exception here and there . . . that being in a different sphere, can understand t'one t'other, and be friends wi'out slavishness o' one hand, or pride o' t'other" (chap. 18, p. 326).

In this society marriage is not an emotionally based arrangement unless it can be of some profitable interest, and the mutual antipathy between the sexes is revealed by Rev. Helstone's "admiration" for unintelligent women and by Caroline and Robert's lack of sympathy for each other. Robert personifies the sort of selfishness that Brontë believes destroys human values and care for people. Business and profit consume Robert's very existence, from his adoption of Whig politics as support for his business interests to his refusal of personal relationships, such as marriage, unless they too prove to be a good business proposition. As he tells Hiram Yorke,

> "I am not in a position to be dreaming of marriage. Marriage! I cannot bear the word: it sounds so silly and utopian. I have settled it decidedly that marriage and love are superfluities, intended only for the rich, who live at ease, and have no need to take thought for the morrow, or desperations, the last and reckless joy of the deeply wretched, who never hope to rise out of the slough of their utter poverty." (chap. 9, p. 164)

However, Robert Moore is not the only one affected by a selfish society. His brother, Louis Moore, despised tutor to the Sympson family, is denied his humanity by his position in a family that barely acknowledges his existence. Louis's attitudes are partially to blame for his social isolation. He represses his feelings out of pride, out of his fear of seeming needy, or in the case of his love for Shirley, out of his fear of rejection by her. This false pride causes misunderstandings and erects barriers of wealth and class that make love almost impossible for him. But Brontë also suggests that the realities of wealth and class generate distorted personalities and feelings in all human beings who are falsely socialized into selfishness and thereby corrupted by such a culture.

Louis and Robert, however, are not the only characters motivated by false pride and class concerns. Shirley also has great pride in herself as the mistress of a great estate; she is a sort of substitute man, lord of the manor, who rules because there is no male heir. This pride makes her insensitive to and ignorant of the feelings and character of her companion Mrs. Pryor, whom she berates for not opening Fieldhead. She also has a tendency to isolate herself from others, as when she refuses to admit her need for help when bitten by the dog Phoebe. Her pride, which causes her to be unsure of Louis's feelings for her, forces her to approach him in a courtship that is oddly mixed of about equal parts of disdain and humility.

Caroline, who appears to possess little pride, can be perceived as a societal victim, an orphan of sorts without knowledge of her mother and relegated to living with an uncle who sees her as a woman he does not need or want to appreciate or respect as an equal. Her place as a respectable woman leaves her with no active duties to perform and no one to understand her. She must remain silent and avoid expressing her love for Robert openly. Caroline's story brings the social and private themes together. Her dreaded spinsterhood placed within and against this contemporary social background makes her a societal victim, symbolic of all classes and peoples who live their lives at the mercy of those who elevate self-interest above all else.

Typically, Brontë suggests that societal salvation lies in balancing the demands of the public and the private life and can be achieved only through the rejection of reserve and pride in favor of sensitivity to others. Robert Moore learns this lesson by seeing the living conditions of the poor and by experiencing Shirley's rejection of his marriage proposal. Not only does Shirley help him reassess his view of marriage and see what is important in such a relationship but she also crushes his pride. Louis and Shirley are also transformed. They attempt to establish a relationship of equals devoid of wealth and class. Shirley asks for Louis's help and relinquishes her prominent position so that Louis can dominate her, which he does when he abandons his pride and proposes. Brontë is able to conclude the novel with the merging of history and private life and thus indicates that the story continues after the book's conclusion. She continues to point to a better society modeled on individual change; she optimistically tries to connect the end of the war to an eradication of individual selfishness.

Although *Shirley* appears to endorse the established church on the surface, the novel places the ideas of political radicalism and religious dissent in a feminist context in which the middle-class woman—either Caroline or Shirley—refuses to embrace Christianity on grounds more intrinsic than orthodoxy or doctrine. As a result the established church is undermined. This feminist dissent is expressed in a threefold way: first, through the questioning of Christianity's views of women; second, through a critique of the nature of Christianity itself; and third, through an alternative view of religion and human nature in which the ability to dissent is expressed positively.[8]

In "The Valley of the Shadow of Death" (chap. 24), the narrator implies that Christianity is the cause of women's problems. This idea emerges in the commentary on the future as a Lazarus—shrouded, unknown, and horrific—an image that essentially questions the reality of the central belief of Christianity, the Resurrection. Earlier the narrator distorts the assurance of salvation by rewriting Luke 11: 9–13 in terms of the female lover's receipt of pain and rejection as an award for loving in contrast to the son's reward of bread and egg:

A lover masculine so disappointed can speak and urge explanation; a lover feminine can say nothing: if she did the result would be shame and anguish, inward remorse for self-treachery. Nature would brand such demonstration as a rebellion against her instincts, and would vindictively repay it afterwards by the thunderbolt of self-contempt smiting suddenly in secret. Take the matter as you find it: ask no questions, utter no remonstrances: it is your best wisdom. You expected bread, and you have got a stone; break your teeth on it, and don't shriek because the nerves are martyrized; do not doubt that your mental stomach—if you have such a thing—is strong as an ostrich's—the stone will digest. You held out your hand for an egg, and fate put into it a scorpion. Show no consternation: close your fingers firmly upon the gift; let it sting through your palm. Never mind: in time, after your hand and arm have swelled and quivered long with torture, the squeezed scorpion will die, and you will have learned the great lesson how to endure without a sob. For the whole remnant of your life, if you survive the test—some, it is said, die under it—you will be stronger, wiser, less sensitive. (chap. 7, p. 105)

This powerfully painful passage questions and ultimately denies the applicability of Christ's promises to women. The irony of the events that occur at the celebration of Whitsuntide also mocks Christianity. The established church members produce political and religious unrest, as seen in the Dissenters' disruption of the parade, and Helstone's responses to the "tongues of fire" that "speak" in the battle of Moore's mill contradicts the peace brought by the original tongues of fire of Pentecost.

Caroline ultimately finds affirmation not in the Christian faith but in her mother, Mrs. Pryor, who has survived male dominance and emerged with greater strength and reserve. Caroline's reunion with her mother results in Shirley's decline because Mrs. Pryor (prior), the "mother" of both, not only perpetuates the dichotomy of female passivity and male self-assertion (seen in Caroline and Shirley respectively) but also defines a mother's role as inherently tragic. Caroline and Shirley's shared sisterhood would appear to be confirmed in their attachments to the Moore brothers. Shirley eventually is wooed and won by Louis, a version of the first man who adopts the spirit of Genius in order to become woman's savior.

The ending of the novel has been criticized for suggesting that women's dissenting voices can be silenced and also appears to reestablish male power in the form of Louis Moore, who usurps Shirley's voice by becoming the novel's final authority and interpreter. For instance, he rewrites the tale of Genius and Eva, originally composed by Shirley, who incorporated her own idea of an uncorrupted Eve:

She felt the world, the sky, the night, boundlessly mighty. Of all things, herself seemed to herself the centre,—a small, forgotten atom of life, a spark of soul, emitted inadvertent from the great creative source, and now burning unmarked to waste in the heart of a black hollow. She asked, was she thus to burn out and perish, her living light doing no good, never seen, never needed, a star in an else starless firmament,—which nor shepherd, nor wanderer, nor sage, nor priest, tracked as a guide, or read as a prophecy? Could this be, she demanded, when the flame of her intelligence burned so vivid; when her life beat so true, and real, and potent; when something within her stirred disquieted, and rest-

lessly asserted a God-given strength, for which it insisted she should find
exercise? (chap. 27, p. 487)

Louis's version makes Genius the originator of life who struggles with
sin and saves Eva for immortality. In Louis's version sin has uncertain
origins—in either the serpent or the woman—that recall the negative
stereotypes about the deceptive nature of woman. Louis's version incorporates masculine power and thereby makes feminine power feeble and
derivative of the stronger and prior male Genius:

> How, by his patience, by his strength, by that unutterable excellence he
> held from God—his Origin—this faithful Seraph fought for Humanity a
> good fight through Time; and when Time's course closed, and Death was
> encountered at the end, barring with fleshless arm the portals of Eter-
> nity, how Genius still held close his dying bride, sustained her through
> the agony of the passage, bore her triumphant into his own home—
> Heaven; restored her, redeemed, to Jehovah—her Maker, and at last,
> before Angel and Archangel, crowned her with the crown of Immortal-
> ity? (chap. 27, p. 490)

Woman becomes in this exchange of linguistic power the blank page for
man to write on, and Shirley concludes the novel by relinquishing her
voice to Louis. Like Eva's marriage to Genius, Shirley's and Caroline's
marriages suggest the loss of feminine power and place women in men's
shadow. They are no longer pure pages but have been defaced by male
dominance and power, which appear to rob them of their voices, names,
and individualities.

Hunger and Wounds

As Gubar first noted, eating disorders in *Shirley* function as a means for
a woman, in a society that deprives her of a voice with which to protest
and express pain, to control her life.[9] Food imagery begins in the very
first chapter, in which the curates mistreat the landlady who serves them
dinner, and continues to develop in Robert Moore's conflict with the
starving, displaced mill weavers as well as in the concluding reference to
Louis as "bon comme le pain" (chap. 37, p. 643). Caroline's and Shirley's
delayed appearances in the novel, which come after all the male characters are introduced, metaphorically imply the insignificance of the
women's lives and further illustrate the prevalence of the hunger motif.

Most dominant, however, in the theme of hunger in the text are Shirley's and Caroline's attempts to deal with their desire for more fulfilling lives by paradoxically starving themselves. Caroline's attempt to become independent of her need for Robert's love leaves her hungry for employment, loyal friendship, and the emotional support lacking in the life of a spinster. As a result, she becomes sick, stops eating, and almost dies. Caroline's decline occurs because she possesses no alternatives other than to resign herself to the narrowness of woman's place. This confinement presents her with two options: to lead the unoccupied and barren life of an old maid or to become an exchange commodity on the marriage market. Caroline's sense of inadequacy is reinforced by Rose Yorke, who believes women's imprisonment is self-inflicted and who looks to the parable of the 10 talents as her motivation for rejecting women's imprisoning self-denial. However, Rose's advocacy of women's entry into the mercantile market is repressive and limiting, for it advocates another form of competition between the sexes that Brontë would have considered destructive to both men and women. As a result, Caroline gives in to her longing for death as a form of escape from both her social and personal dilemmas, for she has been deprived of both physical and emotional food. Her self-induced starvation indicates the sorrow eating away at her and implies her rejection of Christian definitions of communion and redemption, or the value of ever earning the Father's love. Men's selfishness destroys Caroline's belief in paternal benevolence and causes her to question the existence of an afterlife and her purpose in this one. Fasting for both women, then, becomes an act of revolt against patriarchal religion, heterosexual romance, and male domination.

Shirley, on the other hand, fears that her strength may deprive her of love, and as a result she abandons her strength for love. For instance, she knows she must confide in Louis that she fears the dog bite she received from Phoebe may be fatal; by not revealing this fear she starves herself of her need for self-expression and is able to recover only by expressing her fears to Louis and receiving his reassurance: " 'You [Shirley] are very womanish. If the whole affair were coolly examined and discussed, I feel assured it would turn out that there is no danger to your dying at all' " (chap. 28, p. 511).

At first appearance Shirley seems full of strength and energy, believing in the possibilities for herself as a primordial Eve, but like Caroline she also suffers from desire and lack, the external signs of female hunger. Like Caroline, Shirley finds life as an unmarried woman to be an unsavory proposition, and she too hopes to find an equal to marry. Her independence, class, and wealth cannot effectively shield her from being a woman in a male-dominated society. Although Shirley hungers for a male partner who is her equal, she turns to Louis Moore, whose attempts to make her into his image ironically silence her and usurp her voice. Louis himself goes through a strange illness when he hears that Shirley may marry his brother Robert. He also promptly loses his appetite, takes to his bed, and recovers just as quickly when he discovers there will be no wedding for Robert and Shirley.

Caroline's denial of desire for Robert affects her physical appetite, whereas Shirley's starvation is a disruptive force in the text. Shirley does not eat at first due to the dog bite, but her ensuing decline implies that her starvation may be a result of her love for Louis, which, like the dog bite, keeps her silent out of fear of exposing herself to rejection and further pain. Unfortunately, this love makes her see Louis as her chosen intellectual superior, the only kind of man she could marry.[10]

Although both Shirley and Caroline undergo purgation and wounding through the motif of hunger, Robert Moore is literally wounded when he is shot by the Antinomian weaver. Louis Moore experiences symbolic wounds when he is insulted and defamed by Shirley's uncle Sympson, and Shirley is literally wounded by the dog Phoebe. Shirley's response to the potentially fatal bite is to cauterize the wound herself, an act that had deeply autobiographical implications for Brontë because her sister Emily had done the exact same thing to herself. That Shirley cauterizes her wound with a hot iron can be seen as an act of female self-mutilation, a desperately heroic act that at the same time also inscribes the visible mark of female inferiority on her body.

Shirley's courtship by Louis, however, resonates paradoxically with both hyperbolic rhetoric and animal imagery. The description we are given of Shirley in love is a painfully compromised portrait of a woman who has accepted marriage as a new form of servitude to a Nietzschean overlord: she initially addresses Louis as "My master" and then asks him if he will "be good to me, and never tyrannize?" (chap. 36, pp. 622–23). Louis compares her to a "leopardess," and she acknowledges Louis's undisputed power over her: "I am glad I know my keeper, and am used to him. Only his voice will I follow; only his hand shall manage me; only at his feet will I repose. . . . I know you are wise; I feel you are benevolent; I believe you are conscientious. Be my companion through life; be my guide where I am ignorant; be my master where I am faulty; be my friend always!" (chap. 36, pp. 623–24). Shortly before their marriage, Louis looks into Shirley's eyes and sees deep ambivalence in them:

" 'Pantheress!—beautiful forest-born!—wily, tameless, peerless nature!
She gnaws her chain: I see the white teeth working at the steel! She has
dreams of her wild woods, and pinings after virgin freedom' " (chap. 36,
p. 629). The severely tamed Shirley enters her marriage as a virtual
shadow of her former self, and such an image surely suggests Brontë's
deep ambivalence toward a state she both desired and feared for herself.

Quaternity and Doubleness

The four main characters in the novel—Shirley Keeldar, Caroline Helstone, and Robert and Louis Moore—form eerie mirrored personas; the
two women double each other and are in love with two brothers, who
recall the opposed brothers in Brontë's early juvenilia as well as the
Crimsworth brothers in *The Professor*. Brontë's radical commitment to
doubling all of her heroes and heroines extended throughout her career
and was clearly a deeply embedded pattern in her literary imagination.
For instance, in the chapter "Uncle and Niece," we assume that we will
read about the Reverend Helstone and Caroline, who have functioned
until this point in the novel as the dominant uncle and niece in the text.
But instead we are introduced to the very similar dynamics between yet
another uncle and niece, Sympson and Shirley. There are even two dogs,
Phoebe, the dog who bites Shirley, and Tartar, Shirley's devoted guard
dog, modeled on Emily Brontë's beloved dog Keeper.

It appears evident that all four of the main characters struggle to
define themselves in relation to each other but fail to realize that their
delusions of class and gender deprive them of this desired identity.
Robert Moore's allegiance to his business renders him little more than a
machine, and Caroline deceives herself into believing that Robert cares
for her. Shirley also fails in defining her sexual identity; as the narrator
points out, her claim to androgyny through her masculine name is
invalid because her name is a product of her parents' desire for a son and
therefore indicates her status as an inadequate substitute.[11] Although
Shirley believes her name entitles her to such male positions as that of
esquire and gentleman, her sex makes her more of a witness to the male
social positions than an actual participant in them. Shirley's attempts to
cultivate the pose of masculinity mislead Robert into proposing to her
and force her back into asserting her womanhood. Ironically, both heroines in *Shirley* appear to be self-victimized due to their inability to for-
give men for their limited and limiting attitudes toward them.

Brontë plots the novel by focusing on the immobilization and hopelessness that affect all classes and that can best be exemplified in Robert Moore's constant waiting for machinery that never arrives or for a change in his fortune. In order to obtain what he waits for, Robert must use people. He uses his workers to enhance his production, and he uses Caroline as an amusing diversion before rejecting her in favor of the wealthy Shirley. Robert's use and misuse of Caroline links him to the other men in the novel.

Like Robert, Hiram Yorke and the Reverend Helstone both see women as unworthy of respect. Helstone likes women to be silly, and Yorke uses his wife primarily for reproductive purposes. Under these conditions, Mary Cave, for whose attentions Helstone and Yorke were once rivals, personifies women's position in a male-dominated society; that is, all that is required of her is suicidal self-denial. And like Mary Cave, who dies from neglect after marrying Helstone, Caroline lives a physically adequate existence with a measure of social freedom but is unnoticed and unappreciated in Helstone's house.

In her final series of images, Brontë links the figure of Mary Cave— the woman buried by her marriage to an unloving man—with Shirley's invocation of mermaids in order to suggest that men simply cannot see or accept women as they really are. Instead, as she has Shirley state, men can perceive only the radically constructed and misperceived woman of their own imaginings:

> "Men, I believe, fancy women's minds something like those of children. Now, that is a mistake. . . . If men could see us as we really are, they would be a little amazed; but the cleverest, the acutest men are often under an illusion about women; they do not read them in true light; they misapprehend them, both for good and evil: their good woman is a queer thing, half doll, half angel; their bad woman almost always a fiend. Then to hear them fall into extasies with each other's creations, worshipping the heroine of such a poem—novel—drama, thinking it fine—divine! Fine and divine it may be, but often quite artificial—false as the rose in my best bonnet there." (chap. 20, p. 352)

But if men construct such literally powerful images of women, women in turn appear against their best intentions to be seduced by the very fictitiousness of such imagery. Shirley later confesses to Caroline and Mrs. Prior that she would like to set out as a sea captain in order to pursue mermaids:

"She comprehends our unmoved gaze; she feels herself powerless; anger crosses her front; she cannot charm, but she will appal us; she rises high, and glides all revealed, on the dark wave-ridge. Temptress-traitor! monstrous likeness of ourselves! Are you not glad, Caroline, when at last, and with a wild shriek, she dives?" (chap. 13, p. 246)

The unimaginative Caroline can respond only, " 'But, Shirley, she is not like us: we are neither temptresses, nor terrors, nor monsters.' " To which the shrewd Shirley answers, " 'Some of our kind, it is said, are all three. There are men who ascribe to 'woman,' in general, such attributes' " (chap. 13, p. 247).

By focusing incessantly on women as misfits, failures, or mythic constructions, Brontë actually undercuts her feminist purposes in this novel. It would appear that in *Shirley* Brontë's attempt to adopt the stance of a historical novelist confines her to a tradition that makes it especially difficult to write narratives of female strength and survival. The novel's conventionally happy ending actually subverts marriage as just another suspect male institution based on the curtailment of female opportunities. Shirley finds her happiness by relinquishing her power to Louis, whereas Robert allows Caroline to pretend to possess him. Brontë's conclusion to the novel attempts to point out the ironic and deeply problematic connection between hunger, wounds, bread as stones, barren Christianity, and flawed masculine institutions of all sorts.

Narrative Voice

Shirley develops the theme of young women in love at the same time it questions the proper use of female talents. Brontë does not resolve the contradiction but leaves it open through her use of an ambiguous narrative voice. Although *Shirley* concludes optimistically with the unifying picture of a double wedding, the artificiality of such a conclusion has caused numerous accusations by almost all contemporary feminist critics that *Shirley* exhibits unresolvable differences between the public world of war, religion, and business, represented by the book's heroes, and the private world of domesticity and love, represented by the book's heroines. These differences are a result of the narrator's own incoherence and inconsistency.[12]

In her use of the narrative voice in this text Brontë appears to alternately trust her reader, in whom she confides, as in the concluding conversation with Martha; at other times, as in the second paragraph of chapter 1, she condescends to her reader and doubts the reader's ability to comprehend a situation. In still other instances, Brontë seems to lose direction. For example, midway through the novel she changes her analysis of Hiram Yorke's character, while her analysis of Caroline Helstone implies a coherence and understanding between Brontë and the reader that does not exist.

Brontë also relinquishes her authority as storyteller several times, as when Robert Moore narrates Shirley's rejection of his marriage proposal or when Louis Moore records the story of his relationship with Shirley. This leaves the reader with various forms of truth, none of which are complete or final. This uncertainty about knowing what exactly has happened reveals the incompatibility of public and private versions of truth and also emphasizes the importance of the relativity, diversity, and richness of truth that is never absolute. For example, Robert Moore shifts truths when he refuses to give in to the demands of his workers but then provides William Farren with a job. Caroline learns that her belief in Robert's love for her is equally ambiguous. The same sort of discontinuities between perception and reality plague all of the other major characters in the text.

Shirley has recently been subjected to a number of provocative and important reassessments that have attempted to place the novel in its full feminist context. A rich, diffuse, and problematic text, *Shirley* will be viewed increasingly as an important work that contains a full and complex exploration of women's pain and suffering as they emerge from a consistently hostile capitalist society that views them as various forms of property to be exchanged between men. Brontë's attempt to rewrite her own and her sisters' lives in this novel will continue to stand as a testament to her imaginative daring and resolve to use the written word to construct an idealized locus of feminine power.

Chapter Six

"This Heretic Narrative": *Villette*

Villette, Charlotte Brontë's final novel, may well be also her greatest work: it is a complex portrait of a woman living on the margins of her culture, a woman who must make her own way in the world and who cannot expect to be rescued by a benevolent patriarch.[1] As a sustained analysis of the powerless position of unmarried women in Victorian culture, *Villette* may be unequaled in nineteenth-century fiction. Yet its uncompromising portrayal of a single woman's loneliness and alienation also makes this one of Brontë's most challenging novels to read. Both *Villette*'s admirers and detractors have described it as a representation of an individual's ordeal of consciousness, "one long meditation on a prison break," the reflection of a mind "filled with hunger, rebellion, and rage."[2] Even Brontë's friend Harriet Martineau felt that *Villette* burdened readers by exposing them directly to its heroine's despair: "The book is almost intolerably painful. We are wont to say, when we read narratives which are made up of the external woes of life, such as may and do happen every day, but are never congregated into one experience—that the author has no right to make readers so miserable."[3]

Villette affects readers powerfully because it does more than simply report the limitations of Lucy's life. Lucy's first-person narrative engulfs the reader in her psychological dilemmas, immersing him or her in Lucy's experiences of surveillance, limitation, and frustration. Brontë gives us a narrator who equivocates, withholds and elides information from the reader, and at times seems almost to hallucinate—a narrator who seems increasingly unreliable as the novel progresses. Yet Lucy's narrative simultaneously forces us to identify with her, as we recognize the extent to which her duplicitous-seeming discursive strategies are a logical response to the bizarre rules and expectations of her world.[4] *Villette* offers no conventional solutions to the problem of being an intelligent, highly emotional woman who has no appropriate role in patriarchy. Lucy's battle to suppress what is unacceptable, and thus fictionally unrepresentable, about herself results in a novel that is permeated by metaphors of limitation. This longest of Brontë's novels is consumed with waiting and inaction, which are summed up in Lucy's unflinching self-appraisal: "I was born only to work for a piece of bread, to await the pains of death, and steadily through all life to despond."[5]

Villette and *Jane Eyre*

Villette re-envisions the terms of *Jane Eyre,* Brontë's 1847 novel of an unprivileged female orphan finding her way in a hostile world. The shared elements of *Jane Eyre* and *Villette* are easy to identify. Each novel features an ordinary-looking, intelligent orphan whose first-person narrative details her struggle without family or fortune to find her way in the world. Each heroine earns a living as a teacher of young girls and in the process becomes involved in a turbulent affair with an older man whose demands on her are somehow excessive. Each heroine also becomes involved with a handsome but deeply flawed younger man whose attentions she eventually relinquishes as destructive. Each heroine is buffeted by apparently supernatural revelations designed to help her understand her unconscious knowledge. Each learns to master her intense emotions in order to improve her standing in life. Each is rewarded at closure with the undying love of a patriarch she has effectively "tamed" and who has lifted her to a position of social power and emotional fulfillment.

The larger plot parallels between the two novels are reinforced by literal textual echoes, as in the passages that describe the heroines' transitions from adolescence to adulthood. Marking the point in her life when she decides to move from the safety of her childhood "home," Lowood School, into the uncharted waters of adulthood, Jane notes, "This is not to be a regular autobiography: I am only bound to invoke memory where I know her responses will possess some degree of interest; therefore *I now pass a space of eight years* almost in silence: a few lines only are necessary to keep up the links of connection."[6] The "few lines" Jane supplies describe a pattern of the triumph of merit and virtue over evil. As a consequence of the pestilence that killed Helen Burns, she tells us, the hypocritical Brocklehurst was justly deposed, and Lowood School, under Miss Temple's superintendency, became "a truly noble and useful institution" at which Jane became "first girl of the first class; then I was invested with the office of teacher" (chap. 10, p. 73). Having vanquished her enemies and mastered her environment, Jane is now ready to take on greater tasks. Lucy Snowe of *Villette,* in contrast, describes a similar lapse in her narrative in a very different way:

On quitting Bretton . . . I betook myself home. . . . It will be conjec-
tured that I was of course glad to return to the bosom of my kindred.
Well! The amiable conjecture does no harm, and may therefore be safely
left uncontradicted. Far from saying nay, indeed, I will permit the reader
to picture me, *for the next eight years,* as a bark slumbering through hal-
cyon weather, in a harbour still as glass. . . . A great many women and
girls are supposed to pass their lives something in that fashion; why not I
with the rest?

Picture me, then, idle, basking, plump, and happy, stretched on a
cushioned deck, warmed with constant sunshine, rocked by breezes indo-
lently soft. However, it cannot be concealed that there must have been a
wreck at last. I too well remember a time—of cold, of danger, of contention. To this hour, when I have the nightmare, it repeats the rush and
saltness of briny waves in my throat, and their icy pressure on my lungs.
I even know there was a storm, and that not of one hour or one day. For
many days and nights neither sun nor stars appeared; we cast with our
own hands the tackling out of the ship; a heavy tempest lay on us; all
hope that we should be saved was taken away. In fine, the ship was lost,
the crew perished. (chap. 4, p. 94; emphasis added)

Lucy's evasive account of her eight-year lapse illustrates the difference
between Jane's and her experiences—and their narratives. While Jane's
lapse of eight years can be compressed into a few glowing highlights—a
trajectory of successes—Lucy's presumably negative experience during
this time of "cold, of danger, of contention" cannot be summarized or
even described directly. We are left to assume that Lucy omits these eight
years because they are too discouraging to be discussed. Taking an elliptical approach to an ellipse in her own narrative, Lucy enlists the metaphor
of a sea journey to evoke a sense of disaster. Characteristically, though she
describes the destruction of both the "ship" and the "crew," she defers
revealing her own fate. Presumably the sole survivor of an unnameable
catastrophe, Lucy distinguishes her own "life" from the metaphorical
lives of women that novel readers are accustomed to encountering.[7] At
the same time, she neatly foreshadows not only her own journey through
a life of exile in Labassecour but also the fate of her lover Paul Emanuel.
This virtuosic reworking of a key passage from *Jane Eyre* reveals the ways
in which *Villette* will present the story of the fortune-seeking orphan not
as a fairy-tale romance punctuated by a series of conquests and rescues
but as a psychological ordeal of mitigated disaster.

The parallel elements in *Jane Eyre* and *Villette* heighten the contrast
between the two renderings of the orphan's story; each element, as re-

presented in *Villette,* is recast in a cold, pessimistic light and revealed to be somehow vexed. Although both heroines are wanderers, *Villette* is set in a foreign country rather than in a series of strange houses. The foreign setting allows Lucy Snowe to explain her sense of not belonging by defining herself as a British Protestant in opposition to the French Catholics of the imaginary nation of Labassecour.[8] Literally rather than figuratively exiled, Lucy can never be "at home." The teaching that Jane finds so satisfying during her brief tenure at the Morton school proves exasperating for Lucy (chap. 31), who as a teacher finds herself forced simply to accept or even reinforce destructive models of female conditioning rather than able to improve the minds of her pupils. The two suitors whose tendency to exploit women is redressed by the small but powerful Jane Eyre turn up in *Villette* as merely flawed—one, John Graham Bretton, is too shallow to recognize Lucy's merit, and another, M. Paul Emanuel, goads Lucy to fury by controlling and criticizing her. Though both Jane and Lucy inherit legacies, the inheritance Lucy receives from her benefactress, Miss Marchmont, comes too late, in contrast to the £20,000 boon that purchases Jane's freedom and that of her Rivers cousins. Seemingly supernatural forces—mysterious voices in *Jane Eyre* and the ghostly nun of *Villette*—supply each protagonist with intuitive knowledge about herself. Yet whereas supernatural voices direct Jane unerringly toward appropriate action, the ghostly nun of *Villette* turns out to be a ruse deliberately designed to mock Lucy's loneliness and to facilitate the illicit sexual relationship between Alfred de Hamal and Ginevra Fanshawe.

The female characters who people the worlds of *Jane Eyre* and *Villette* share many attributes. Bertha Mason Rochester and Madame Beck, for example, both perform the task of surveilling the heroines and attempting to prevent their marriages to patriarchs, but Madame Beck, like all of the female characters in *Villette,* lacks Bertha's status as a victim of male rapacity. She is a tool of the culture that is trying to suppress Lucy rather than an emblem of outlaw female rage. Perhaps the most significant difference in the texts' shared elements lies in the their first-person narratives. Whereas Jane is an implacable "I" whose perceptions and actions are always the central focus of her autobiography, Lucy's narrative is diffused and displaced and at times does not even read like her own story. Though she is what narrative theorist Gerard Genette would call the novel's "focalizer"—the person through whose eyes we see its action—Lucy devotes much of her story to the histories of other women, such as Paulina Mary Home Bassompierre, Miss Marchmont, Ginevra

Fanshawe, Madame Beck, Madame Walravens, and the first and second Justine Marie. Her story is delivered through the filters of these conventional, more socially acceptable women's stories, stories that frame Lucy's unconventional and consequently unrepresentable personal history.

Villette as Autobiography

The existential tone and severe realism of *Villette* reflect the circumstances of its composition. A series of emotional deprivations and personal losses devastated Charlotte Brontë in the six years between the publication of *Jane Eyre* and this work. In 1851, when she began work on *Villette,* Brontë suffered from what would probably now be diagnosed as clinical depression, an illness that left her so drained that she suffered a four-month bout of intellectual paralysis that she referred to in a letter to Harriet Martineau as "months of bad days."[9] Foremost among the tragedies of these years were the deaths of Branwell, Emily, and Anne within less than 12 months of one another. Her siblings had been more than her childhood companions; they had been her coauthors, her readers, her co-conspirators in the imaginative worlds they had created together and apart. The isolation of Haworth parsonage that had contributed to their family insularity now seemed intolerable to Brontë, who leaned more heavily than ever on her old friend Ellen Nussey and reached out to her newer circle of friends in London. Though she had received several marriage proposals and her father's curate Arthur Bell Nicholls continued hotly to pursue her, Brontë was unwilling to settle for a marriage she regarded as merely a domestic partnership rather than a true marriage of minds. Deeply romantic since her teenage days, she continued to hope for the emergence of a soul mate.

But Brontë's literary fame brought her disappointment as well as solace during these years. Still smarting from some critics' derision of *Jane Eyre* as coarse, unfeminine, and rebellious, Brontë constructed *Shirley* in part as an answer to their complaints, focusing her presentation on abstract issues in order to avoid the emotionalism of *Jane Eyre.* But her critics were not appeased; the accusations of coarseness and excessive passion continued with the publication of *Shirley* in 1849. Moreover, because of her overwhelming shyness and severity of manner, Brontë failed to make a positive impression in the London literary circles to which she was introduced. Though she was repeatedly treated with awed respect, Brontë simply did not know what to make of London society; having grown up in an isolated country parsonage, she was unprepared for the literati's sleek sophistry. Brontë was particularly disappointed in the behavior of William Makepeace Thackeray, the novelist to whom she had dedicated the second edition of *Jane Eyre*. The cosmopolitan, sociable Thackeray, frustrated by Brontë's inability to affect a sanguine manner at fashionable gatherings, began to distance himself from her in a series of passive-aggressive incidents, as when he jokingly introduced Brontë to his mother as "Jane Eyre," an offense Brontë resented bitterly.

Villette, though not strictly speaking an autobiography, abounds with autobiographical traces of the sufferings and revelations of Charlotte Brontë's adult life. Foremost among these is her sense of the loss of family members, which left her profoundly depressed. Lucy Snowe's narrative resounds with the orphan's sense of hopeless isolation, as when she wonders what to do after Miss Marchmont's death leaves her homeless and jobless, with no clear vocation and little but a month's wages to live on: "All at once my position rose upon me like a ghost. Anomalous; desolate, almost blank of hope, it stood. What was I doing here alone in great London? What should I do on the morrow? What prospects had I in life? What friends had I on earth? Whence did I come? Whither should I go? What should I do?" (chap. 5, p. 107). In *Villette,* the trope of exile may well reflect the persistent sense of social and geographical isolation Brontë felt living on at Haworth with only the family servant Tabitha Aykroyd and her antisocial and demanding father as companions.

Though she had explored the subject earlier in her still-unpublished first novel, *The Professor,* Brontë returned in *Villette* to the theme of her experiences in Brussels at the Pensionnat Heger, where she and Emily had studied from 1842 to 1844 and Charlotte had taught English in 1844.[10] Brontë's complex relationships with the two principals of the school, Mme. and M. Heger, are fully explored in *Villette* in the characters of Madame Beck and M. Paul Emanuel. Her sense of competition with the beautiful, powerful Mme. Heger and her probably unrequited love for M. Heger are presented unsentimentally and analytically in *Villette*. In *The Professor,* Brontë's portrait of Mme. Heger in particular as Mlle. Zoraide Reuter was skewed by her still-unresolved sense of injury over M. Heger's gradual failure to respond to her impassioned letters after Brontë returned to England from Brussels. Her mature willingness to present both Madame Beck and M. Paul Emanuel as complex—both admirable and flawed—lends *Villette* a sense of maturity, honesty, and detachment missing from *The Professor*. Brontë's rendering of her intense attachment to M. Heger is also reflected in *Villette*'s recurring motif of letters, which Lucy eagerly anticipates, cherishes, and in some cases even buries in order to safeguard the emotions they ignite.

A third key autobiographical element in *Villette* is Brontë's rendering of John Graham Bretton and his mother, Louisa Bretton, characters based on Brontë's publisher George Smith and his mother. George Smith, the young, unmarried head of the publishing house of Smith, Elder, welcomed Brontë into the household he shared with his mother. The trio became friends, and the Smiths squired Brontë around London and extended her hospitality when she traveled from Haworth. Brontë eventually fell in love with Smith but discerned that her publisher felt only friendship for her. Her dissatisfaction with George Smith's subtle rejection of her is articulated in her handling of the relationship between John Graham Bretton and Paulina Home de Bassompierre of *Villette*. George Smith was quick to recognize the parallels, and after Brontë had sent him the finished manuscript, he delayed commenting for several months, telegraphing his disapproval through silence. After *Villette*'s publication, Brontë became completely alienated from the Smiths when Mrs. Smith wrote tactlessly to announce her son's impending marriage to an attractive but unremarkable young woman. In 1854, Brontë severed her ties with her longtime publisher.

Villette as Critique of Women's Roles

Villette reflects Brontë's midlife conviction that her culture tended to ostracize women who failed to fit into a narrow paradigm of appropriate attitudes and behaviors. The inadequacy of conventional female roles is reflected in the novel in themes of women being taught, through visual and verbal texts, how to behave properly—how literally to freeze themselves into tableaux that men deem safe and unthreatening. The twentieth-century feminist theorist Hélène Cixous derides the persistence of this cultural tendency in her essay "The Laugh of the Medusa," noting that even in contemporary culture, women continue to be exhorted to "[h]old still; we're going to do your portrait so you can start looking like it right away."[11] Consequently *Villette,* unlike *Jane Eyre,* is not simply the autobiography of a nonconformist who manages simultaneously to critique and conform to social norms. It also focuses on Lucy's attempt to understand the roles available to her by observing and evaluating a series of female characters who embody the roles their culture deems acceptable. The title *Villette* itself implies the history not of an individual but of a "little city," in this case the mostly female community at Madame Beck's school in the Rue Fossette. The other women's stories warn Lucy of the dangers of conformity even as they confirm her failure to fit a predesigned mold.

Lucy displaces herself from the narrative from the beginning, which concentrates on Paulina and Graham's relationship at the exclusion of Lucy's experiences and feelings. The woman who intrudes only briefly to identify herself as "I, Lucy Snowe" remains a marginal, shadowy presence who rarely comments on the events she witnesses but relies instead on the reader to determine their significance. Lucy's marginality reflects her social insignificance as well as her nonconformity, which Ginevra later bluntly confirms: "I suppose you are nobody's daughter . . . you have no relations; you can't call yourself young at twenty-three; you have no attractive accomplishments; no beauty. . . . Though you might have your own heart broken, no living heart will you ever break" (chap. 14, pp. 215–16). Social status for women is conferred by youth, beauty, a wealthy and socially respectable family lineage, qualities that enable a woman to attract high-status men. Qualities like intelligence, integrity, and wit are nonnegotiable: a woman like Lucy who lacks the key feminine attributes is a "nobody," a "cypher." Brontë had already addressed this issue in *Jane Eyre,* in a scene in which the heroine enlists the metaphor of the portrait to affirm her shortcomings:

> "Listen, then, Jane Eyre, to your sentence: to-morrow, place the glass before you, and draw in chalk your own picture, faithfully, without softening one defect; omit no harsh line, smooth away no displeasing irregularity; write under it, 'Portrait of a Governess, disconnected, poor, and plain.' " (chap. 16, p. 141)

Unlike Jane Eyre, however, Lucy Snowe fails completely to transcend these culturally inscribed limitations. Rather, Lucy self-consciously "frames" her own story through the pictures she presents of other women, contrasting her own representations to others' narratives and portraits of ideal women. Literalizing the metaphor of the role, she renders women as actresses, figures in paintings, or fictive characters seeking male approval. Though Lucy despises their conformity, she admires their ability to accommodate themselves to the roles that have been designed for them. Thus, though she despises Ginevra's flighty sensuality, Lucy admires her ability to play the part of the heartless coquette, admitting that "Ginevra became for me a sort of heroine" (chap. 15, p. 230). Ultimately, however, Lucy's narrative implies that women are stunted, deformed, or destroyed by the process of objectification. At one end of the spectrum, Paulina is transformed from "a pure, fine flame" into a "mouse" and a "spaniel"; at the other, women are literally consumed, destroyed, by conformity (chap. 32, p. 467; chap. 36, p. 510). The costs of objectification are evident to Lucy when she visits Mme. Walravens's house and is confronted not with the original Justine Marie but with her portrait "in a nun's dress" (chap. 34, p. 483). To Lucy, the portrait, which is accompanied by a "little romantic narrative" of Justine Marie's life supplied by Père Silas and Mme. Walravens, is clearly a representation designed to idolize a woman dead because of her inability to assert herself (chap. 34, p. 484):

> The mild Marie had neither the treachery to be false, nor the force to be quite staunch to her lover; she gave up her first suitor, but, refusing to accept a second with a heavier purse, withdrew to the convent, and there died in her noviciate. (chap. 34, p. 485)

Each of the "other women" of *Villette* is pictured as a familiar stereotype: ingenue, coquette, spinster, successful but lonely businesswoman, doting mother, hag. Each woman seems locked into playing out a script that buys her social security in exchange for self-distortion. Two obvious points of focus in Lucy's narrative are the younger women whose stories embody two versions of the romance paradigm for women: the ingenue who guards her sexuality and the coquette who shrewdly markets hers. Paulina, who enacts the role of the ingenue, is at first presented as the perfect virgin. Later, however, Lucy derides Paulina's willing self-subjugation to her father and husband. The coquette par excellence, Ginevra Fanshawe strings along as many men as possible while she is still young and pretty and ultimately marries the wealthy, superficial de Hamal. The coquette is one of the key roles for women in *Villette*. Lucy presents most of the students at the pensionnat as heartless, duplicitous flirts; the only thing that sets Ginevra above this "score of self-possessed self-sufficing misses and mesdemoiselles" is a bluntness Lucy attributes to Ginevra's innately Protestant skepticism (chap. 27, p. 406). To Lucy, Ginevra readily acknowledges the falsity of her role: "I am far more at my ease with you, old lady—you, my dear crosspatch—who take me at my lowest, and know me to be coquettish, and ignorant, and flirting, and fickle, and silly, and selfish, and all the other sweet things you and I have agreed to be part of my character" (chap. 9, p. 155). The emotions, rather than the concept of conquest, that Lucy associates with love are completely absent from Ginevra's calculus. Lucy is amazed by Ginevra's anesthetized sensibilities: "By true love was Ginevra followed: never could she be alone. Was she insensible to this presence?" (chap. 15, p. 230).

Equally influential are the older women whose intelligence and maturity mark them as Lucy's peers. The older women should serve as guides and role models for Lucy, but their investment in patriarchal norms overrides their responsibility for the well-being of a friendless, homeless woman. The first older woman Lucy encounters, Miss Marchmont, is a wealthy, embittered spinster who presents herself as having wasted her life worshiping the memory of a fiancé killed in a riding accident. Miss Marchmont has actually "lived" only during the period described in her story of Frank's death; the remainder of her existence has been storyless, an endless period spent in bed as the victim of a tragic narrative. Though Lucy is left unmoored and rudderless by Miss Marchmont's sudden demise, she also acknowledges that the prospect of spending her life attending to this bedridden employer is tantamount to self-immolation.

Madame Modeste Maria Beck, the widowed directress of the pensionnat, spends her life indoctrinating and surveilling the girls and women under her care. Though Lucy admires Mme. Beck's managerial abilities, she is repelled by the older woman's emotional coldness and by her willingness to sacrifice others in her self-interest. Even more significant is Mme. Beck's inability to attract the attentions first of John Graham Bretton and later M. Paul Emanuel, male peers to whom Lucy also is sexually attracted. Although the attractive, capable widow's lack of appeal facilitates Lucy's own affair with M. Paul, it convinces Lucy that the successful businesswoman is a lonely businesswoman—a fate Lucy will later share when she becomes the mistress of her own educational establishment.

Mrs. Louisa Bretton, modeled on the mother of George Smith, provides the second stereotype of the widow: the mother whose life revolves around her son, who is "master and must be obeyed" (chap. 17, p. 253). Mrs. Bretton is oedipally protective of sexual threats to her maternal primacy. When John Graham Bretton complacently surveys his marriage prospects as he looks around at the concert audience, Mrs. Bretton only half-jokingly rejects the notion and retorts, "You will bring no goddess to La Terrasse: that little chateau will not contain two mistresses" (chap. 20, p. 288). Mrs. Bretton, like Mme. Beck and Miss Marchmont, has no story of her own but lives exclusively through and for her son. Her lack of an existence is suggested in the letter she writes to Lucy, which, like Lucy's narrative itself, elides her thoughts and actions to focus on the exploits of the son she deferentially calls "my lord" (chap. 24, pp. 355–56).

The final older woman presented in Lucy's narrative is the stereotypical hag, or crone, Mme. Walravens, the keeper of the myth of Justine Marie, colluder with Père Silas, gatekeeper of the heart of M. Paul Emanuel. Lucy, repelled by Mme. Walravens's deformed appearance, derides her: "Cunegonde, the sorceress! Malevola, the evil fairy" (chap. 34, p. 489). The long-dead young woman whose story she safeguards, the first Justine Marie, was engaged to marry M. Paul Emanuel, but Mme. Walravens's opposition to the impoverished young man's suit resulted in Justine Marie's betrayal and subsequent death. The high priestess of patriarchy, Mme. Walravens represents all of the forces constraining women: the pressure to marry appropriately, the penalties for failing to do so, the myths created to honor women who die rather than risk breaking the culture's rules of proper feminine conduct. The first Justine Marie shared the fate of the ghostly nun rumored to have been buried alive "for some sin against her vow" beneath the pear-tree in the garden of the Rue Fossette (chap. 12, p. 172). Yet both Justine Marie and the ghostly nun have one thing in common: their myths must be kept alive by the collective guilt of the culture that has wronged them. As Lucy discovers, both are little more than fraudulent stories designed to permit men to perpetuate myths about women.

The "ghostly nun" that haunts the pensionnat—a nun who both does and does not exist—mirrors Lucy's repressed, androgynous, and therefore indescribable status. Lucy identifies both with the buried-alive nun and, albeit unknowingly, with Ginevra's suitor Alfred de Hamal, who masquerades as the nun in order to gain access to his lover.[12] Yet neither of these identities is satisfactory: Lucy is terrified by the nunlike, renunciatory aspects of her personality, and though she enjoys her momentary experience of androgyny while acting the part of the young man in the school play, she renounces the experience immediately afterward (chap. 14, p. 211). The nun operates as a nightmare vision that confirms Lucy's worst fears about herself: that she is poor, plain, doomed to a life of renunciation and unfulfilled desire, and in imminent danger of being brutally sacrificed because of her inability to keep her vows—that is, her inability to suppress her overwhelming, outlaw emotions. The scenario of the nun is so terrifying that Lucy refuses to describe it to others, both for fear of being thought mentally unstable and because she does not want to give her fears the power of words. After sighting the nun when her letter has mysteriously disappeared, Lucy tells John Graham Bretton,

> "I will never tell exactly what I saw," said I, "unless some one else sees it too, and then I will give corroborative testimony; but otherwise, I shall be discredited and accused of dreaming." (chap. 22, p. 328)

Lucy's refusal to describe the nun to John Graham Bretton mirrors her refusal to describe to the reader her own image at the theater when a mirror reveals to her a glimpse of herself, attired in the pink dress given her by Mrs. Bretton. Lucy is so disturbed by this image that she dissociates from it momentarily. She describes herself in the third person and then quickly rejects the image her conscious mind forces her to confront:

> I noted them all—the third person as well as the other two—and for the fraction of a moment, believed them all strangers, thus receiving an impartial impression of their appearance. But the impression was hardly felt and not fixed, before the consciousness that I faced a great mirror, filling a compartment between two pillars, dispelled it: the party was our own party. Thus for the first, and perhaps only time in my life, I enjoyed the "giftie" of seeing myself as others see me. No need to dwell on the result. It brought a jar of discord, a pang of regret; it was not flattering, yet, after all, I ought to be thankful: it might have been worse. (chap. 20, p. 286)

Lucy gradually relinquishes her identification with the nun as her heart is healed by M. Paul Emanuel's love and as she gradually renounces her affection for the heartless John Graham Bretton, who is Ginevra's male counterpart in coquetry. As the novel progresses, Lucy's sexual and emotional desires, having found an appropriate object in M. Paul Emanuel, require less and less suppression. During her visit to Mme. Walravens, Lucy confronts the myth of Justine Marie, Paul Emanuel's first love. Listening to Père Silas's story and looking at Justine Marie's portrait, Lucy realizes that Justine's renunciation of her true love arose not from strength of character but from an inability to honor the validity of her emotions and to assert herself against authority. This recognition, coupled with Lucy's discovery of the nun's habit that de Hamal and Ginevra have hidden in her dormitory bed, allows Lucy to cease identifying with the nun, who is revealed figuratively and literally to be little more than another patriarchal myth designed to control women's desires and behavior. The night Lucy uncovers the nun's habit in her bed, she sets herself free by deliberately thwarting Mme. Beck's attempt to subdue her. Her subsequent opiated journey through the park allows her to observe the entire "village" of the Rue Fossette as they truly are, and she finally recognizes M. Paul Emanuel's love for her:

> I said, "Truth, you are a good mistress to your faithful servants! While a Lie pressed me, how I suffered! Even when the Falsehood was still sweet, still flattering to the fancy and warm to the feelings, it wasted me with hourly torment. . . . Truth stripped away Falsehood, and Flattery, and Expectancy, and here I stand—free!" (chap. 39, p. 566)

After this revelatory experience, Lucy notes that "nothing remained now but to take my freedom to my chamber, to carry it with me to my bed and see what I could make of it" (chap. 39, p. 566). There she confronts the effigy of the nun, whom Ginevra's elopement note imparts to have been de Hamal's costume on his midnight visits. This sets to rest her paranoia about the nun, who now literally is revealed to be little more than cloth and stuffing, a costume that Lucy—like the fop de Hamal— can cast off at will.

As Lucy fleshes out and ultimately rejects the roles the conscribed female characters of *Villette* represent, she learns that she is more androgynous than feminine—that is, she possesses a combination of stereotypically male and female qualities. Lucy receives a strong intimation of this early in the novel when she accepts the role of the male protagonist in the school play and performs opposite Ginevra, who has been cast as the ingenue. Though Lucy initially refuses to participate, she accedes to M. Paul Emanuel's command, which encodes his recognition of her ability to perform and of her innate identification with the male role: "Play you must. I will not have you shrink, or frown, or make the prude. I read your skill, the night you came; I see your moyens: play you can; play you must" (chap. 14, p. 202). Lucy proves him correct by mastering the role in a single day. Yet when the time comes to perform, Lucy deliberately refuses to follow the script, which features the rivalry of two suitors, one "a gallant but unpolished man, a sort of diamond in the rough; the other . . . a butterfly, a talker, and a traitor: and I was to be the butterfly, talker, and traitor" (chap. 14, p. 203). First, she refuses to don a completely male costume, instead fashioning a hybrid outfit that incorporates both men's and women's garments. Then, though Lucy has diligently mastered the part as written, during the performance she collaborates with Ginevra to "half-change . . . the nature of the role, gilding it from top to toe. . . . Ginevra was tender; how could I be otherwise than chivalric?" (chap. 14, p. 210). Throwing herself into the role, Lucy-as-suitor defines herself in opposition to her "gallant but unpolished" opponent, whom she recognizes as John's type, and glories in her ability to "rival and outrival him": "I knew myself but a fop, but where *he* was outcast *I* would please" (chap. 14, p. 210). Lucy's transformation by costume and role into someone capable of expressing ambition, competition, and sexual desire for another woman makes this series of scenes one of the most remarkable in nineteenth-century literature.

As if recognizing the unspeakableness of such androgynous strength, Lucy quickly suppresses the possibilities presented by her theatrical triumph, minimizing the transformation as little more than the expression of "a keen relish for dramatic expression" (chap. 14, p. 211). She notes severely that "to cherish and exercise this new-found faculty might gift me with a world of delight, but it would not do for a mere looker-on at life: the strength and longing must be put by; and I put them by, and fastened them in with the lock of a resolution which neither Time nor Temptation has since picked" (chap. 14, p. 211). She continues:

> What I felt that night, and what I did, I no more expected to feel and do, than to be lifted in a trance to the seventh heaven. Cold, reluctant, and apprehensive, I had accepted a part to please another; ere long, warming, becoming interested, taking courage, I acted to please myself. Yet the next day, when I thought it over, I quite disapproved of these amateur performances; and though glad that I had obliged M. Paul, and tried my own strength for once, I took a firm resolution never to be drawn into a similar affair. (chap. 14, p. 211)

Lucy's deliberate suppression of the selves that were allowed to emerge during her performance appears to arise from a deep suspicion of theatricality, which Lucy identifies as the dominant trope of culturally mandated femininity.[13] In Lucy's eyes, all of the novel's women are actresses engaged in the process of miming correct behavior; in consequence, they lose their ability to recognize and act on their own feelings and desires. The pressure for all women to be "female impersonators" is overwhelming; the penalties for failing to conform (like the nun Justine Marie's harsh punishment) are severe. It takes Lucy a long time to resign herself to the fact that her ability to impersonate will enable her to survive emotionally. As her skill at impersonation grows, she shares her sense of mastery with the reader:

> "Is it," I said with a tone and manner whose consummate chariness and frostiness I could not but applaud. It was so seldom I could properly act out my own resolution to be reserved and cool when I had been grieved or hurt, that I felt almost proud of this one successful effort. That "Is it?" sounded just like the manner of other people. I had heard hundreds of such little minced, docked, dry phrases, from the pursed-up coral lips of a score of self-possessed, self-sufficing misses and mesdemoiselles. (chap. 27, p. 406)

While Lucy distrusts theatricality, she recognizes the power of impersonation. Her lack of a well-defined role often works to her advantage: by camouflaging herself as a nonentity and by fading into the background of the pensionnat, she is able to master her situation. From her countersurveillance of Mme. Beck—miming sleep, Lucy watches her supervisor rifle through her possessions—to her monitoring of others' emotional lives, Lucy watches constantly and learns much.[14] When Ginevra acknowledges, "If you are really the nobody I once thought you, you must be a cool hand," Lucy parries, "Who am I indeed? Perhaps a personage in disguise. Pity I don't look the character" (chap. 27, p. 393). Yet Lucy's response to Ginevra is disingenuous, for Lucy uses costume with great regularity to shift her identity. Her everyday style of dress is deliberately inconspicuous, as we discover when she accidentally receives the note addressed metonymically to "la robe grise et le chapeau de paille"—the gray dress and the straw hat— which describes the uniform of many adult women at the pensionnat, from Lucy to Rosine.

Stereotypically masculine costumes allow Lucy to express the "masculine" aspects of her identity. Lucy's self-styled, gender-hybrid costume at a dramatic performance during the *vaudeville de pensionnat*—a costume half-male, half-female—comes closer than any other in *Villette* to expressing Lucy's sexually ambiguous persona and her powder keg of free-floating desire. Everyone at the fête, including M. Paul Emanuel, is awed by the way Lucy is transformed by her costume and role. John

Graham Bretton later admires her: "I saw [Lucy] enact, with no little spirit, the part of a very killing fine young gentleman" (chap. 15, p. 215). Another apparel item that reinforces Lucy's androgyny is the cigar case she receives as a lottery prize and that she refuses to trade with John, who has received as his prize a blue turban (chap. 20, p. 300). John, embarrassed, cannot figure out what to do with his very feminine prize. After Lucy refuses to exchange her gift for his, Mrs. Bretton guards the turban for him, and he later considers giving this "lady's headdress" to Ginevra (as a complement to his earlier gift of a blue silk sash). Though Mrs. Bretton later jokingly transforms the blue turban into an orientalized symbol of John's male dominance by placing it on his head while he sleeps, Lucy's refusal to surrender her cigar case is an unrepentantly masculine gesture, particularly in a novel in which M. Paul Emanuel's courtship gifts to Lucy are marked by the distinctively masculine fragrance of cigars.

More problematic for Lucy, because it is more closely identified with the idealized femininity she has learned to resist, is the pink dress Mrs. Bretton buys her as a gift (chap. 20, p. 283). This dress, with its unmistakable implications of youth and sexual vulnerability, makes Lucy erotically self-conscious at a time when she is barely able to suppress her desire for John Graham Bretton. Lucy feels completely foreign in the dress, to the point that she admits, "I would almost as soon clothe myself in the costume of a Chinese lady of rank" (chap. 20, p. 283). A large part of her discomfort derives from the fact that the pink dress alone is unable to make her beautiful enough to satisfy the desires of John Graham Bretton, who straightforwardly has announced his preference for conventionally beautiful women. Pink dress or not, Lucy still lacks the mask of perfect femininity and consequently continues to see herself as invisible, imperfect, an impostor.

Aside from Lucy's performance in the school fête, the consummate image of problematic theatricality in *Villette* is the performance of the actress Vashti, whom Brontë modeled on the contemporary French actress Rachel Félix. John Graham Bretton surprises Lucy by taking her to see Vashti's performance at a moment in Lucy's life when she is negotiating an uneasy truce between her reason and her strong emotions and struggling to overcome her increasingly strong affection for John (chap. 23, p. 335). At the performance, Lucy identifies with Vashti's emotional intensity and finds her admirable and horrible simultaneously—a response that mirrors Lucy's confusion about her own divided self, which is "neither of woman nor of man":

For awhile . . . I thought it was only a woman, though an unique
woman, who moved in might and grace before this multitude. By and by
I recognized my mistake. Behold! I found upon her something neither of
woman nor of man: in each of her eyes sat a devil. These evil forces bore
her through the tragedy, kept up her feeble strength—for she was but a
frail creature; and as the action rose and the stir deepened, how wildly
they shook her with their passions of the pit! They wrote HELL on her
straight, haughty brow. They tuned her voice to the note of torment.
They writhed her regal face to a demoniac mask. Hate and Murder and
Madness incarnate, she stood.
    It was a marvellous sight: a mighty revelation.
    It was a spectacle low, horrible, immoral. (chap. 23, p. 339)

Lucy demonizes Vashti's frank display of forbidden emotions because
Lucy is struggling so hard to suppress her own negative emotions—
especially her rage at the injustice of her powerless position. What seems
most repellent about Vashti's performance is the way suffering, which
this actress is able to summon and display for her culture only in the
context of a formal performance, is presented as an unresolved process.
Yet Lucy finds Vashti's performance—as readers are meant to find
Lucy's life, as incarnated in her own performances—to display authentic
emotion and to be effective, well-executed art. Lucy contrasts Vashti's
performance with the pictures in the art gallery: "Suffering had struck
that stage empress; and she stood before her audience neither yielding
to, nor enduring, nor in finite measure, resenting it: she stood locked in
struggle, rigid in resistance. . . . Where was the artist of the Cleopatra?
Let him come and sit down and study this vision" (chap. 23, p. 339).
Lucy finds, however, that she is alone in her admiration of, and identification with, Vashti. John Graham Bretton condemns Vashti "as a
woman, not an artist: it was a branding judgment" (chap. 23, p. 342).
The reader cannot help but contrast Bretton's negative reaction with
M. Paul Emanuel's response to Lucy's vaudeville performance: "Were
you not gratified when you succeeded in that *vaudeville*? I watched you,
and saw a passionate ardour for triumph in your physiognomy. What
fire shot into the glance! Not mere light, but flame; je me tins pour
averti" (chap. 15, p. 226). The outlaw emotions reflected and unleashed
in Vashti's performance, in John Graham Bretton's view, should remain
unarticulated.
    As if to confirm the destructive power of unleashed female emotion, a
fire breaks out in the theater after Vashti's performance. In the crush that
follows, Lucy learns indirectly of the fate of her relationship with John

Graham Bretton. In the panic that arises after the cries of "Fire," Bretton rushes to save the young woman whom we later discover to be Paulina Mary Home de Bassompierre, who has fainted in the press of the crowd. Lucy is ironically brushed aside when someone asks John whether or not he is accompanied by a lady; he responds that he is but that "she will be neither hindrance nor incumbrance" (chap. 23, p. 343). Paulina, whose "feminine" frailty renders her a hindrance and incumbrance, is thus a worthy focus of Bretton's attention and ministrations. Lucy is rendered invisible and, for the second time in the novel, takes her place at the margins of a romantic scene pairing the strong, superior John Graham Bretton with the infantilized Paulina.

The Unwritable Text

Villette is an anti-romance—the story not of love fulfilled but of love deferred. The traditional women's "love stories" of *Villette,* namely the narratives of Ginevra and Paulina, are sharply if indirectly critiqued by the rest of the narrative, which focuses on the unfulfilled emotional lives of such women as Mrs. Bretton, Mme. Beck, Justine Marie, and Lucy herself. *Villette* fails to fit the romance paradigm as did *Jane Eyre* and most other Victorian novels purporting to describe women's experiences. Lucy recognizes that such stories are generally "romantic rubbish" (chap. 12, p. 173), yet she is unable fully to describe such feelings as loneliness, rage, and despair because others—including readers who will identify with John Graham Bretton—will find these emotions to be coarse and subversive. Brontë signals this dilemma by frequently highlighting the difference between the real and the romantic, wryly acknowledging her readership's resistance to the imperatives of the "rude Real," which "burst[s] coarsely in—all evil, grovelling and repellent as she too often is" (chap. 12, p. 177). Yet without heterosexual romance—the lack of which Lucy identifies with "that insufferable thought of being no more loved" (chap. 15, p. 232)—Lucy's life seems meaningless. She signals this sense of emptiness when John Graham Bretton fails to demonstrate love for her by writing her letters: "Following that eventful evening at the theatre, came for me seven weeks as bare as seven sheets of blank paper: no word was written on one of them; not a visit, not a token" (chap. 24, p. 349).

Brontë uses several indirect rhetorical techniques to subvert the limitations of a genre that forces women to adhere to a few shopworn scripts. For example, Lucy frequently uses humor to simultaneously mask and express her rage; Kate Millett notes that *Villette* is "one of the wittier novels in English and one of the rare witty books in an age which specialized in sentimental comedy" (chap. 9, p. 147). A favorite target of Lucy's wit is the bourgeois convention of eroticizing feminine voluptuousness: her descriptions of Ginevra's weightiness and of the blowsy Rubens painting of Cleopatra are both witty and contemptuous; they defamiliarize and hence debunk the attributes fetishized by male culture. When she despises a particular representation, such as the works in the art museum, Lucy enlists hyperbole to mock it indirectly, damning with excessive praise: "It was impossible to keep one's attention confined to these masterpieces" (chap. 19, p. 278). She also tempers the harshness of her judgments with self-deprecating humor, poking fun at others' impressions of her, as when she admits to learning to take the married Ginevra's cries for help with a grain of salt: "I was frightened at first, and wrote back pathetically, but I soon found there was more cry than wool in the business, and relapsed into my natural cruel insensibility" (chap. 40, p. 577).

Another of Brontë's indirect rhetorical strategies is her frequent use of untranslated French when the characters discuss forbidden emotions or ideas. Lucy accuses Ginevra of "always [having] recourse to French when she was about to say something specially heartless or perverse" (chap. 9, p. 155), but Lucy herself and the other characters frequently enlist French for the same reasons. When M. Paul Emanuel acknowledges Lucy's blazing triumph in the *vaudeville de pensionnat,* he begins in English but lapses into French to describe the dangerous extent to which Lucy's performance has moved him: "I watched you, and saw a passionate ardour for triumph in your physiognomy. What fire shot into the glance! Not mere light, but flame; je me tins pour averti" ("I took this as a warning"; chap. 15, p. 226). Concepts Brontë views as peculiarly French—especially issues related to the linked themes of Catholicism, surveillance, and duplicity—are often discussed in French terms, as when Mme. Beck informs Lucy that "Désirée a besoin d'une surveillance toute particulière" ("Désirée is particularly in need of surveillance"; chap. 10, p. 158). The illicit sexuality from which M. Paul Emanuel seeks to shield Lucy at the art museum also lends itself to French; M. Paul lauds the Rubens Cleopatra as "Une femme superbe—une taille d'imperatrice, des formes de Junon," but then advises Lucy, "[M]ais une personne dont je ne voudrais ni pour femme, ni pour fille, ni pour soeur. Aussi vous ne jeterez plus un coup d'oeil de sa côté" (chap. 19, p. 280). Translated, the passage reads, "[She is] a superb woman—an imperial figure, with the form of a Juno, but she is a person whom I would not like as a wife, daughter, or sister; accordingly, you will not take another glance in that direction." M. Paul Emanuel's frank acknowledgment of the sexual double standard and his directive to suppress Lucy's female curiosity are sufficiently risqué to require the veil of French.

Surveillance is both a theme and a narrative strategy in *Villette*. Although nineteenth-century realists prided themselves on their ability to re-create the appearance of social reality, Brontë recognizes that realistic mimetic strategies ironically objectify and consequently distort the reality they strive faithfully to represent. From the moment she sets foot in Labassecour (when she is threatened by the unwanted pursuit of two strangers) to the novel's close, when the priest Père Silas informs her that "never have I for a day lost sight of you" (chap. 34, p. 487), Lucy feels constantly watched, spied on, scrutinized, especially by the Labassecouriens. Throughout her narrative Lucy reports feeling violated by the surveillance, which she views as duplicitous, disrespectful, and threatening. She complains, "What should I do to prevent [surveillance]? In what corner of this strange house was it possible to find security or secrecy? Where could a key be a safe-guard, or a padlock a barrier?" (chap. 26, p. 379). Madame Beck is the novel's past master of espionage:

> Madame had her own system for managing and regulating this mass of machinery; and a very pretty system it was: the reader has seen a specimen of it, in that small affair of turning my pocket inside out, and reading my private memoranda. "Surveillance," "espionage,"—these were her watch-words. (chap. 8, p. 135)

Though she feels violated by Madame Beck's probe of her possessions, Lucy seems to appreciate, and even encourage, surveillance from men. There are cultural reasons for this apparently illogical double standard. In Western culture, in which a woman's appearance signals her sexual attractiveness, to be looked at appreciatively and visually objectified by others, especially by men, is an index of a woman's social power. To be perceived as beautiful, women must conform to a culturally defined standard of fair, frail physical ideality that accentuates smallness, whiteness, hairlessness, and other childlike qualities (chap. 21, p. 314). Any natural deficit of these qualities must be compensated for by artifice, an imperative that forces most girls and women into habitual duplicity. After teaching a single lesson in the pensionnat, Lucy begins

"rightly to see the wide difference that lies between the novelist's and
the poet's ideal 'jeune fille' and the said 'jeune fille' as she really is"
(chap. 8, p. 142). The pupils named Blanche, Virginie, and Angelique
fail to live up to the promise of their names ("white," "virginal,"
"angelic"); instead, they learn to please by lying. Lucy condemns
Madame Beck's sanctions of female duplicity:

> Not a soul in Madame Beck's house, from the scullion to the directress
> herself, but was above being ashamed of a lie; they thought nothing of it;
> to invent might not be precisely a virtue, but it was the most venial of
> faults. "J'ai menti plusiers fois" ["I have lied many times"] formed an
> item of every girl's and woman's monthly confession; the priest heard
> unshocked, and absolved unreluctant. (chap. 9, p. 145)

Whether it comes naturally or must be manufactured through artifice, physical beauty—the quality that attracts the male gaze—endows
women with social power and hence an identity. Women who lack
beauty, because they are unlikely to attract male attention and protection, are doomed to more than loneliness: because social status for
women consists of establishing a relationship to a man, they are
doomed to social death. John Graham Bretton confirms this when he
tells Lucy, who has just sighted the nun, "Lucy, was she a pretty nun?
Had she a pretty face? You have not told me that yet; and *that* is the
really important point" (chap. 21, p. 332). Later, when John Graham
Bretton tries to soothe Lucy by assuring her that he would go out of his
way not to hurt her because she is "a being inoffensive as a shadow," she
responds,

> I smiled, but I also hushed a groan. Oh!—I wished he would just let me
> alone—cease allusion to me. These epithets—these attributes—I put
> from me. His "quiet Lucy Snowe," his "inoffensive shadow," I gave him
> back; not with scorn, but with extreme weariness: theirs was the coldness
> and the pressure of lead; let him whelm me with no such weight. (chap.
> 27, p. 403)

To Lucy, whose ordinary appearance and subdued manner have doomed
her to receive little notice from others, the male gaze sometimes seems
like positive attention. She despairs at her inability to capture the attention of such men as the good Samaritan (whom she later reveals to have
been John Graham Bretton) who aids her on her arrival in Labassecour: "I

was turning away, in the deep consciousness of all absence to claim to look for further help from such a one as he" (chap. 7, p. 124).

Yet the male gaze often turns out to be harshly evaluative, even threatening. Mme. Beck, when considering whether or not to hire Lucy, invites M. Paul Emanuel to scrutinize the shape of her head in consonance with the nineteenth-century pseudoscience of phrenology, which held that an individual's character could be read from the bumps and depressions of the skull (chap. 7, p. 129). M. Paul Emanuel's initial judgment of Lucy is repeated again and again in *Villette,* from his close monitoring of Lucy's performance in the vaudeville to his interference in her intellectual life. Often, M. Paul Emanuel's surveillance takes the form of censorship: he steers her away from the Cleopatra, cuts out the racy parts from the novels he leaves in her school desk, and tells her what and how to study. He argues that his surveillance is necessary because Lucy is so inherently powerful that she must be constantly watched. He tells her, "You are one of those beings who must be kept down. I know you! I know you! Other people in this house see you pass, and think that a colorless shadow has gone by. As for me, I scrutinized your face once, and it sufficed" (chap. 15, p. 226). This passage can be construed as both a tribute to Lucy's integrity and a sign that M. Paul Emanuel is attracted to Lucy's appearance—it was a glance at her face, after all, that "sufficed" to convince him of Lucy's power. Though the independent Lucy often rebels against M. Paul Emanuel's basilisk gaze, she accepts it as a sign of love and eventually capitulates to M. Paul's suit.

Lucy's expressed distaste for Mme. Beck's surveillance strategies, which she finds understandable but not morally justifiable, is undermined by the fact that Lucy too enlists surveillance—in order to present "reality" to the reader. Just as Lucy silently countersurveils Mme. Beck when her employer gently sifts through her personal possessions in the midnight darkness of the dormitory, Lucy makes herself marginalized and inconspicuous the better to record the details of the other characters' emotional lives. From the initial chapters, in which Lucy elides her own thoughts and feelings in order to highlight her description of the relationship between John Graham Bretton and Paulina Home, to Lucy's opiated flight through the park when she eavesdrops on the plots of the "junta" of Labassecour, Lucy is consistently watching and listening to others, trying to get to the bottom of everyone else's secrets. Sometimes her gaze is stereotypically masculine, as when she stares desirously at John Graham Bretton:

It was not perhaps my business to observe the mystery of his bearing, or
search out its origin or aim; but, placed as I was, I could hardly help it.
He laid himself open to my observation, according to my presence in the
room just that degree of notice and consequence a person of my exterior
habitually expects: that is to say, about what is given to unobtrusive articles of furniture, chairs of ordinary joiner's work, and carpets of no striking pattern. Often, while waiting for Madame, he would muse, smile,
watch, or listen like a man who thinks himself alone. I, meantime, was
free to puzzle over his countenance and movements, and wonder what
could be the meaning of that peculiar interest and attachment—all
mixed up with doubt and strangeness, and inexplicably ruled by some
presiding spell—which wedded him to this demi-convent, secluded in
the built-up core of a capital. He, I believe, never remembered that I had
eyes in my head; much less a brain behind them. (chap. 10, p. 162)

At other times, Lucy's plainness is not quite enough to camouflage her
completely. In one scene, Lucy must conceal herself behind a door in
order to eavesdrop on a conversation between John Graham Bretton
and the portress Rosine:

I heard a giddy treble laugh in the little cabinet; close by the door of
which I stood—that door half-unclosed; a man's voice in a soft, deep,
pleading tone, uttered some words, whereof I only caught the adjuration,
"For God's sake!" Then, after a second's pause, forth issued Dr. John, his
eye full-shining; but not with either joy or triumph; his fair English
cheek high-coloured; a baffled, tortured, anxious, and yet a tender meaning on his brow. (chap. 11, p. 168)

What distinguishes Lucy's surveillance and espionage from those of
Madame Beck? Little enough, as Lucy acknowledges; most of her tributes to Mme. Beck are prompted by watching her in the midst of espionage: "I will not deny that it was with a secret glee I watched her. Had
I been a gentleman, I believe madame would have found favour in my
eyes she was so handy, neat, thorough in all she did: some people's
movements provoke the soul by their loose awkwardness, hers—satisfied by their trim compactness" (chap. 13, p. 186). The primary difference seems to be one of form. Whereas Mme. Beck is in the business of
managing social fictions, Lucy is purportedly constructing something
more important: a formal fiction in which the reader, as co-conspirator,
understands why Lucy is compelled to spy on others.

This brings us to a series of indirect narrative strategies that are even more clearly duplicitous than is Lucy's habit of surveillance: Lucy's systematic elision of key points of information from the reader. These omissions take a few characteristic forms. The most obvious ones occur when Lucy announces that she is about to leave something out of her narrative: "The polite tact of the reader will please to leave out of the account a brief, secret consultation on this point in Madame's own chamber" (chap. 14, p. 196). Such elisions highlight the arbitrariness and unreliability of the fictionalizer's prerogative; if Lucy is withholding *this* incident from me, wonders the reader, what else is she keeping back? Such lacunae subject the reader to precisely the same kinds of censorship that M. Paul Emanuel imposes on the novels he presents to Lucy: if a scene is too troubling or potentially too arousing of the reader's curiosity, it must be cut out, pruned back. The reader must either pass over the omission or "fill in the blanks," taking responsibility for re-creating events or emotions Lucy's culture has marked as off limits for discussion.

Her burgeoning affection first for John Graham Bretton and later for M. Paul Emanuel is subject to the same kinds of elision, probably because Lucy fears her love will go unrequited and thus should never be articulated. Instead of discussing her emotions, she endows objects with tremendous metonymic power, focusing on John's letters and M. Paul Emanuel's chocolates, novels, and flowers without explaining directly why these tokens have become so significant to her. It takes Lucy many chapters to admit to the reader that she has fallen in love with John, and she teases the reader along with the suitor by refusing for many pages to reveal the name of the recipient of the watch-case she makes for M. Paul Emanuel. The men themselves are the last to find out what Lucy thinks and feels; she seems to have no compunction about lying to protect herself from the emotional risk of unrequited love. At one point, Lucy gloats,

> "I am not conscious of you, monsieur, or of any other having excited such emotion as you indicate" was my answer; and in giving it, I again surpassed my usual self, and achieved a neat, frosty falsehood. (chap. 27, p. 406)

Lucy's other elisions are more subtle because they are unannounced; typically, she omits to reveal the identity of a key player in the scene and only much later uncovers for us a pattern of connection she has known all along. This technique reinforces her superior control of the reality she shares with the reader while it confirms her social invisibility. Typically, although she recognizes the identity of others, such as John Graham Bretton, Mrs. Bretton, Paulina Home de' Bassompierre, and Messrs. Boissec and Rochemorte, they fail to recognize her. John Graham Bretton fails to "see" Lucy both when he assists her after her arrival in Labassecour and long after he has become the official physician of the Rue Fossette. The reader also is left in the dark: only the heretofore inexplicable inclusion of the "Bretton" chapters with the rest of Lucy's narrative has prepared the reader for the coincidental reemergence of the Brettons and the Home de Bassompierres in Labassecour.

Finally, Lucy typically elides her own presence from key scenes, as in the opening chapters, when she omits mention of herself in order to focus on the relationship between Paulina and John Graham Bretton. Lucy's relative absence from this scene effectively highlights the significance of this one-sided love affair, which serves as a model for the position of all women in Lucy's culture. Yet the scene also deceives us as to Lucy's status. One of the few remarks she makes about herself is to define herself in opposition to Paulina, asserting, "I, Lucy Snowe, plead guiltless of that curse, an overheated and discursive imagination," which she then labels as resulting in "that monomaniac tendency I have ever thought was the most unfortunate with which man or woman can be cursed" (chap. 2, p. 69). This assertion is disingenuous: Lucy's imagination is at times "overheated" and is nearly always "discursive," and the "monomaniac tendency," unfortunate or not, is both an indicator of her emotional intensity and a key source of her strength as an artist insofar as it spurs her to investigate her world. As Lucy correctly points out, "[T]he multitude have something else to do than to read hearts and interpret dark sayings" (chap. 38, p. 545), but she, as an artist, is not the multitude, and we are the better for it.

Perhaps the most evocative series of elisions occurs at the end of the novel, when Lucy rejects the romance paradigm by refusing to tell us what has happened to M. Paul Emanuel. The opening sentences of the final chapter, "Man cannot prophecy. Love is no oracle. Fear sometimes imagines a vain thing" (chap. 41, p. 591), constitute a warning as much to the reader as to Lucy that the long-anticipated marriage may now not take place—and that this may be for the best. The reader, expecting Lucy's emotional fulfillment to hinge on marriage and sexual fulfillment, is surprised to read Lucy's assertion that M. Paul Emanuel's absence results in "three of the happiest years of my life." Evidently Lucy's happiness has been more contingent on her establishment as directress of her own school than on M. Paul Emanuel's love. This calls into question much that she has told us about their relationship; perhaps all her wily endurance of his taunts about women's inferiority have been little more than a ruse designed to engineer her own freedom. Lucy's elliptical conclusion gives rise to the possibility that she is happiest as long as M. Paul Emanuel expresses his love in letters but remains far enough removed to keep from dominating her. These profoundly antipatriarchal feelings, however, are unrepresentable. Consequently Lucy concludes with a moment of silence, exhorting the reader to "pause: Pause at once. There is enough said. Trouble no more, kind heart; let sunny imaginations hope" (chap. 42, p. 596). This conclusion allows the reader to construct multiple possible conclusions, as does Lucy's parting comment to the reader, simply "Farewell" (chap. 42, p. 596).

Chapter Seven

"All Turned Up in Tumult": The Poetry and Letters

Close to the end of her life, Brontë looked back on her poetry and made the ruthlessly honest assessment that her published poems in the 1846 volume were composed "before [my] taste was chastened or judgement matured—accordingly they now appear to me very crude" (*SHB LFC*, III, 86). Further, she told Elizabeth Gaskell that her poems were "chiefly juvenile productions; the restless effervescence of a mind that would not be still. In those days the sea too often 'wrought and was tempestuous,' and weed, sand, and shingle—all turned up in tumult" (*SHB LFC*, III, 162). Brontë's poetry has received surprisingly little attention apart from its role in reconstructing her creation of the Angrian saga with Branwell, and her letters, although important as biographical documents, have also received scant attention from literary critics.

The major problem with examining the texts of the poetry and the letters, however, which is the same in both cases, is that Brontë's literary heirs and greedy editors have contaminated and corrupted them. We cannot discuss either the poetry or the letters without rehearsing the pathetic tale of those incredibly corrupt entrepreneurs T. J. Wise and Clement Shorter, the former being one of the "editors" of the so-called definitive *Shakespeare Head Brontë*. This chapter will examine the textual damage done to both the poetry and the letters and will then look at both oeuvres in light of their importance as documents that shed light on the composition of the mature novels.

The Publication History of the Poetry

Apart from the 19 poems Brontë published with her two sisters in their 1846 volume, along with three other short poems, all of her other poetic texts went through the hands of either her husband or her first editors, Thomas J. Wise and Clement Shorter, and seriously suffered as a result. The damage done to her original poetic manuscripts has been one of the most extensive in the history of modern literary production. It is necessary here to rehearse the major problems so that students of Charlotte Brontë can appreciate how difficult it has been to assemble anything like a definitive edition of either her poetry or her letters. That it was more than 100 years before a Brontë scholar was able to produce an almost-complete standard edition of her poetry, the volume edited by Victor Neufeldt and published in 1985, suggests how daunting the project has been. As Neufeldt notes, of the 206 poems, verse translations, and fragments in the now-standard edition of Brontë's poetry, only 22 were published in her lifetime.[1]

The story of the serious damage done to her early poetic texts begins in 1895, when Clement Shorter, acting on behalf of T. J. Wise, bought a substantial number of Brontë manuscripts from the Reverend Nicholls. Wise had wanted to purchase all the Brontë manuscripts but was unable to do so. What he did manage to acquire, however, was so badly muddled and mutilated by Wise, Shorter, and the well-meaning but destructive Nicholls that it has taken several generations of Brontë scholars to undo the damage. Neufeldt credits the efforts of Fannie Ratchford, Davidson Cook, C. W. Hatfield, and Mildred Christian with restoring the Brontë poetic canon. Surely he is being modest, for without his meticulous research and extensive detective work there would be no standard edition of the poetry at all.

The next stage in the sad publication saga occurred when T. J. Wise began his infamous career as a Brontë "scholar" by publishing a series of privately printed and very expensive editions of Brontë poems; however, the poems in these volumes were assembled in a cobbled, random manner, and some of Charlotte's poems were attributed to Emily and some of Anne's attributed to Charlotte. Wise's *Shakespeare Head Brontë* included only 141 of the 206 poems we know to exist, and several of the poems included could be verified by Wise in facsimile reproduction only. Because of their desecration, their random and haphazard sale, and the butchering they suffered at many hands, the original manuscripts for 17 poems included in the Neufeldt edition are lost or inaccessible. Of those 17, 11 were last seen in the library of Sir Alfred Law of Honresfeld. After Sir Alfred's death in 1939 his family denied access to his library to all Brontë scholars. Other Brontë manuscripts are scattered over 19 sites in both the United States and Great Britain.

The next problem encountered in deciphering Brontë's poetic manuscripts concerns their original production. Brontë produced the majority of her poems in a tiny handwritten script that can be read only with the aid of a magnifying glass. In addition to the water damage such productions incurred, the booklets were also often ripped apart; single pages were pulled out of their original context and sold as if separate and complete in themselves. Both Neufeldt and Brontë's other contemporary poetry editor, Tom Winnifrith, place the blame for this carelessness on the head of one man alone—Thomas J. Wise.[2]

But Wise is not the only culprit. Brontë's naive husband, the Reverend Arthur Nicholls, also participated in scattering the corpus among his family and Elizabeth Gaskell. In 1856, one year after Charlotte's death, Nicholls gave Gaskell "a whole *heap* of those minute writings,"[3] and Gaskell later remarked in her biography, "I have had a curious packet confided to me, containing an immense amount of manuscript, in an inconceivably small space; tales, dramas, poems, romances, written principally by Charlotte" (chap. 5). Before Nicholls moved to Ireland with all the manuscripts returned to his possession, he transcribed some of the poems of all three Brontë sisters, including 24 of Charlotte's. As Neufeldt points out, Nicholls was "not only a careless copyist, he also 'edited' poems at times," and on other occasions he copied two poems as one. When Clement Shorter published an edition of the poetry in 1910, he used Nicholls's transcriptions and thereby continued the tradition of printing incorrect and unreliable texts as "definitive."[4]

Once in Ireland, Nicholls began giving a number of manuscripts away, seemingly as gifts, to at least two of his cousins, a Miss Bell and a Mrs. Bolster. In addition to the substantial manuscripts sold in 1895 to Shorter and Wise, 33 Brontë manuscripts were sold at auction at Sotheby's in 1907 and 1914. On another occasion the Nicholls family sold one poem of Charlotte's in three different sections, all coincidentally purchased by Henry Bonnell and pieced together by him in the act of transcription. By selling the manuscripts as well as the copyright to Wise and Shorter, however, Nicholls did the most damage to the poems' future publication history. Wise was not motivated by the best scholarly intentions but rather by greed and profit. As Tom Winnifrith states,

> Once it has been established that financial gain rather than the disinterested pursuit of knowledge was the mainspring behind Wise's activities, a whole area of uncertainty is opened up, since Wise exercised such a monopoly in Brontë affairs. . . . By selling Branwell's manuscripts as Charlotte's, by selling manuscripts which he had promised to bequeath to the nation, by binding manuscripts together which had no connection, but which might result in a more profitable sale, and by editing inefficiently the Brontë manuscripts he had squandered Wise has surely won himself an immortal place in Brontë studies.[5]

In addition to selling manuscripts in a shameless manner, Wise also exchanged them for other manuscripts and used them as gifts to friends. Wise was a major bidder at each of the two Sotheby's auctions, and those manuscripts that came into his hands were treated as the earlier ones had been. The final charge against Wise concerns his transcriptions of the original manuscripts. He employed a variety of scribes, and some were more careful and professional than others. In addition, some of his transcriptions are full of errors, and in others he left a blank space when he could not decipher a word or phrase. In short, the transcriptions that his expensive limited editions were based on were flawed or incomplete or both.

Another major culprit in the Brontë manuscript travesty is Clement Shorter, a journalist by profession, who also was not motivated by issues of scholarly accuracy or completeness. When Shorter published his expensive private editions, he simply used whatever printed text was already available to him without checking it for accuracy. In this way the errors were simply compounded from volume to volume, lending an air of validity to the editions, which were large money-makers for both Shorter and Wise. When serious Brontë scholars, such as Hatfield, attempted to check the accuracy of printed poems against the Brontë manuscripts, Shorter denied access on any number of occasions.

By the time of Shorter's death in 1926, serious Brontë scholars were raising a number of concerns and were questioning the accuracy of the so-called definitive edition, *The Shakespeare Head Brontë*. Neufeldt summarizes the charges made against the editors of this volume, Wise and J. A. Symington, as follows:

(a) poems for which the manuscripts were known to be extant [were] omitted;

(b) poems [were] attributed to the wrong author and [were] misdated;

(c) words, lines, and whole stanzas [were] omitted;

(d) [there were] many serious misreadings;

(e) uncanceled variants [were] ignored completely or inconsistently noted—i.e., sometimes Charlotte's first version is given as the preferred reading, sometimes the later variant;

(f) notes [referred] to non-existent alternate drafts, or confus[ed] the chronological sequence of alternate drafts.[6]

Wise and Symington ignored all of these problems, which were sufficiently serious to give any reader or student of the Brontës pause, in their drive to solidify their reputations as the world's premier Brontë scholars. They have left behind a legacy that has taken more than 50 years to unravel and set straight. Because of the flaws in their *Shakespeare Head Brontë*, students of Brontë's poetry should use Neufeldt's edition of the poetry for the most accurate and reliable texts.

The Poems

Because there are so many poems and because more than 60 percent of them relate directly to the complicated juvenilia Charlotte wrote with Branwell, the Glass Town saga, we will examine here only a few representatives of this vast output. It would be foolhardy to try to claim that Brontë had a great talent for poetry or that this early poetry is crucial for understanding her mature novels. As most critics have noted and as Brontë herself admitted, her poetry is largely juvenile—it is florid, melodramatic, and highly derivative. Between 1830 and 1850, Brontë produced more than 200 poems and verse fragments, far exceeding the output of both of her sisters combined. Neufeldt claims that her poetic career is marked by three periods of intensive composition: 1829 through 1830, 1833 through 1834, and 1837 through 1838.[7] In the first period Brontë produced 65 poems, 12 of them in collaboration with Branwell, and the play she called "The Poetaster," in which she mocks Branwell's literary pretensions. These early poems also reveal her literary sophistication and her experimentation with a variety of literary forms. Included in the output are a pindaric ode, a blank verse drama, open and closed couplet forms, a variety of stanzaic forms and rhyme schemes, and the ballad form. Christine Alexander has claimed that all of Brontë's early poems relate to the Glass Town saga, but Neufeldt qualifies that assertion by pointing out that just over half of the poems relate to the genii and the development of Glass Town.[8]

As Neufeldt observes, the high point of Brontë's poetic career occurred in 1830, when she was 14 years old. During that year she produced more poems than she would at any time in her life, so it is fair to conclude that poetry was clearly an apprentice activity for an artist whose true métier was prose fiction. The early poems are concerned with the nature of genius, art, and poetry itself.[9] Clearly inspired by the romantic movement, these early works are self-referential and discuss nature's inspiration in her growing sense of herself as a poet. A typical poem from this period, "The Violet," is signed by the Marquis of Douro and was obviously intended to be part of the Angrian saga. The speaker praises the poetic tradition of "Aeolian music" and lauds the literary luminaries Homer, Sophocles, and Virgil. Revealing the influence of Shelley's *Alastor* and Keats's *Hyperion* poems, this text calls on the "Mighty Mother's ear" to grant the poet's request to be among the chosen ones.

The second period of great poetic intensity, from 1833 through 1834, coincides with Brontë's return to collaboration with Branwell in the construction of the Glass Town saga. Thirty-two poems and verse fragments relating to the Duke of Zamorna's infidelities and political intrigues consumed her efforts during this year. The only poem written during this period that is not related to the Angrian cycle is titled "Richard Coeur de Lion & Bondel." Brontë appears to have bound this poem with four others, "Death of Darius Codomanus," "Saul," "Memory," and "Morning," in order to present her prying father with a sample of some of her literary creations. Neufeldt speculates that she did not want him near the Glass Town saga, so she constructed this more conventional offering, written not in her usual minuscule hand but in a large legible hand expressly for her father's failing eyes.[10] Two poems— "Memory" and "Reason"—are typical of the sort of faculty psychology she engaged in throughout *The Professor*, in which William Crimsworth holds debates between a variety of split-off tendencies in his own mind. Depressing and self-pitying, "Reason" attempts to examine her limited options in a life without passion or optimism:

> No syren-Beauty is not mine
> Affection's joys I ne'er shall know
> Lonely will be my life's decline
> Even as my youth is lonely now
> Come Reason—Science—Learning—Thought
> To you my heart I dedicate
> I have a faithful subject brought
> Faithful because most desolate. (ll. 17–24)

Another poem from this period reflects her growing anxiety about the siblings' mutual immersion in the creation of their fantasy world Glass Town, "We wove a web in childhood." Like that of her *Farewell to Angria*, the tone of this poem is one of almost religious guilt and shame, evident in the words that suggest decay and corruption: "blighted," "withered," "mouldered," and "faded." For all of Brontë's self-conscious condemnation of the escapist tendencies of obsessive activity, she also reveals in this poem the pull, the attraction, that kept her drawn to the creation of the silly Zamorna and his mistresses:

> The vision's spell had deepened o'er me
> Its lands its scenes were spread before me
> In one short hour a hundred homes
> Had roofed me with their lordly domes
> And I had sat by fires whose light
> Flashed wide o'er halls of regal height
> And I had seen those come & go
> Whose forms gave radiance to the glow (ll. 83–93)

The world of Angria is a world of very active, powerful, attractive people—an inverse, mirror world of the Haworth parsonage, which was quiet, dull, powerless, and unattractive. In creating such a bustling world Brontë peoples her own barren inner life with artificial beauty and activity. She is the ultimate God, the creator, the genius who has the power to bestow life and to undo the sting of death. The fantasy was a powerful wish fulfillment. It was also, however, also a recompense for loneliness, for in spending her days compulsively telling the same stories over and over again Brontë could blot out from her consciousness the realization that her life was going nowhere, her own chances for adventure and love negligible.

During her final period of poetic creativity, from 1837 through 1838, Brontë produced 60 poems, approximately two-thirds of which are Angrian in nature. Byron's influence can be noted in several of these poems, as it can be in a number of the poems she wrote in 1836. Brontë's growing anxiety about the fantasy world she and Branwell had created and that had a stranglehold on her imagination comes through in a number of poems, as does her growing religious angst about the amorality of this fantasy kingdom and of her intense attraction to and psychic immersion in it. Whereas her earlier poems survive in "fair copy" form, clean and final drafts with no canceled sections, these later poems survive only in rough-draft form, with numerous blank spaces and canceled lines and stanzas. Neufeldt claims that the quality of Brontë's poetry "declines noticeably from about mid-1837 on," and most contemporary critics would agree. Winifred Gérin has suggested that the reason for this decline can be found in Brontë's shift from "unself-conscious dreaming to critical artistic composition and self-critical evaluation."[11] As Brontë became more aware of her strengths and weaknesses as a literary artist, she shifted her efforts to her prose, and her desire to write verse declined. Another plausible explanation can be located in her increasingly sophisticated ability to use prose to explore her psychic pains and traumas.

In 1838 Brontë produced several short lyrics, all but one being Angrian and seven being parts of prose narratives. Between 1838 and Brontë's departure for Brussels in February 1842, she wrote only six poems, four of which deal with the continuing Angrian saga. In 1840 she wrote the "Valentine" poem, and in 1841 she produced the first draft of "Passion," a poem ostensibly based on the Napoleonic Wars in Spain. Sounding like Keats as well as Byron, "Passion" looks toward death with bravado:

> I'd die when all the foam is up,
> The bright wine sparkling high;
> Nor wait till in the exhausted cup
> Life's dull dregs only lie.
> Then Love thus crowned with sweet reward,
> Hope blast with fulness large,
> I'd mount the saddle, draw the sword,
> And perish in the charge! (ll. 46–53)

While living in Brussels in 1842 she wrote a poem on the death of her friend Martha Taylor and copied a number of her earlier poems into a copy book found by Ernest Nys and sold by him to the British Museum. When Brontë returned from Brussels she was convinced that her writing career was finished, and she poured her grief and sense of betrayal by M. Heger initially into her letters to him. When he did not respond to her overtures, she turned once again to the creative outlet with which she was most familiar—poetry.

Brontë stumbled on her sister Emily's poems and then insisted that all three sisters publish their poetry together in one volume, the 1846 collection that began their careers, paradoxically, as novelists. As Neufeldt notes, most of Charlotte's poems published in the volume are slight revisions of poems she had written years before, in some cases as many as 10 years earlier. Charlotte's poetry was not considered as strong as Emily's, and Charlotte went on after the publication of the 1846 volume to write only a handful of poems. Of the 19 poems Brontë selected for inclusion in the 1846 volume, "Gilbert," "Preference," "The Missionary," and "The Wood" were written before her stay in Brussels. Neufeldt believes that "Preference" and "The Wood" are probably reworkings of earlier Angrian poems, and that Brontë simply changed the names of the characters in order to conceal the poetry's origins. Only "Gilbert" and "The Missionary" were written in 1845, whereas all of the other poems are much older, some dating back to 1836.[12]

"The Missionary" has certain affinities with the character St. John Rivers in the later *Jane Eyre,* as does the "The Teacher's Monologue." "The Missionary," which is told from a man's point of view, recounts his painful decision to leave his beloved Helen behind in England while he pursues his destiny converting "pagan-priests, whose creed is Wrong" (p. 67):

> And I—who have the healing creed,
> The faith benign of Mary's Son;
> Shall I behold my brother's need
> And, selfishly, to aid him shun? (ll. 71–74)

The poem's religious intensity and the seriousness with which the missionary takes both the man's vocation and his presumed death suggest that the St. John Rivers figure in *Jane Eyre* has to be taken seriously as a recurring masculine type that Brontë found intensely attractive.

Similarly, "The Teacher's Monologue" suggests not simply the despair of Jane Eyre or Lucy Snowe as erstwhile instructors of unruly girls but the more autobiographical sources of Brontë's own depression while teaching at Roe Head. Feeling her youth wasted, she expresses in this poem her mourning for a more active and meaningful life:

> And Patience, weary with her yoke,
> Is yielding to despair,
> And Health's elastic spring is broke
> Beneath the strain of care.
> Life will be gone ere I have lived;
> Where now is Life's first prime?

> I've worked and studied, longed and grieved,
> Through all that rosy time.
> To toil, to think, to long, to grieve,—
> Is such my future fate? (ll. 74–84)

In "Gilbert" a solitary man strolls alone through a garden placed "in a city-heart" (p. 9). We recall immediately William Crimsworth's foray through *The Professor*'s *"allée défendue,"* but this poetic melodrama quickly shifts the scene in order to explore significantly different territory. "Gilbert" is a quasi-ballad about a suicidal demon lover who returns after many years to claim the financially successful and arrogant Gilbert as her mate. Just as Gilbert rejected his first love, who then committed suicide by drowning, so now does that "ashy-white" woman come back to cause Gilbert's suicide. The heavy-handed moral of the poem is stated baldly: " 'The measure thou to her didst mete, / To thee shall measured be!' " (ll. 391–92). What follows is Gilbert's wildly theatrical end:

> Across his throat, a keen-edged knife
> With vigorous hand he drew;
> The wound was wide—his outraged life
> Rushed rash and redly through.
> And thus he died, by a shameful death,
> A wise and worldly man,
> Who never drew but selfish breath
> Since first his life began. (ll. 401–8)

It is interesting to consider the poem "Frances" in light of Emily's creation of Frances Hindley in her later novel *Wuthering Heights*. But apart from this sort of intertextuality, there is little of interest in these poems except for the Brontë aficionado.

In 1847 Brontë composed "Jane" for inclusion in *The Professor;* that same year she also composed "He saw my heart's woe," about the frustration she felt in her unrequited love for M. Heger, and in 1848 and 1849 she wrote poems on the deaths of Emily and Anne respectively. "He saw my heart's woe" is so nakedly frank, so unrelievingly depressing that it is almost painful to read. Referring to the letters she promised to send M. Heger only once a year, she writes that he never responded: "He was mute as was the grave—he stood stirless as a tower / At last I looked up and saw I prayed to stone." The intense sense of rejection and the imagery of idolatry is, of course, replayed differently in the relationship of Lucy Snowe and M. Paul Emanuel, and one recalls the stone obelisk in *Villette* as one reads this meditation on frustrated love. Clearly poetry writing was a form of therapy for Brontë, a way for her to rework her manifold longings and to shape and control her disappointments and trauma. When she learned that she could do the same therapeutic work in prose fiction, and on a much grander scale, she abandoned her poetic muse.

The Publication History of the Letters

Brontë wrote lengthy and revealing letters her entire adult life to her girlhood friend Ellen Nussey, and these letters have provided the source of most of what we know about Brontë's life. As such, these letters are vital to our understanding of Brontë's mind, moods, and psychological and emotional development, from the very first, written in 1831 when Brontë was 15 years old, to the last, composed just weeks before her death. Brontë clearly valued the letters she wrote to her two closest friends, Nussey and Mary Taylor, and she also strongly appreciated receiving letters: "I thank you again for your last letter which I found as full or fuller of interest than either of the preceding ones—it is just written as I wish you to write to me—not a detail too much—a correspondence of that sort is the next best thing to actual conversation—though it must be allowed that between the two there is a wide gulph still—I imagine your face—voice—presence very plainly when I read your letters" (Brontë to Nussey, 19 January 1847). Brontë aimed to produce the sort of letters she praises here, and reading her long and detailed correspondence with Nussey provides us with just this sort of glimpse of her face, voice, and very presence.

The publication history of Brontë's letters bears, unfortunately, numerous similarities to the unsavory publication history of her poetry. Not surprisingly, the copyright to her letters was owned by Brontë's husband, who finally sold that copyright to Shorter along with the bulk of the literary manuscripts in his possession in 1895. The key player in the history of Brontë's letters, however, is her major correspondent and lifelong friend Ellen Nussey. We might wish that Nussey had shown more sense or prudence in her possession of Brontë's valuable letters, but unfortunately that was not the case. Nussey recapitulated many of the same mistakes Patrick Brontë and Arthur Nicholls made with the poetic manuscripts. Nussey's cutting and selling of autographs and portions of the letters began almost immediately after Brontë's death. It has taken many years and the painstaking work of numerous modern editors to piece together the letters to Nussey and others as they were originally written. Some letters, no one is certain how many, are permanently lost.

The definitive edition of Brontë's letters was finally published in 1995, by the respected modern Brontë scholar Margaret Smith. The first volume of Brontë's letters—the only edition available thus far—covers the period of 1829 to 1847. Smith groups the letters chronologically, and her introduction traces Brontë's life through these epistles to Nussey. There are a much smaller number of letters to Robert Southey, her publishers, her sisters and father, M. Heger, and eventually Nicholls. Brontë's other close girlhood friend, Mary Taylor, destroyed all of the letters she received from Brontë. Elizabeth Gaskell, like Brontë's father and husband, began the dispersal and mutilation of the letters written to her as early as 1863. For instance, Gaskell contributed Brontë letters in her possession to an auction to benefit the Union cause during the American Civil War, and both Patrick Brontë and Arthur Nicholls began around the same time to cut Brontë's autograph off of letters for little gifts to visitors and friends. One letter in Smith's volume, written on the occasion of Anne Brontë's death, was pieced together from fragments found in five locations—Haworth, Dublin, Texas, New York, and Pennsylvania.[13]

The letters were first published, highly edited, and selectively pruned by Gaskell in her *Life*. After that, Nussey made at least three attempts to publish the letters in her possession, once even proposing to M. Heger that he collaborate with her in the venture. He demurred. Frightened about the legal complications and threats—veiled or otherwise—she felt she had received from Nicholls, in 1892 Nussey sold the 380 intimate letters written to her by Brontë to Clement Shorter, who presented himself to her as a serious Brontë scholar with the resources to publish the material in a manner that Nussey felt was fitting to the memory of her lifelong friend. Shorter quickly passed the letters on to the unscrupulous Wise, and the wholesale desecration of the letters began in earnest. They were next published in the volume *Charlotte Brontë and Her Circle*, edited by Shorter and published in 1896. Shorter claimed that he had corrected all of the errors and expurgations Gaskell made in *Life*, but in fact he did not catch many of Gaskell's changes and also went on to make several of his own. In one letter, for instance,

Brontë refers to "Penn & the Quakers"; Shorter transcribed the phrase as "Penn on the Marshes." As Smith points out, these letters were then used as the basis of the *Shakespeare Head Brontë* published in 1932 by Wise and Symington.[14] It has taken Smith and numerous other Brontë scholars more than 60 years to reexamine what remains of the original letters and to produce a definitive edition.

The Letters to Ellen Nussey

Shortly after Brontë's marriage, she was instructed by her husband to stop writing such revealing and personal letters to her dear friend Nussey. Brontë responded to this demand by expressing her sense of frustration with her new husband's lack of understanding in yet another letter to Nussey: "Men don't seem to understand making letters a vehicle of communication—they always seem to think us incautious. I'm sure I don't think I have said anything rash—however you must *burn* it when read. Arthur says such letters as mine never ought to be kept—they are dangerous as lucifer matches—so be sure to follow a recommendation he has just given 'fire them'—or 'there will be no more.' . . . I can't help laughing—this seems to me so funny; Arthur however says he is quite serious and looks it, I assure you" (Brontë to Nussey, 27 October 1854). Surely Brontë's statements support the contention of numerous contemporary feminist scholars that letters are an authentic form of writing for nineteenth-century women writers.

The earliest letters, written between 1829 and 1835, reveal little of Brontë's secret writing life with Branwell that we know was her obsession during this period. Instead, the letters are the product of a precocious schoolgirl who sprinkled them liberally and perhaps pretentiously with references to Byron, Scott, Milton, Southey, Coleridge, and Burns. The next period of intense letter writing, 1836 to 1838, occurred while Brontë was a teacher at the Roe Head school (1836–37). The letters of this period reveal a stark contrast between Brontë's mundane tasks as a sort of drill sergeant of young girls and her rich immersion in her imaginary, secret Angrian world. As we know from her Roe Head journal, she frequently escaped at the end of every day's tedious work to her bedroom, where she indulged in escapist and erotic daydreams:

> [I] crept up to the bed-room to be *alone* for the first time [and resigned myself] to the Luxury of twilight & solitude . . . the toil of the Day succeeded by this moment of divine leisure—had acted on me like opium &

was coiling about me a disturbed but fascinated spell such as I never felt before. What I imagined grew morbidly vivid. I remember I quite seemed to see with my bodily eyes, a lady standing in the hall of a Gentlemen's house as if waiting for some one. . . . She was very handsome— it is not often we can form from pure idea faces so individually fine.[15]

It was during this period also that Brontë's attachment to Nussey grew particularly obsessive, perhaps out of sheer loneliness and desperation. The letters display a tone of spiritual despair and a bout of hypochondria that recalls both William Crimsworth in *The Professor* and Lucy Snowe's depression during the long holiday she spent alone with a cretin in *Villette*. To Nussey, Brontë writes that she has a "longing for holiness which I shall *never, never* obtain . . . darkened in short by the very shadows of Spiritual Death!" (5–6 December 1836). The letters also reveal her envy of more worldly and fashionable women as well as uniformly suggest a young woman consumed with self-hatred, self doubts, and self-absorption.

The next period of letter writing, from 1839 through 1841, occurred when Brontë returned home from Roe Head for five months before taking a position as a governess to the White children of Rawdon, near Leeds. A new self-confidence is revealed in these letters to Nussey, written while Brontë was composing the novelettes "Henry Hastings," "Caroline Vernon," "Ashworth," and finally the "Farewell to Angria." In many ways the letters suggest the development of ideas, themes, and techniques that are found in Brontë's major novels. There is a new tone of satire and gentle sarcasm on a number of subjects, most notably the folly of curates that was later developed in the first chapter of *Shirley,* "Levitical." For instance, when Brontë describes the "shower of curates" falling on England like a plague, we hear very much the same voice— humorous and slightly mocking the shortcomings of greedy and gluttonous clergy who should be more concerned for their flocks than for their stomachs.

Brontë's next productive period of letter writing was from 1842 through 1844, years Brontë spent in Brussels studying with and eventually teaching for the Hegers. These letters to Nussey initially begin in optimism and delight at having such a brilliant and learned man as her tutor and intellectual mentor. Brontë's first year in Brussels, however, was also the year that her friend Martha Taylor died and was buried in the Protestant cemetery outside of the gates of Louvain, an event Brontë was to recreate in both *The Professor* and *Shirley.* The early letters from

Brussels also reveal "brief attacks of home-sickness" and depict three particularly difficult fellow students: "singularly cold, selfish, animal and inferior—they are besides very mutinous and difficult for the teachers to manage" (Brontë to Nussey, July 1842). Brontë's intense sensitivity toward these students would cause her to portray them unflatteringly in both *The Professor* and *Villette*.

By the second year in Brussels, however, depression and despair set in as Brontë seemed to struggle with confessing and yet simultaneously denying her love for M. Heger. Claiming not to understand why Mme. Heger is cool to her, she complains that M. Heger has "withdrawn the light of his countenance" (29 May 1843), and in another letter to her sister Emily she admits that her depression drove her to make a "real confession" in a Catholic cathedral (19 December 1843).

In 1845 Brontë composed her famous letters to M. Heger. This was also the year during which she learned of her brother Branwell's sexual disgrace with Lydia Robinson and mourned the loss of her close friend Mary Taylor, who was to depart shortly for New Zealand. Despite or perhaps because of her despair over these events, Brontë returned to writing a story about two brothers that she had begun before she left for Brussels—the novel that would become *The Professor*. Brontë's frustration over her thwarted relationship with M. Heger comes through in her letters to Nussey, who could not have suspected the actual source of Brontë's intense disequilibrium. In one letter written during this period, Brontë expresses to Nussey her sense of being buried alive, a feeling she was to embody literally in the figure of Bertha Rochester in *Jane Eyre:*

> I can hardly tell you how time gets on here at Haworth . . . life wears away—I shall soon be 30—and I have done nothing yet—sometimes I get melancholy—at the prospect before and behind me—yet it is wrong and foolish to repine—undoubtedly my Duty directs me to stay at home for the present. . . . I feel as if we were all buried here—I long to travel—to work to live a life of action. (24 March 1845)

In the autumn of this painful year, Brontë discovered Emily's poems, and the famous Bell brothers began their literary careers as poets with a volume of 61 poems, published with their own funds in May 1846. Throwing herself into the revision of her earlier poetry, removing all references to Angria and Gondal, Brontë staved off a bit longer her pain over receiving nothing but silence from M. Heger.

In 1846 Brontë corresponded with different publishers—Chambers & Co., Aylott and Jones, and Henry Colburn, among many others—in a futile attempt to find outlets for the first novels the Bells produced. *The Professor* was rejected time after time, and Brontë told Gaskell that she had received one rejection on the very day her father was to have cataract surgery in Manchester—25 August 1846. Gaskell observed in her *Life* that Brontë "had the heart of Robert Bruce within her, and failure upon failure daunted her no more than him. Not only did "The Professor" return again to try his chance among the London publishers, but she began, in this time of care and depressing inquietude,—in those grey, weary, uniform streets . . . there and then, did the brave genius begin "Jane Eyre" (Gaskell, *Life*, p. 245). Because Brontë wanted to keep her professional writing ambitions from Nussey, there is no mention of any of her aspirations in the letters she wrote during this period. Instead, she dwells on the problems Nussey had with her mentally ill brother George, a dilemma that Brontë could understand given the rapidly deteriorating condition of her own brother Branwell. Brontë writes to Nussey: "Poor George! time passes—winter, spring and summer, and his ?natural self delays to return—How can his brothers decline to give assistance in his case?" (MS BPM Bon 189). Ironically, as it is only fair to observe, Brontë was at the same time less than sympathetic to her own brother's growing addictions and erratic and self-destructive behavior.

In 1847—the Brontës' *annus mirabilis*—*Jane Eyre, Wuthering Heights,* and *Agnes Grey* were published. That same year Brontë also wrote numerous letters to her publisher, George Smith, the man who would eventually be portrayed in the fiction of *Villette* as Dr. John Graham Bretton. When Smith definitively rejected Brontë's first attempt at fiction, *The Professor,* Brontë called the book her "martyrised MS" and wrote sarcastically to him, "Of course my feelings towards it can only be paralleled by those of a doting parent towards an idiot child" (Brontë to Smith, 5 February 1851). But when she accepted Smith's advice to set aside *The Professor* and try her hand at another story, Brontë turned out *Jane Eyre,* which she described as "true" to Smith: "Perhaps too the first part of "Jane Eyre" may suit the public taste better than you anticipate—for it is true and Truth has a severe charm of its own" (12 September 1847). The publication of *Jane Eyre* began Brontë's public persona and widely enlarged her circle of correspondents. She continued her correspondence with Nussey, but those letters are remarkably free of Brontë's professional concerns and literary ambitions.

The Letters to Heger

Although only four letters from Brontë to M. Constantin Heger survive, these mutilated and stitched-together epistles revolutionized understanding of Brontë's life and novels when they first became known in 1913. Heger himself had shown the letters to Gaskell when she visited in May 1856 on a research trip to complete her *Life,* but Gaskell had decided to whitewash the relationship in an attempt to present Brontë as a Christian heroine. We know that letters are missing because after Brontë initially left Brussels she wrote M. Heger twice a week. It was Mme. Heger who responded, informing Brontë that she would be permitted to send a letter once every six months. At some point M. Heger tore up and threw out the surviving letters, but Mme. Heger retrieved them, sewed or glued them together, and decided to keep them as evidence in the event of a legal threat made against them by Brontë. Mme. Heger told her children that when Brontë left Brussels, she had spit out the words "Je me vengerai" ("I shall avenge myself"). The writing of *Villette* was perhaps the fulfillment of that threat, but Mme. Heger was taking no chances on what the infatuated British tutor might yet try to inflict on her family.

Because of persistent rumors about how the Heger family had wronged Brontë, two of the Heger children, Louise and Paul, donated the letters to the British Museum in 1913 in an effort to set the record straight. These letters were first published in the *Times* on 29 July 1913, with a translation and analysis by Marion H. Spielmann, an art critic and close friend of the Heger family. T. J. Wise quickly pirated the letters and published them in an expensive volume entitled *The Love Letters of Charlotte Brontë to Constantin Heger* (1914). Also without copyright permission, Shorter published the letters in his 1914 edition of *The Brontës and Their Circle.*

In the letters Brontë confesses everlasting "affection" for M. Heger, although she herself changed that word to "respect." Written in frustration and with an increasing sense of impotence and rejection, the letters show that the relationship was one-sided and that Brontë was pathetically wrapped up in an attempt to prove herself worthy of yet another distant and unattainable father-figure. In the letter written on 24 July 1844, Brontë tells M. Heger that she has received support from Southey and Coleridge to pursue her literary career, but this was not the case. She goes on in a confessional mode to beg forgiveness for her emotional excesses:

Ah Monsieur! I once wrote you a letter [now missing] which was hardly rational, because sadness was wringing my heart, but I shall do so no more—I will try to stop being egotistical and though I look on your letters as one of the greatest joys I know, I shall wait patiently to receive them until it pleases and suits you to send them.[16]

Claiming that her eyes are so weak she cannot pursue a career in writing, she goes on to sketch out her plan to establish a private school in the parsonage, in direct imitation of the school that Mme. Heger had successfully instituted in Brussels:

Nevertheless I have made a plan: (when one lives in seclusion one's brain is always active—one longs to be busy—one longs to launch out into an active career) Our Parsonage is a fairly large house—with some alterations—there will be room for five or six boarders—if I could find that number of children from respectable families—I would devote myself to their education. . . . So all that remains is to find the pupils—a rather difficult matter—for we live a long way from towns and people hardly wish to take the trouble of crossing the mountains which form a barrier round us—but the task which lacks difficulty almost lacks merit—it is very rewarding to surmount obstacles—I do not say that I shall succeed but I shall *try* to succeed—the effort alone will do me good *I fear nothing so much as* idleness—*lack of employment—inertia—lethargy of the faculties— when the body is idle, the spirit suffers cruelly.*[17]

As if to justify her abdication of a literary career that the literary luminaries of Britain were supposedly encouraging her to pursue, Brontë then claims to be suffering from a form of blindness remarkably similar to that afflicting her father: "—if I wrote a line I would become blind. This weakness of sight is a terrible privation for me—without it, do you know what I would do, Monsieur?—I would write a book and I would dedicate it to my literature master—to the only master that I have ever had—to you Monsieur."[18] Again, the need to compete with a powerful maternal figure and win the father-lover's approval would be almost pathetic had the wound not resulted in the major novels that reworked that pain for the heroines and their author.

Miscellaneous Letters

The earliest existing letter Brontë wrote to someone outside her close circle of family and friends is her letter of introduction to the famous poet Robert Southey, an early literary hero of Brontë and her siblings. This letter, written to the elderly Southey on 28 December 1836 and no longer available, expresses the fledgling poet's desire for an objective opinion on the merit of her poems. Its contents have been deduced from the response that Brontë received from Southey. Awash in a feverish bravado, the letter reveals Brontë's desire to be "for ever known" as a poetess who begs merely for the exalted Southey to "stoop from a throne of light & glory" to speak to her. Southey more cautiously advised that such hyperbolic fantasies could cause only "a distempered state of mind" and then went on to pronounce that self-important injunction: "Literature cannot be the business of a woman's life" (Southey to Brontë, 12 March 1837). For all the pain that Southey's letter caused Brontë, she was later able to say to Gaskell that "Mr. Southey's letter was kind and admirable; a little stringent, but it did me good" (Gaskell, *Life*, p. 124).

Another important letter, written to refuse Henry Nussey's marriage proposal, reveals Brontë's cool powers of observation and discernment. She tells Henry that she has studied his character and determined that she would not be the sort of woman who would make him a good wife. Instead, she tactfully suggests that he should marry a "mild" and pious woman whose "personal attractions" should "please your eye and gratify your just pride" (5 March 1839). The emphasis on a marriage of like minds and similar temperaments anticipates in many ways the marriages her heroines made in the four major novels, but most particularly in *Jane Eyre*.

Brontë also wrote a letter to Hartley Coleridge on 10 December 1840 in which she asked for his literary opinion about one of her Angrian short stories. Brontë adopts in this letter the style and tone of her male persona Charles Townshend, and she makes numerous references to her knowledge of the novels of Samuel Richardson, whose influence is obvious in the composition of *The Professor, Jane Eyre,* and *Shirley:*

> I am pleased that you cannot quite decide whether I belong to the soft or the hard sex—and though at first I had no intention of being enigmatical on the subject—yet as I accidentally omitted to give the clue at first, I will venture purposely to withhold it now—as to my handwriting, or the ladylike tricks you mention in my style and imagery—you must not draw any conclusion from those—Several young gentlemen curl their hair and wear corsets—Richardson and Rousseau—often write exactly like old women—and Bulwer and Cooper and Dickens and Warren like boarding-school misses.[19]

Mocking her own literary ambitions was perhaps the safest position for her to take, given her paucity of opportunities: "I wonder you took the trouble to read and notice the demi-semi novelette of an anonymous scribe who had not even the manners to tell you whether he was a man or woman or whether his common-place 'C.T.' meant Charles Tims or Charlotte Tomkins."[20] This second attempt to appeal to a major literary figure of her culture for help, however, betrays how serious Brontë was about her career even at this early date.

Two letters written to her former schoolmistress Miss Wooler reveal how intensely Brontë needed her as a maternal substitute. Coincidentally, Wooler had a brother who also suffered from mental illness, and one of the most revealing letters to her concerns Brontë's sympathy for this brother's bouts with the "tyranny of Hypochondria." Using a phrase she had employed just a few months earlier in the Red Room scene of *Jane Eyre,* Brontë tells Wooler that she too has experienced the "preternatural horror" of hypochondria (November–December 1846).

W. S. Williams became another correspondent who assumed importance to Brontë as her literary success increased. Throughout 1848 and 1849 Brontë wrote him a number of personal letters that shared her grief over the deaths of Branwell, Emily, and Anne. On the death of Emily, Brontë wrote,

> Emily is nowhere here now, her wasted mortal remains are taken out of the house. We have laid her cherished head under the church aisle beside my mother's, my two sisters'—dead long ago—and my poor, hapless brother's. But a small remnant of the race is left—so my father thinks. Well, the loss is ours, not hers, and some sad comfort I take, as I hear the wind blow and feel the cutting keenness of the frost, in knowing that the elements bring her no more suffering; their severity cannot reach her grave; her fever is quieted, her restlessness soothed, her deep, hollow cough is hushed for ever; we do not hear it in the night nor listen for it in the morning; we have not the conflict of the strangely strong spirit and the fragile frame before us—relentless conflict—once seen, never to be forgotten. A dreary calm reigns round us, in the midst of which we seek resignation.[21]

Brontë was considerably more restrained and less poetic in reporting to Williams Anne's death: "My poor sister is taken quietly home at last. She died on Monday. With almost her last breath she said she was happy, and thanked God that death was come, and come so gently. I did not think it would be so soon."[22]

The letters to Williams are also significant for what they tell us about Brontë's reading habits and tastes as well as about the compositional history of all of her novels. When Williams asked her to revise the preface to *Shirley,* she responded, "I cannot change my preface. I can shed no tears before the public, nor utter any groan in the public ear. The deep, real tragedy of our domestic experience is yet terribly fresh in my mind and memory. It is not a time to be talked about to the indifferent; it is not a topic for allusion to in print."[23] Later, when Williams tried to lure her out of her seclusion and into the literary life of London, she responded,

> You mention the literary coteries. To speak the truth, I recoil from them, though I long to see some of the truly great literary characters. However, this is not to be yet—I cannot sacrifice my incognito. And let me be content with seclusion—it has its advantages. In general, indeed, I am tranquil, it is only now and then that a struggle disturbs me—that I wish for a wider world than Haworth. When it is past, Reason tells me how unfit I am for anything very different.[24]

But "Reason" also told Brontë how limited her life was, like the lives of so many middle-class women. To Williams she confided her frustration:

> Lonely as I am, how should I be if Providence had never given me courage to adopt a career—perseverance to plead through two long, weary years with publishers till they admitted me? How should I be with youth past, sisters lost, a resident in a moorland parish where there is not a single educated family? In that case I should have no world at all: the raven, weary of surveying the deluge, and without an ark to return to, would be my type. As it is, something like a hope and motive sustains me still. I wish all your daughters—I wish every woman in England, had also a hope and motive. Alas! there are many old maids who have neither.[25]

Other literary correspondents would later include George Henry Lewes, Gaskell, Thackeray, and Harriet Martineau. Never comfortable with the London literary scene, however, Brontë would increasingly retreat from all but Gaskell, a safely maternal figure.

Brontë's last letters, written largely to Nussey, concern her decision to marry Nicholls, their wedding, their honeymoon in Ireland, and their brief married life. The letter to Nussey most frequently quoted contains the only description we have in Brontë's own hand about her married state. This cryptic passage, written on 9 August 1854, reads,

> During the last six weeks the colour of my thoughts is a good deal changed: I know more of the realities of life than I once did. I think many false ideas are propagated, perhaps unintentionally. I think those married women who indiscriminately urge their acquaintances to marry, much to blame. For my part, I can only say with deeper sincerity and fuller significance, what I always said in theory, "Wait God's will." Indeed, indeed, Nell, it is a solemn and strange and perilous thing for a woman to become a wife. Man's lot is far, far different.[26]

This letter seems to suggest some difficulty in accepting the sexual realities of marriage, the physical demands of pregnancy, and the threatening nature of childbirth. Given its heavily censored tone, however, it is difficult to assert anything definitive about Brontë's adjustment to the marriage or about her attitude toward an impending pregnancy.

Brontë's poetry and letters have traditionally formed the absent chapter—the silent text—for most of the literary discussions we have of her novels. Although no one would claim that the poetry is sophisticated or profound, the poems present in miniature what appear to be etchings of pain and longing that would surface again on a broader canvas in the novels. As Brontë wrote to Lewes, "Can there be a great Artist without poetry?" (18 January 1848).

Notes and References

Chapter One

1. Author's preface to Charlotte Brontë, *Jane Eyre,* ed. Richard Dunn (New York: W. W. Norton, 1971; rpt. 1987), 1–2. Brontë lauds Thackeray as "a man . . . who speaks truth as deep, with a power as prophet-like and as vital—a mien as dauntless and as daring. . . . I see in him an intellect profounder and more unique than his contemporaries have yet recognised. . . . I regard him as the first social regenerator of the day—as the very master of that working corps who would restore to rectitude the warped system of things" (p. 2).

2. Rebecca Fraser, *The Brontës: Charlotte Brontë and Her Family* (New York: Crown, 1988), 285.

3. Gaye Tuchman and Nina Fortin, *Edging Women Out* (New Haven: Yale University Press, 1988), 8. Tuchman and Fortin chart the ways in which rising female writers were subtly but systematically excluded from book publishing, whereas increasing numbers of men became professional fiction writers from 1840 until the end of the nineteenth century.

4. Robert Southey to Charlotte Brontë, March 1837. Quoted in Winifred Gérin, *Charlotte Brontë: The Evolution of Genius* (Oxford: Oxford University Press, 1967), 110.

5. E. S. Dallas, *Blackwood's* 87 (1853): 19.

6. G. H. Lewes, "The Lady Novelists," *Westminster Review,* n.s., 2 (1852): 133.

7. Virginia Woolf, *A Room of One's Own* (New York: Harcourt Brace & World, 1929), 4, 108.

8. Catherine Hamilton, *Women Writers: Their Works and Ways* (London: Lock, Bowden & Co., 1892), quoted without page attribution in Elaine Showalter, *A Literature of Their Own: British Women Novelists from Brontë to Lessing* (Princeton, N.J.: Princeton University Press, 1977), 85.

9. Fraser, *The Brontës: Charlotte Brontë and Her Family,* ix–x.

10. T. J. Wise and J. A. Symington, eds., *The Brontës: Their Lives, Friendships, and Correspondences,* vol. 2 (Oxford: Shakespeare Head Press, 1938), 218.

11. Quoted in Elizabeth Gaskell, *The Life of Charlotte Brontë,* ed. and intro. Alan Shelston (New York: Penguin, 1975), 161.

12. Tom Winnifrith and Edward Chitham, *Charlotte and Emily Brontë: Literary Lives* (New York: Macmillan, 1989), 2.

13. W. M. Thackeray to Lucy Baxter, 11 March 1853, in Gordon Ray, ed., *The Letters and Private Papers of William Makepeace Thackeray,* 4 vols. (Cambridge, Mass.: Harvard University Press, 1946). Reprinted in Miriam Allott,

ed. and intro., *Charlotte Brontë: "Jane Eyre" and "Villette": A Casebook* (London: Macmillan, 1973), 93.

14.   "A Few Words about Jane Eyre," *Sharpe's London Magazine*, n.s., 5 (June 1855): 339–42.

15.   A good overview of Gaskell's biography is provided in Alan Shelston's introduction to Gaskell, *The Life of Charlotte Brontë* (Harmondsworth, England: Penguin, 1975), 9–37; analyses of Gaskell's biography include Margaret Lane, "The Hazards of Biography: Mrs. Gaskell and Charlotte Brontë," *Cornhill Magazine* 993 (Summer 1950): 351–75, and Arthur Pollard, "Mrs. Gaskell's *Life of Charlotte Brontë*," *Bulletin of the John Rylands Library* 47 (n. d.): 453–88.

16.   Alan Shelston, introduction to Gaskell, *The Life of Charlotte Brontë*, 13.

17.   Gaskell, *The Life of Charlotte Brontë*, 334.

18.   Gaskell, *The Life of Charlotte Brontë*, ed. Alan Shelston, appendix A, 527–28.

19.   Ellen Nussey, "Reminiscences of Charlotte Brontë," *Scribner's Monthly Magazine* (May 1871): XXX; rpt. *Brontë Society Transactions* 2.10 (n. d.): 58–83.

20.   George Smith, "The Brontës," *Cornhill Magazine* X (July 1873): 54–71.

21.   Mrs. Oliphant, "The Literature of the Last Fifty Years," *Blackwood's* 141 (January 1887): 757–58.

22.   Algernon Charles Swinburne, *A Note on Charlotte Brontë* (London: Chatto & Windus, 1877). Reprinted in part in Allott, ed., *The Brontës: The Critical Heritage*, (London: Routledge and Kegan Paul, 1974), 404–12. Hereafter, *The Critical Heritage*.

23.   Leslie Stephen, "Charlotte Brontë," in Stephen, *Hours in a Library* (London: Smith, Elder, 1878), 325–64. First published in *Cornhill Magazine* (December 1877): 723–29. Reprinted in part in Allott, *The Critical Heritage*, 413–23.

24.   Peter Bayne, "Charlotte Brontë and Her Sisters," in Bayne, *Two Great Englishwomen: Mrs. Browning and Charlotte Brontë* (London: James Clark & Co., 1881), 155–340.

25.   Mary Augusta [Mrs. Humphrey] Ward, prefaces to *The Life and Works of Charlotte Brontë and Her Sisters,* Haworth edition, 7 vols. (London: Smith, Elder, 1899–1900).

26.   Allott, ed. and intro., *The Critical Heritage,* 43.

27.   E. F. Benson, *Charlotte Brontë* (London: Longmans, 1932).

28.   Quoted in Margot Peters, "Charlotte Brontë: A Critico-Bibliographic Survey, 1945–1974," *British Studies Monitor* 6 (1976): 20.

29.   A. C. Benson, *A Life of Edward White Benson, Late Archbishop of Canterbury* (London: n. p., 1895).

30. Quoted in Margot Peters, *Unquiet Soul: A Biography of Charlotte Brontë* (Garden City, N.Y.: Doubleday, 1986), 176.

31. Lord David Cecil, *Early Victorian Novelists: Essays in Revaluation* (New York: Bobbs-Merrill Co., 1935), 119–54; reprinted in part in Judith O'Neill, ed., *Critics on Charlotte Brontë* (Coral Gables, Fla.: University of Miami Press, 1968), 20, 22, 23, 24.

32. Winifred Gérin, *Charlotte Brontë: The Evolution of Genius* (New York: Oxford University Press, 1967), xv. Gérin has also published, through the Longman Writers and Their Work series (Harlow: Longman) two biographical pamphlets that are particularly useful for student use: *The Brontës: The Formative Years* (1973) and *The Brontës: The Creative Work* (1974).

33. Gérin, *Charlotte Brontë: The Evolution of Genius,* xvi.

34. Peters, *Unquiet Soul,* 34.

35. Peters, *Unquiet Soul,* 414.

36. Tom Winnifrith, *The Brontës and Their Background: Romance and Reality* (New York: Barnes, 1973), ix.

37. Ibid.

38. Ibid., 3.

39. Ibid., 5.

40. Helene Moglen, *Charlotte Brontë: The Self Conceived* (New York: Norton, 1976), 78. Moglen's book contains individual chapters on the four major novels. Her biographical analysis can be found in the first chapter, "Survival," which focuses on Brontë's life through 1845.

41. Fraser, *The Brontës: Charlotte Brontë and Her Family,* ix.

42. Ibid., x.

43. Ibid.

44. Juliet Barker, *The Brontës* (New York: St. Martin's Press, 1995), xix.

45. Ibid., xx.

46. Robert B. Martin, *Accents of Persuasion: Charlotte Brontë's Novels* (New York: Norton, 1966), 18, 16.

47. Barker, *The Brontës,* xx.

Chapter Two

1. Charlotte Brontë, "Roe Head Journal" (5 January 1843), Brontë Parsonage Museum, Haworth, England.

2. Elizabeth Gaskell, *The Life of Charlotte Brontë,* ed. and intro. Alan Shelston, 111–12.

3. Fannie Ratchford, *The Brontës' Web of Childhood* (New York: Columbia University Press, 1941), xi.

4. Charlotte Brontë, *Five Novelettes,* edited and transcribed from the original manuscripts by Winifred Gérin (London: Folio, 1971).

5. Frances Beer, ed., *The Juvenilia of Jane Austen and Charlotte Brontë* (Harmondsworth, England: Penguin, 1986). Hereafter, *The Juvenilia.*

6. Gérin, ed., *Five Novelettes,* 23.

7. Beer, ed., *The Juvenilia,* 19.

8. Gérin, ed., *Five Novelettes,* 16.

9. Christine Alexander, *The Early Writings of Charlotte Brontë* (Buffalo, N.Y.: Prometheus Books, 1983), 243.

10. Gérin, ed., *Five Novelettes,* 17.

11. Alexander, *The Early Writings,* 19.

12. See Alexander, *The Early Writings,* chapter 1, "Childhood Influences," 11–26, and chapter 31, "The Visual Imagination," 234–43; see also Gérin, *Charlotte Brontë: The Evolution of Genius,* 24–29.

13. Alexander, *The Early Writings,* 18.

14. Beer, ed., *The Juvenilia,* 22.

15. Gérin, ed., *Five Novelettes,* 18.

16. Ibid., 143.

17. Ibid., 165.

18. Beer, ed., *The Juvenilia,* 228.

19. Ibid., 275.

20. Ibid., 20.

21. T. J. Wise and J. A. Symington, eds., *The Brontës: Their Lives, Friendships, and Correspondences* (Oxford: Shakespeare Head Press, 1938), vol. 2, 218. Hereafter, *SHB LFC.*

22. Gérin, ed., *Five Novelettes,* 19.

23. Ibid., 20.

24. Charlotte Brontë, *The Professor,* ed. Margaret Smith and Herbert Rosengarten (Oxford, England: Oxford University Press, 1987; rpt. 1992), 1.

25. Brontë, *The Professor,* 1.

Chapter Three

1. Mary Augusta Ward, introduction to the Haworth edition of *The Professor* (New York: Harper and Brothers, 1899–1903), xiii–xvii.

2. Laura Hinkley, *The Brontës: Charlotte and Emily* (New York: Haskell House, 1945), 249.

3. "Novels by the Authoress of 'John Halifax,' " *North British Review* 29 (1858): 474–75.

4. Charlotte Brontë, *The Professor,* ed. Margaret Smith and Herbert Rosengarten (Oxford, England: Oxford University Press, 1987; rpt. 1992), 13. All quotations from *The Professor* are from the 1992 edition; chapter citations and page numbers are provided in parentheses in the text.

5. Charles Burkhart, *Charlotte Brontë: A Psychosexual Study of Her Novels* (London: Gollancz, 1973), 48.

6. Ibid., 49, 213.

7. Ibid., 49.

8. Brontë, preface to *The Professor,* ed. Smith and Rosengarten, 1.

9. Ibid., 2.

10. J. A. V. Chapple and Arthur Pollard, eds., *The Letters of Mrs. Gaskell* (Cambridge: Harvard University Press, 1967), 401, 403, 409–10, 417.

11. For a representative sampling of early criticism of *The Professor,* see J. A. Falconer, *"The Professor* and *Villette," English Studies* 9 (1927): 33–37; M. M. Brammer, "The Manuscript of *The Professor," Review of English Studies* 11 (1960): 157–70; and Michael Wheeler, "Literary and Biblical Allusion in *The Professor," Brontë Society Transactions* 17 (1976): 46–57.

12. W. A. Craik, *The Brontë Novels* (London: Methuen, 1968), 49, and Margaret Blom, *Charlotte Brontë* (Boston: Twayne, 1977).

13. Blom, *Charlotte Brontë,* 83.

14. Ibid., 81.

15. Burkhart, *Charlotte Brontë: A Psychosexual Study of Her Novels,* 50.

16. Earl Knies, *The Art of Charlotte Brontë* (Athens: Ohio University Press, 1969), 88, 92–94, 98.

17. Robert B. Martin, *Accents of Persuasion,* 49, 25, Fannie E. Ratchford, *The Brontës' Web of Childhood,* 190–200.

18. See the valuable discussion of autobiographical elements in *The Professor* in Annette Tromley, *The Cover of the Mask: The Autobiographers in Charlotte Brontë's Fiction* (Victoria, B.C.: English Literary Studies Monograph Series, 1982), 20–41.

19. Tromley suggestively claims that *"The Professor* is not, above all, Brontë's unmediated autobiography. It is, however, William Crimsworth's autobiography. A careful examination of *The Professor* reveals a primary interest in the motives and processes of self-presentation; the book is informed by its exploration of the issue" (p. 21).

20. Bettina L. Knapp, *The Brontës: Branwell, Anne, Emily, Charlotte* (New York: Continuum, 1991), 138–39, 143.

21. Helene Moglen, *Charlotte Brontë: The Self Conceived,* 88, 86.

22. Dianne F. Sadoff, *Monsters of Affection: Dickens, Eliot, and Brontë on Fatherhood* (Baltimore: Johns Hopkins University Press, 1982), 119; 121.

23. Ibid., 127.

24. Ibid., 127, 168–69.

25. See the valuable chapter "A Secret, Inward Wound: *The Professor's* Pupil," in Sandra M. Gilbert and Susan Gubar, *The Madwoman in the Attic: The Woman Writer and the Nineteenth-Century Literary Imagination* (New Haven: Yale University Press, 1979), 311–35.

26. Ibid., 331. Consider the authors' suggestive observation that "Crimsworth is anxious not only to kill the dog [Yorke] but to kill what the dog represents. Now fully a patriarch and professor, he sees Yorke Hunsden, as well as the dog Yorke, as a diseased, rabid element in his life" (p. 334).

27. See Rebecca Rodolff, "From the Ending of *The Professor* to the Conception of *Jane Eyre," Philological Quarterly* 61 (1982): 71–89. A brief overview, with feminist sympathies, of the heroine of *The Professor* can be found in Sue

Ann Betsinger, "Charlotte Brontë's Archetypal Heroine," *Brontë Society Transactions* 19 (1989): 301–9.

28. Consider Rodolff's conclusion: "The idea of the subject of *Jane Eyre* and of the feminine point of view—the idea, in short, of entering the soul of a retiring but inwardly passionate woman struggling for social independence and emotional fulfillment—was likely grasped in the act of writing the end of *The Professor*" (p. 72).

29. See Judith Williams, *Perception and Expression in the Novels of Charlotte Brontë* (Ann Arbor, Mich.: UMI Press, 1988), 7–18.

30. Williams makes the interesting observation that "Hunsden treats William as William treats Frances, and Frances is a more real and sympathetic female double of William; thus the centers of male and female power in this novel are to be found in Hunsden and Frances respectively—two figures between whom the flat and uninteresting William is a barrier, or perhaps a conduit" (p. 14).

Chapter Four

1. Fraser, *The Brontës: Charlotte Brontë and Her Family,* 262–84.

2. William Smith Williams to Brontë, 28 January 1848, T. J. Wise and J. A. Symington, eds., *SHB LFC,* vol. 2, 183–84.

3. Thackeray to William Smith Williams, 23 October 1847, T. J. Wise and J. A. Symington, eds., *SHB LFC,* vol. 2, 149.

4. From an unsigned review, *Atlas* (23 October 1847): 719. Reprinted in part in Miriam Allott, ed. and intro., *The Critical Heritage,* 67.

5. George Henry Lewes, "Recent Novels, French and English," *Fraser's Magazine* (December 1847): 690–93.

6. See Donna Marie Nudd, "Rediscovering *Jane Eyre* Through Its Adaptations," in Diane Long Hoeveler and Beth Lau, eds., *Approaches to Teaching 'Jane Eyre'* (New York: Modern Language Association Press, 1993), 139–47, for an essay with an annotated filmography.

7. See, for example, the untitled, unsigned review in *Spectator* (6 November 1847); reprinted in part in Allott, *The Critical Heritage,* 74–75.

8. [Elizabeth Rigby], "*Vanity Fair*—and *Jane Eyre*." Unsigned review in the *Quarterly Review* 84 (December 1848/March 1849): 153–85.

9. Several harsh reviews of *Jane Eyre* so distressed Brontë, who was particularly wounded by accusations of heresy, that she answered them in her preface to the second edition of *Jane Eyre:* "Conventionality is not morality. Self-righteousness is not religion. To attack the first is not to assail the last. To pluck the mask from the face of the Pharisee, is not to lift an impious hand to the Crown of Thorns." Brontë, *Jane Eyre,* ed. Dunn, 1).

10. In postwar twentieth-century fiction, "romances" or "romance novels" signify mass-market, formulaic courtship novels. Since the middle ages, the word

romance has been used to describe a wide variety of narratives. Here we use the term in its contemporary sense to refer to a novel focused on courtship.

11.   These two stories are extremely well known, having been told and retold for centuries all over Europe and the world; in addition, versions of "Cinderella" exist in many cultures. See Alan Dundes, *Cinderella: a Casebook* (New York: Wildman Press, 1983).

12.   *Jane Eyre* reflects the influence of the gothic genre, born in the eighteenth century and increasingly popular in the nineteenth. Gothic romances, especially the subgenre critics have called the "female gothic," describe women's journey to sexual maturity as traumatic and portray male sexuality as violent and duplicitous. Most gothic romances follow the familiar "Bluebeard" paradigm: an innocent young woman comes under the power of a sexually experienced man whose worldly attractiveness conceals a predilection for violating and destroying women. The action of the story takes place inside a house that is ancient, luxurious, and prisonlike and whose forbidden chambers contain traces or symbols of male sexual violence. The heroine's task is to save herself and to stop the cycle of violence by eliminating the dangerous man; later she is often rewarded with a younger, gentler husband. See Ellen Moers, *Literary Women: The Great Writers* (New York: Doubleday & Company, 1976), 90–110.

13.   For an analysis of the ways in which fiction by women has been read in terms of its conformity—or failure to conform—to the limitations of the courtship plot, see Nancy K. Miller, "Emphasis Added: Plots and Plausibilities in Women's Fiction," in Elaine Showalter, ed., *The New Feminist Criticism: Essays on Women, Literature, and Theory* (New York: Pantheon Books, 1983), 339–60.

14.   See Donald Ericksen, "Imagery as Structure in *Jane Eyre*," *Victorian Newsletter* 30 (Fall 1966): 18–22; Eric Solomon, "*Jane Eyre:* Fire and Water," *College English* 25 (December 1963): 215–17; Nina Auerbach, "Charlotte Brontë: The Two Countries," *Toronto Quarterly* 42 (Summer 1973): 328–42; David Lodge, "Fire and Eyre: Charlotte Brontë's War of Earthly Elements," in Lodge, *The Language of Fiction* (London: Routledge and Kegan Paul, 1966), 114–43.

15.   The term "political criticism" to describe critiques based on issues of race, class, and gender is borrowed from Terry Eagleton, *Literary Theory: An Introduction* (Minneapolis: University of Minnesota Press, 1982), 194–218.

16.   Virginia Woolf, "*Jane Eyre* and *Wuthering Heights,*" in Woolf, *The Common Reader* (New York: Harcourt Brace Jovanovich, 1925), 219–27. Reprinted in part in Brontë, *Jane Eyre,* ed. Dunn, 455–57.

17.   Mary Wollstonecraft, *A Vindication of the Rights of Woman,* (1792; reprint, with an introduction and edited by Miriam Brody Kramnick, New York: Penguin Books, 1982). The Mills, who were husband and wife, were well

known for supporting women's emancipation; John Stuart Mills's *The Subjection of Women,* however, was not published until 1869. For an example of the Millses' contemporaneous writings about feminism, see Harriet Taylor Mill [unattributed], "The Enfranchisement of Women," *Westminster Review* (July 1851): 149–61. This article in the liberal *Westminster Review* (whose assistant editor was then Mary Ann Evans, later the novelist George Eliot) criticizes female writers who disclaim equality with men and seek male approval.

    18.   Rich draws this quotation from Phyllis Chesler, *Women and Madness* (New York: Doubleday & Company, 1972).

    19.   Adrienne Rich, *"Jane Eyre:* The Temptations of a Motherless Woman," in Rich, *On Lies, Secrets, and Silence: Selected Prose, 1966–1978* (New York: W. W. Norton & Company, 1979), 89–106.

    20.   For other readings that emphasize the importance of Bertha, see Helene Moglen, *Charlotte Brontë: The Self Conceived,* 124–26, 140–41; Richard Chase, "The Brontës: Or Myth Domesticated," in *Forms of Modern Fiction: Essays in Honor of Joseph Warren Beach,* ed. William Van O'Connor (Minneapolis: University of Minnesota Press, 1848), 107–8; Carolyn Heilbrun, *Toward a Recognition of Androgyny* (New York: Alfred A. Knopf, 1973), 59; Patricia Yaeger, *Honey-Mad Women: Emancipatory Strategies in Women's Writing* (New York: Columbia University Press, 1988), 39; John Maynard, *Charlotte Brontë and Sexuality* (Cambridge, England: Cambridge University Press, 1984), 126. Laurence Lerner's "Bertha and the Critics," *Nineteenth-Century Literature* (1989): 273–300, argues that critics have exaggerated Bertha's significance.

    21.   See, for example, Elaine Showalter, *A Literature of Their Own: British Women Novelists from Brontë to Lessing,* 113.

    22.   Sandra M. Gilbert and Susan Gubar, *The Madwoman in the Attic,* 336–71.

    23.   See M. Jeanne Peterson, "The Victorian Governess: Status Incongruence in Family and Society," in Martha Vicinus, *Suffer and Be Still: Women in the Victorian Age* (Bloomington, Ind.: Indiana University Press, 1972), 3–19. See also Terry Eagleton, *Myths of Power: A Marxist Study of the Brontës* (London: Macmillan, 1975).

    24.   Mary Poovey, *Uneven Developments: The Ideological Work of Gender in the Victorian Novel* (Baltimore: Johns Hopkins University Press, 1988).

    25.   Ibid., 43.

    26.   Henry James, "The Turn of the Screw," Norton Critical Edition, ed. Robert Kimbrough (New York: W. W. Norton, 1966). For a psychoanalytical reading of the dynamics of this story, see Shoshana Felman, "Turning the Screw of Interpretation," in Felman, ed., *Literature and Psychoanalysis: The Question of Reading: Otherwise* (Baltimore: Johns Hopkins University Press, 1980), 94–207.

    27.   The phrase originated in Sir Walter Scott's 1827 *Life of Napoleon* but later was widely used to describe Victorian imperialism.

    28.   Gayatri Spivak, in "Three Women's Texts and a Critique of Imperialism," *Critical Inquiry* 12 (1985): 243–61, argues that the colonialist perspec-

tive subsumes the feminist perspective. See also Laura E. Donaldson, "The Miranda Complex: Colonialism and the Question of Feminist Reading," *Diacritics* 18 (1988): 65–77; Parama Roy, "Unaccommodated Woman and the Poetics of Property in *Jane Eyre*," *Studies in English Literature* 29 (Autumn 1989): 713–27; Susan L. Meyer, "Colonialism and the Figurative Strategy of *Jane Eyre*," *Victorian Studies* 33 (1990): 247–68.

    29.   Jean Rhys, *Wide Sargasso Sea* (London: Penguin, 1966). See also Joyce Carol Oates, "Romance and Anti-Romance: From Charlotte Brontë's *Jane Eyre* to Rhys's *Wide Sargasso Sea*," *Virginia Quarterly Review* 61 (Winter 1985): 44–58.

    30.   Richard Chase, "The Brontës, or Myth Domesticated," in *Forms of Modern Fiction,* ed. William V. O'Connor (Minneapolis: University of Minnesota Press, 1948), 102–13.

    31.   Jacques Lacan, *Écrits: A Selection,* trans. Alan Sheridan (New York: W. W. Norton, 1977).

Chapter Five

    1.   Charlotte Brontë, *Shirley,* ed. Herbert Rosengarten and Margaret Smith (Oxford, England: Oxford University Press, 1979; rpt. 1981), chap. 1, p. 5. All quotations from *Shirley* are from the 1981 edition; chapter and page citations are provided in parentheses in the text.

    2.   For the most theoretically informed discussion of the conflict between realism and romanticism in *Shirley,* see Elizabeth Langland, "Dialogic Plots and Chameleon Narrators in Novels of Victorian Women Writers: The Example of Charlotte Brontë's *Shirley*," *Papers in Comparative Studies* 5 (1987): 23–37.

    3.   For a fuller discussion of the role and function of the "old maids" in the novel, see Roslyn Belkin, "Rejects of the Marketplace: Old Maids in Charlotte Brontë's *Shirley*," *International Journal of Women's Studies* 4 (1981): 50–66.

    4.   For a fuller discussion of the motif of the paired heroine, see Margaret Kirkham, "Reading the Brontës," in *Women Reading Women's Writing*, ed. Sue Roe (New York: St. Martin's Press, 1987), 61–82.

    5.   On the issue of labor in *Shirley,* see Karen F. Reifel, " 'And What Is Your Reading?': Self-Definition in Charlotte Brontë's *Shirley*," *Cahiers-Victoriens et Edouardiens* 34 (1991): 31–45; and Igor Webb, *From Custom to Capital: The English Novel and the Industrial Novel* (Ithaca, N.Y.: Cornell University Press, 1981).

    6.   See the valuable reading of *Shirley* that emphasizes its complicated and unconventional religious vision in Kate Lawson, "The Dissenting Voice: *Shirley*'s Vision of Women and Christianity," *SEL: Studies in English Literature* 29 (1989): 729–43.

    7.   Readings that emphasize the split between private and public issues can be found in Arnold Shapiro, "Public Themes and Private Lives: Social

Themes in *Shirley*," *Papers in Language and Literature* 4 (1969): 74–84. A more valuable recent reading of the same issue can be found in Helen Taylor's "Class and Gender in Charlotte Brontë's *Shirley*," *Feminist Review* 1 (1979): 83–93.

8. Lawson observes that the voice of feminist dissent in *Shirley* is a species of what Derrida calls "*différance*": "The voice of feminist dissent heightens the language of *Shirley*, attracts the reader's attention by its *différance*, by its refusal to be incorporated calmly into narrative sequence." Lawson, "The Dissenting Voice: *Shirley*'s Vision of Women and Christianity," *SEL: Studies in English Literature* 29 (1989): 742.

9. See Gubar, "The Genesis of Hunger According to *Shirley*," *Feminist Studies* 3 (1976): 5–21; reprinted in Gilbert and Gubar, *The Madwoman in the Attic,* 372–98.

10. See Gilbert and Gubar's observation that "Women will starve in silence, Brontë seems to imply, until new stores are created that confer upon them the power of naming themselves and controlling their world. Caroline's fasting criticizes female providing and male feasting, even as it implies that a Father whose love must be earned by well-invested talents is not worth having." Gilbert and Gubar, *The Madwoman in the Attic,* 391.

11. See Joseph A. Dupras, "Charlotte Brontë's *Shirley* and Interpretive Engineering," *Papers in Language and Literature* (1988): 301–16, for a discussion of the gender complications in the text.

12. See Janet Freeman, "Unity and Diversity in *Shirley*," *Journal of English and German Philology* (1988): 558–75, for an insightful analysis of Brontë's convoluted narrative voice.

Chapter Six

1. See, for example, Robert Colby's "*Villette* and the Life of the Mind," *PMLA* 75 (September 1960): 410–19, in which Colby argues that *Villette* is not only Brontë's greatest accomplishment but a key precursor of the great psychologically oriented narratives of the twentieth century.

2. Kate Millett, *Sexual Politics* (New York: Avon Books, 1970), 140; Matthew Arnold, letter to Mrs. Forster, 14 April 1853, in *Letters of Matthew Arnold,* vol. 1 of 2, collected and arranged by George W. E. Russell (New York: Macmillan, 1895), 33–34.

3. Miriam Allott, ed. and intro., *The Critical Heritage,* 75–76.

4. *Villette*'s narrative strategies are discussed in Janice Carlisle, "The Face in the Mirror: *Villette* and the Conventions of Autobiography," *ELH* 46 (Summer 1979): 262–89; Patricia E. Johnson, " 'This Heretic Narrative': The Strategy of the Split Narrative in *Villette*," *Studies in English Literature 1500–1900* 30, no. 4 (Autumn 1990): 617–31; Nancy Sorkin Rabinowitz, " 'Faithful Narrator' or 'Partial Eulogist': First-Person Narration in Brontë's *Villette*," *Journal of Narrative Technique* 15 (Fall 1985): 244–55.

5. Charlotte Brontë, *Villette*, ed. Mark Lilly and intro. Tony Tanner (Harmondsworth, England: Penguin, 1979), chap. 21, p. 307. All subsequent references are to this edition and are included parenthetically in the text with chapter numbers.

6. Brontë, *Jane Eyre*, ed. Dunn, 2nd edition, chap. 10, p. 72; emphasis added. All subsequent references are to this edition and are included parenthetically in the text with chapter numbers.

7. In "Charlotte Brontë's *Villette*: Forgeries of Sex and Self," *Studies in the Novel* 26, no. 3 (Fall 1994): 218–35, Laura Ciolkowski argues that Brontë's questioning of Victorian concepts of gender identity in *Villette* is a source of serious discomfort to generations of readers. She suggests that Brontë manipulates the conventions of the female bildungsroman to create a new Victorian feminine identity.

8. Rosemary Clark-Beattie analyzes Brontë's handling of Catholicism in "Fables of Rebellion: Anti-Catholicism and the Structure of *Villette*," *ELH* 53, no. 4 (Winter 1986): 821–47.

9. Quoted but not fully cited in Winifred Gérin, *Charlotte Brontë: The Evolution of Genius,* 462.

10. For an analysis of Brontë's transformation of her Brussels experience into her fiction, see Donald Williams Bruce, "Charlotte Brontë in Brussels: *The Professor* and *Villette*," *Contemporary Review* 254, no. 1481 (June 1989): 321–28.

11. Hélène Cixous, "The Laugh of the Medusa," trans. Keith Cohen and Paula Cohen, *Signs: A Journal of Woman in Culture and Society* 1 (1976): 892.

12. Two early studies of the nun's influence on *Villette* are Charles Burkhart, *Charlotte Brontë: A Psychosexual Study of Her Novels,* and E. D. H. Johnson, " 'Daring and Dread Glance': Charlotte Brontë's Treatment of the Supernatural in *Villette*," *Nineteenth-Century Fiction* 20 (March 1966): 325–36.

13. For a discussion of the implications of theatricality see Litvak's *Caught in the Act: Theatricality and the Nineteenth-Century Novel* (Berkeley: University of California Press, 1992). Chapter 1, "The Infection of Acting," provides a poststructuralist approach to the metaphors of theater and acting; chapter 2, "The Governess As Actress," focuses on *Jane Eyre;* and chapter 3, "Scenes of Writing and Instruction," focuses on *Villette*.

14. In "Depolicing *Villette*: Surveillance, Invisibility, and the Female Erotics of a 'heretic narrative,' " *Novel* 26, no. 1 (Fall 1992): 20–43, Joseph A. Boone enlists Foucauldian theory to reveal that Lucy's invisibility both debilitates and empowers her, and provides an analysis of the connection between self-surveillance and self-discipline. Margaret Shaw's "Narrative Surveillance and Social Control in *Villette*," *Studies in English Literature 1500–1900* 34, no. 4 (Autumn 1994): 813–34, argues that Lucy's concerns with surveillance highlight the novel's thematic preoccupation with the ideas that seeing is knowledge and knowledge is power; Lucy's narrative both undercuts and appropriates the traditionally male power of what psychoanalytical and film theorists have called "the gaze."

Chapter Seven

1. *The Poems of Charlotte Brontë: A New Text and Commentary,* ed. Victor Neufeldt (New York: Garland, 1985), xxii.

2. Neufeldt, *The Poems of Charlotte Brontë,* xxiii; Tom Winnifrith, *The Brontës and Their Background,* 200–201.

3. Gérin, *Charlotte Brontë: Evolution of Genius,* 579.

4. Neufeldt, *The Poems of Charlotte Brontë,* xxiv.

5. Winnifrith, *The Brontës and Their Background,* 200–201.

6. Neufeldt, *The Poems of Charlotte Brontë,* xxx.

7. Ibid., xxxiv.

8. Christine Alexander, *The Early Writings of Charlotte Brontë,* 66; Neufeldt, *The Poems of Charlotte Brontë,* xxxv.

9. Neufeldt, *The Poems of Charlotte Brontë,* xxxiii.

10. Ibid., xxxvi.

11. Ibid., xxxix; Gérin, *Charlotte Brontë: Evolution of Genius,* 118.

12. Neufeldt, *The Poems of Charlotte Brontë,* 278–79.

13. *The Letters of Charlotte Brontë, with a Selection of Letters by Family and Friends,* ed. Margaret Smith, vol. 1: 1829–1847 (Oxford, England: Clarendon, 1995), 32.

14. Ibid., 59.

15. Ibid., 5.

16. Ibid., 357.

17. Ibid., 358.

18. Ibid., 357–58.

19. Ibid., 241.

20. Ibid., 241.

21. Clement Shorter, ed., *The Brontës: Their Lives and Letters,* 2 vols. (1886; 1908; rpt., New York: Haskell House, 1969), vol. 2, 16.

22. Ibid., 51.

23. Ibid., 67.

24. Ibid., 69.

25. Ibid., 59.

26. Ibid., 367.

Selected Bibliography

PRIMARY SOURCES

Collected Editions

Beer, Frances, ed. and intro. *The Juvenilia of Jane Austen and Charlotte Brontë.*
Harmondsworth, England: Penguin, 1986. Selections of Brontë's juvenilia from 1829 to 1839, tracing the evolution of the two central male
figures whose conflict underlies Angrian political struggles. Strong focus
on Brontë's development of female characters.

Brontë, Charlotte. *The Shakespeare Head Brontë (SHB).* Edited by T. J. Wise and
J. A. Symington. 19 vols. Oxford: Shakespeare Head Press, 1931–38.
Until recently the definitive edition: novels, 11 vols.; biography and letters, 4 vols.; poems, 2 vols.; miscellaneous and unpublished writings,
including juvenilia, 2 vols.

—————. *Five Novelettes.* Edited and transcribed from the original manuscripts
by Winifred Gérin. London: Folio, 1971. This beautifully produced volume was the first published edition of the short novels Charlotte composed in early adulthood (1836–39): *Passing Events, Julia, Mina Laury,
Henry Hastings,* and *Caroline Vernon.* Gérin supplies an informative general introduction, headnotes, textual notes, a brief list of people and
places in the Angrian chronicles, and color and monochrome plates of the
watercolor and pen-and-ink maps and illustrations by Branwell and
Charlotte.

—————. *The Clarendon Edition of the Novels of Charlotte Brontë.* Edited by Jane
Jack, Herbert Rosengarten, and Margaret Smith. 5 vols. Oxford: Clarendon-Oxford University Press, 1975–87. The definitive edition of the
novels.

—————. *An Edition of the Early Writings of Charlotte Brontë,* edited by Christine
Alexander. 3 vols. have been published so far: volume 1, *The Glass Town
Saga, 1826–1832* (Oxford: Blackwell, 1983); volume 2, part 1, *The Rise
of Angria, 1833–1834* (Oxford: Blackwell, 1987); volume 2, part 2, *The
Rise of Angria, 1834–1835* (Oxford: Blackwell, 1991). See also the Penguin edition, *The Juvenilia of Jane Austen and Charlotte Brontë* (Harmondsworth, England: 1986), edited by Frances Beer.

Individual Novels

Brontë, Charlotte. *Jane Eyre: An Autobiography: Edited by Currer Bell.* London:
Smith, Elder and Company, 1847. 3 vols. Besides the Clarendon edition,

edited by Jane Jack and Margaret Smith (Oxford: Clarendon-Oxford University Press, 1969; corrected edition, 1975), see the more accessible Norton Critical edition, edited by Richard J. Dunn (New York: W. W. Norton, 1971; second edition, 1987), which is based on the third edition of 1848, the last corrected by Charlotte Brontë. See also the Penguin edition, edited by Q. D. Leavis (Harmondsworth, England: Penguin, 1966), and the Oxford World's Classics edition, edited by Margaret Smith (Oxford: Oxford University Press, 1975).

————. *Shirley: A Tale*. London: Smith, Elder and Company, 1849. 3 vols. Besides the Clarendon edition, edited by Herbert Rosengarten and Margaret Smith (Oxford: Clarendon-Oxford University Press, 1979), there is the more accessible Penguin edition, edited by Andrew and Judith Hook (Harmondsworth, England: Penguin, 1974).

————. *Villette*. London: Smith, Elder and Company, 1853. 3 vols. Besides the Clarendon edition, edited by Herbert Rosengarten and Margaret Smith (Oxford: Clarendon-Oxford University Press, 1984), there is the more accessible Penguin edition, edited by Mark Lilly and with an excellent introduction by Tony Tanner (Harmondsworth, England: Penguin, 1979).

————. *The Professor*. London: Smith, Elder and Company, 1857. 2 vols. Besides the Clarendon edition, edited by Herbert Rosengarten and Margaret Smith (1987), there is the more accessible Penguin edition, edited by Heather Glen (Harmondsworth, England: 1989).

Letters and Poetry

Brontë, Charlotte. *The Poems of Charlotte Brontë: A New Text and Commentary*. Edited by Victor A. Neufeldt. New York: Garland, 1985. The definitive edition of Brontë's poetry. Contains a valuable historical overview of the problems Neufeldt encountered in locating and verifying the original manuscripts of the poetry.

————. *The Poems of Charlotte Brontë*. Edited by Tom Winnifrith. Oxford: Basil Blackwell, 1984.

————. *The Letters of Charlotte Brontë, with a Selection of Letters by Family and Friends*. Edited by Margaret Smith. Vol. 1: 1829–47. Oxford: Clarendon Press, 1995. The definitive modern edition of Brontë's letters; recounts the history of the muddled and corrupt publication of the letters by Brontë's family and friends, primarily Rev. Nicholls and Ellen Nussey. Contains biographical sketches of all of Brontë's correspondents and reprints Ellen Nussey's essay "Reminiscences of Charlotte Brontë by 'a Schoolfellow,'" originally published in *Scribner's Monthly* (May 1871): 18–24.

Shorter, Clement, ed. *The Brontës: Their Lives and Letters*. 2 vols. First published in 1886 as *Charlotte Brontë and Her Circle,* then in 1908 as *The Brontës: Life and Letters* and again in 1914 as *The Brontës and Their Circle*. Reprint, New York: Haskell House, 1969. Selected letters are grouped by subject; the achronological format and unreliable texts make this less useful than the Shakespeare Head edition. The preferred edition of the letters published through 1847 is the Smith edition.

Wise, T. J., and J. A. Symington, eds. *The Brontës: Their Lives, Friendships, and Correspondences*. 4 vols. Oxford: Shakespeare Head Press, 1931–1938. Currently the only complete edition of the letters but will be supplanted by the Smith edition (cited earlier) when it is completed.

SECONDARY SOURCES

Biographies

Barker, Juliet. *The Brontës*. New York: St. Martin's Press, 1994. Seeks to incorporate new materials from primary sources and to psychoanalyze the relationships between the family members.

Bayne, Peter. *Two Great Englishwomen: Mrs. Browning and Charlotte Brontë*. London: James Clark & Co., 1881, 155–340. Praises Emily at Charlotte's expense.

Benson, E. F. *Charlotte Brontë*. London: Longmans, 1932. This influential biography, based largely on the letters, debunks Gaskell's heroic treatment of Brontë and focuses on negatives, such as tensions between the siblings over Branwell's behavior and Charlotte's obsession with M. Heger, which Gaskell minimized or elided. Benson presents Brontë as neurotic and hypercritical.

Bentley, Phyllis. *The Brontës and Their World*. New York: Viking, 1969. A brief, well-written pictorial study illustrated with a wide variety of black and-white plates that depict Brontëana and Brontë places.

Fraser, Rebecca. *The Brontës: Charlotte Brontë and Her Family*. New York: Crown, 1988. A revisionist narrative biography that depicts Charlotte as a feminist pioneer whose paradoxically ordinary and yet revolutionary life was characterized by a passion for self-expression.

Gaskell, Elizabeth. *The Life of Charlotte Brontë*. London: Smith, Elder and Co., 1857. Rpt. New York: Penguin, 1975. Edited by Alan Shelston. Published with the assistance but not the approval of Patrick Brontë, this early biography by Brontë's friend and colleague distinguishes between the writer Currer Bell and the woman Charlotte Brontë. Gaskell casts Brontë as a heroic character torn by the tension between the pragmatic and romantic aspects of her complex personality. Throughout the nineteenth century, Gaskell's biography was considered definitive.

Gérin, Winifred. *Charlotte Brontë: The Evolution of Genius*. New York: Oxford University Press, 1967. Gérin, who has also written biographies of Emily, Anne, and Branwell, makes exhaustive use of source material in an attempt to connect Brontë's life closely to her fictional works. The sections on Cowan Bridge School, Roe Head, and Brussels are particularly effective.

Gordon, Lyndall. *Charlotte Brontë: A Passionate Life*. London: Chatto & Windus, 1994. An uneven and often derivative treatment that fails to supersede Peters and Gérin.

Moglen, Helene. *Charlotte Brontë: The Self Conceived*. New York: W. W. Norton, 1976. This spare and somewhat speculative literary biography presents Brontë as an analogue of her characters, a feminist literary pioneer struggling against insuperable obstacles.

Peters, Margot. *Unquiet Soul: A Biography of Charlotte Brontë*. Garden City, N.Y.: Doubleday, 1986. A more straightforwardly feminist complement to Gérin's biography that reads Brontë's life as a struggle against patriarchal oppression.

Reid, Thomas Wemyss. *Charlotte Brontë: A Monograph*. London: Macmillan, 1877. First published as a series of articles in *Macmillan's Magazine* in 1876, this biography follows Gaskell's tone except in its call for reconsideration of Emily's works.

Smith, George. "Charlotte Brontë." *The Cornhill Magazine* (9 December 1900): 778–95. Guarded retrospection by Brontë's erstwhile friend and publisher.

Swinburne, Algernon Charles. *A Note on Charlotte Brontë*. London: Chatto & Windus, 1877. Reprinted in part in Miriam Allott, *The Critical Heritage* (London: Routledge and Kegan Paul, 1974), 404–12. Written in response to Reid's monograph on Brontë.

Stephen, Leslie. "Charlotte Brontë." In Stephen, *Hours in a Library* (London: Smith, Elder, 1878), 325–64. First published in *Cornhill Magazine* (December 1877): 723–29. Reprinted in part in Allott, *The Critical Heritage*, 413–23. Stephen's cool response to Swinburne's emotionally charged defense of Charlotte Brontë.

Ward, Mary Augusta [Mrs. Humphrey]. Prefaces to *The Life and Works of Charlotte Brontë and Her Sisters*. Haworth edition. 7 vols. London: Smith, Elder, 1899–1900. Treats Brontë's writings as a reflection of her Irish and Yorkish ancestry.

Wilks, Brian. *The Brontës*. New York: Viking, 1976. A pictorial biography that focuses on the Haworth milieu; color and monochrome plates.

Bibliographical Guides

Alexander, Christine. *A Bibliography of the Manuscripts of Charlotte Brontë*. Haworth: Brontë Society-Meckier, 1982.

Christian, Mildred. "The Brontës." In *Victorian Fiction: A Guide to Research*. Edited by Lionel Stevenson. Cambridge: Harvard University Press, 1966, 214–44.

Crump, Rebecca W. *Charlotte and Emily Brontë: A Reference Guide*. 3 vols. Boston: G. K. Hall, 1982–86. An exhaustive annotated bibliography that covers the period of 1846 to 1983 and comprises more than 3,000 entries.

Passel, Anne. *Charlotte and Emily Brontë: An Annotated Bibliography*. New York: Garland, 1979.

Peters, Margot. "Charlotte Brontë: A Critico-Bibliographic Survey, 1945–1974." *British Studies Monitor* 6 and 7 (1976–77).

Rosengarten, Herbert J. "The Brontës." In George H. Ford, ed., *Victorian Fiction: A Second Guide to Research*. New York: Modern Language Association of America, 1978, 172–203.

General Critical Collections

Allott, Miriam, ed. and intro. *The Brontës: The Critical Heritage*. London: Routledge & Kegan Paul, 1974. Provides a general introduction, excerpts and analysis of the critical receptions to the works of the Brontë sisters from 1846 to 1900. Includes many contributions from G. H. Lewes and many of Brontë's contemporaries, including Arnold, D. G. Rossetti, Pater, Oliphant, and Trollope. Concludes with a brief section on twentieth-century reception to Brontë's works.

Allott, Miriam, ed. and intro. *Charlotte Brontë: "Jane Eyre" and "Villette": A Casebook*. London: Macmillan, 1973. A useful introduction to contemporary criticism of Brontë's two greatest novels, with an overview essay and excerpts from influential reviews and essays by Lord David Cecil, Colby, Heilman, Scargill, R. B. Martin, and others.

Bloom, Harold. *Modern Critical Interpretations: The Brontës*. New York: Chelsea, 1987. A collection of well-known critical essays on all three Brontë sisters.

Gates, Barbara Timm, ed. *Critical Essays on Charlotte Brontë*. Boston: G. K. Hall, 1990. Valuable collection of recent essays, as well as standard earlier ones, on all of the major novels.

Gregor, Ian, ed. *The Brontës: A Collection of Critical Essays*. Twentieth-Century Views Series. Englewood Cliffs, N.J.: Prentice-Hall, 1970. About half the essays in this now rather dated collection are devoted to Charlotte Brontë; among the best are Philip Drew's examination of Charlotte Brontë's editing of *Wuthering Heights,* Robert Heilman's ground-breaking essay on Brontë's "new gothic," and David Lodge's analysis of Brontë's use of naturalistic metaphors.

Lloyd Evans, Barbara and Gareth. *The Scribner Companion to the Brontës*. New York: Charles Scribner's Sons, 1982. An exhaustive encyclopedic guide that provides information on the Brontës and their works, including character synopses and plot summaries.

Pinion, F. B. *A Brontë Companion: Literary Assessment, Background, and Reference*. New York: Harper & Row/Barnes and Noble, 1975. Features character

studies of all family members, a general essay on each novel and the juvenilia, an annotated list of people and places in the Brontës' works, a glos-
sary of Yorkshire dialect and some French words used in the novels, and
a short but informative annotated bibliography. Useful appendixes chart
references in the novels to Charlotte Brontë's readings and Gaskell's cen-
soring of the third edition of her biography in response to lawsuits that
arose after *Jane Eyre*'s publication.

General Studies: Books

Eagleton, Terry. *Myths of Power: A Marxist Study of the Brontës*. London: Macmillan, 1975. Argues that Brontë's novels reveal a conflict between rebellion
and conventionality that mirrored contemporary political conflicts between
property owners and the working class.
Hinkley, Laura. *The Brontës: Charlotte and Emily*. New York: Haskell, 1945.
Typical of the impressionist criticism on the Brontës being published
mid-century.
Keefe, Robert. *Charlotte Brontë's World of Death*. Austin: University of Texas
Press, 1979. Sees Brontë's novels as suffused with unresolved mourning
for her mother and siblings.
Knapp, Bettina L. *The Brontës: Branwell, Anne, Emily, Charlotte*. New York: Con-
tinuum, 1991. A Jungian interpretation of the works of all four Brontës.
Kucich, John. *Repression in Victorian Fiction: Charlotte Brontë, George Eliot, and
Charles Dickens*. Berkeley: University of California Press, 1988. Brontë's
novels reveal that reserve, romanticized as self-control, both inhibited Vic-
torians' social activism and enhanced the intensity of their emotional lives.
Linder, Cynthia A. *Romantic Imagery in the Novels of Charlotte Brontë*. London:
Macmillan, 1975. Traces imagery patterns to their sources in Brontë's
reading of the major British romantic poets.
Peters, Margot. *Charlotte Brontë: Style in the Novel*. Madison: University of Wisconsin Press, 1973. Argues that Brontë's unique knotty, uneven prose
style reflects the author's ideological and personal conflicts.
Winnifrith, Tom. *The Brontës and Their Background: Romance and Reality*. London: Macmillan, 1973. A heavily researched textual analysis of the inter-
connections between the Brontës' novels and juvenilia and a discussion of
the influence of Victorian culture, especially religious belief, on their
works. The chapter entitled "Texts and Transmissions" summarizes the
history of Brontë scholarship to about 1970.

General Studies: Articles and Chapters

Chase, Richard. "The Brontës, or Myth Domesticated." In *Forms of Modern Fiction,* edited by William Van O'Connor. Bloomington: Indiana University
Press, 1959, 102–19. Argues that Brontë's works endowed familiar Vic-

torian themes with mythical status and presented a Byronic masculine universe challenged by strong women who ultimately fail to transform it.

Michie, Helena. "That Stormy Sisterhood: Portrait of the Brontës." In *Sororaphobia*. New York: Oxford University Press, 1992. Discusses the Brontës as a familial writing unit.

Peterson, M. Jeanne. "The Victorian Governess: Status Incongruence in Family and Society." In Martha Vicinus, *Suffer and Be Still: Women in the Victorian Age*. Bloomington: Indiana University Press, 1972, 3–19. Argues that governesses were anathematized because they emblematized Victorian women's economic and social insecurity.

Special Issues: Feminist Criticism

Christ, Carol T. "Imaginative Constraint, Feminine Duty, and the Form of Charlotte Brontë's Fiction." *Women's Studies* 6, no. 3 (1979): 287–96. Reads Brontë's fiction as a perennial struggle against the norm of the "angel of the house," the symbol of constructed femininity created by Coventry Patmore and invoked as a symbol of oppression by Virginia Woolf.

Ewbank, Inga-Stina. *Their Proper Sphere: A Study of the Brontë Sisters as Early Victorian Novelists*. London: Edward Arnold, 1965. An early analysis of the influence of gender on the novels' composition.

Gilbert, Sandra M., and Susan Gubar. *The Madwoman in the Attic: The Woman Writer and the Nineteenth-Century Literary Imagination*. New Haven: Yale University Press, 1979. Chapters on *The Professor, Jane Eyre, Shirley,* and *Villette* reveal Brontë's techniques for simultaneously conforming to and subverting patriarchal standards of conduct and of narrative discourse.

Millett, Kate. *Sexual Politics*. New York: Avon Books, 1970. Reads *Villette* as an account of the damage patriarchy inflicts on able, intelligent women (see pp. 140–47) and portrays Lucy as subtly prevailing over a culture determined to suppress her.

Moers, Ellen. *Literary Women: The Great Writers*. New York: Doubleday & Company, 1976. Reprint, New York: Oxford University Press, 1985. Argues that literature by women reflects women's social position and results in the creation of new genres and topics. See especially chapter 5, "The Female Gothic," pp. 90–112.

Special Issues: Gothic and Genre Criticism

Beaty, Jerome. *Misreading 'Jane Eyre.'* Columbus, OH: Ohio State University Press, 1996.

Dickerson, Vanessa. "Spells and Dreams, Hollows and Moors: Supernaturalism in *Jane Eyre* and *Wuthering Heights*." In *Victorian Ghosts in the Noontide*. Columbia: University of Missouri Press, 1996.

Heilman, Robert B. "Charlotte Brontë's New Gothic." In *From Jane Austen to Joseph Conrad,* ed. Robert Rathburn and Martin Steinman Jr. (Minneapolis: University of Minnesota Press, 1958), 118–132. Reprinted in part in *Jane Eyre,* ed. Richard Dunn, 2nd edition, 458–462. Argues that Brontë transformed hackneyed gothic conventions that had previously been used simply for shock effect by enlisting them to articulate her heroines' forbidden passions.

Massé, Michele. "Looking Out for Yourself: The Spectator and *Jane Eyre.*" In *In the Name of Love: Women, Masochism, and the Gothic.* Ithaca: Cornell University Press, 1992.

Special Issues: Psychology and Sexuality

Burkhart, Charles. *Charlotte Brontë: A Psychosexual Study of Her Novels.* London: Victor Gollancz, 1973. Argues that Brontë's works manifest a pervasive unconscious sexual frustration.

Gezaric, Janet. *Charlotte Brontë and Defensive Conduct.* Philadelphia: University of Pennsylvania Press, 1992.

Maynard, John. *Charlotte Brontë and Sexuality.* Cambridge: Cambridge University Press, 1984. Resists reductionist psychobiographical diagnoses of Brontë as traumatized and neurotic and presents Brontë and her texts as complex and ambiguous in their representations of sexuality and desire.

Momberger, Philip. "Self and World in the Works of Charlotte Brontë." *English Literary History* 32 (1965): 349–69. Reads Brontë's protagonists as outcasts seeking to establish a stable identity in relation to an antagonistic world.

Sadoff, Dianne F. *Monsters of Affection: Dickens, Eliot, and Brontë on Fatherhood.* Baltimore: Johns Hopkins University Press, 1982. An interpretation of Brontë's major novels that employs Lacanian and Kristevan psychoanalytic theories.

Shuttleworth, Sally. *Charlotte Brontë and Victorian Psychology.* London: Cambridge University Press, 1996. A contextual analysis of Victorian constructions of psychology, sexuality, and insanity that traces Brontë's handling of Victorian debates about psychology.

Stockton, Kathryn Bond. *God Between Their Lips: Desire Between Women in Irigaray, Brontë, and Eliot.* Stanford: Stanford University Press, 1994.

Individual Works

JUVENILIA AND SHORT NOVELS

Alexander, Christine. " 'That kingdom of gloom': Charlotte Brontë, the Annuals, and the Gothic." *Nineteenth-Century Literature* 47, no. 4 (March 1993): 409–32. Traces the contemporary sources of gothic elements in Brontë's early works and argues that Brontë's so-called new gothic was actually a reworking of contemporary gothic influences that allowed her to both enlist and critique gothic tropes.

————. *The Early Writings of Charlotte Brontë*. Buffalo, N.Y.: Prometheus Books, 1983. This scrupulously researched volume by the most authoritative transcriber of the juvenilia provides detailed commentary on Brontë's early writings. Three sections analyze the juvenilia; a fourth relates the juvenilia to the later works and resists earlier writers' speculative claims for a direct connection. The appendixes provide a list of Angrian characters and a chronology of Brontë's early prose manuscripts.

Ratchford, Fannie. *The Brontës' Web of Childhood*. New York: Columbia University Press, 1941. The first full-length study of the juvenilia; focuses primarily on works written after 1836 because so few of the manuscripts had at that time been transcribed. Though Ratchford's work has been influential, Alexander's *Early Writings* is more textually reliable and less speculative in its claims about the influence of the early writings.

THE PROFESSOR

Blom, Margaret. *Charlotte Brontë*. Twayne English Authors Series. Boston: G. K. Hall, 1977. Blom's discussion of the novel emphasizes its "tripartite structure": "self-improvement," "temptation," and "reclamation." Blom reads *The Professor* as a religious reworking of the theme of Adam's fall into sexual temptation and eventual salvation through the idealized Frances, and she believes that the novel's value is its status as a "bridge between the writings of her childhood and early adulthood, and her mature work" (p. 79).

Brammer, M. M. "The Manuscript of *The Professor*." *Review of English Series*, n.s., 11 (1960): 157–70. A detailed and extremely technical analysis of all the revisions Brontë and her husband made to the manuscript. Brammer concludes that several sections of the original manuscript can never be recovered because Nicholls excised with a penknife any language he considered objectionable.

Falconer, J. A. "*The Professor* and *Villette*: A Study of Development." *English Studies* 9 (1927): 33–37. An early and straightforward comparison of the similarities and differences between the two novels that emphasizes how Brontë reworked the earlier novel to produce the later and superior one from the same materials: "It is in the character of the hero that the most interesting change is perceptible. Resemblance between Crimsworth and M. Paul ceases with the relationship to the heroine. Crimsworth is not a character but a stick, a woman's ideal of the strong male" (p. 34).

Rodolff, Rebecca. "From the Ending of *The Professor* to the Conception of *Jane Eyre*." *Philological Quarterly* 61 (1992): 71–89. One of the most important critical reassessments of the role that *The Professor* played in shaping Brontë's writing career.

Tromly, Annette. *The Cover of the Mask: The Autobiographers in Charlotte Brontë's Fiction*. Victoria, B.C.: English Literary Studies, 1982. Contains a valuable discussion of *The Professor* as a complex species of autobiography.

Wheeler, Michael D. "Literary and Biblical Allusion in *The Professor.*" *Brontë Society Transactions* 17 (1976): 46–57. A detailed and valuable discussion of the sources and uses of allusion in the novel, primarily those drawn from *Pilgrim's Progress* and the Genesis and Psalms sections of the Bible.

Williams, Judith. *Perception and Expression in the Novels of Charlotte Brontë.* Ann Arbor, Mich.: UMI Press, 1988. "We sense in [Crimsworth] a narrator who has been drained of imaginative energy as a result of his author's attempt to discipline her imagination, and we have an unfair tendency to be uneasy with him, even blame him, for being a block or damper on that imagination" (p. 8).

JANE EYRE

Adams, Maurianne. "*Jane Eyre:* Woman's Estate." In *The Authority of Experience: Essays in Feminist Criticism.* Edited by Arlyn Diamond and Lee R. Edwards. Amherst: University of Massachusetts Press, 1977, 137–59. An early materialist reading of Jane's gradual acquisition of property.

Berg, Maggie. *Jane Eyre: Portrait of a Life.* Boston: Twayne, 1987. Designed to facilitate close classroom study of *Jane Eyre.*

Gilbert, Sandra M., and Susan Gubar. "'A dialogue of Self and Soul': Plain Jane's Progress." Chapter 10 of *The Madwoman in the Attic: The Woman Writer and the Nineteenth-Century Literary Imagination* (New Haven: Yale University Press, 1979), 336–71. Sees Jane's "auto-biography" as the Bunyanesque pilgrimage of a feminist pioneer whose victory is at least partly bought at the cost of another woman—Bertha Mason Rochester.

Hoeveler, Diane Long, and Beth Lau, eds. *Approaches to Teaching 'Jane Eyre.'* New York: Modern Language Association Press, 1993. A collection of 20 essays that explore various aspects of teaching the novel.

Rich, Adrienne. "*Jane Eyre:* The Temptations of a Motherless Woman." In Rich, *On Lies, Secrets and Silence: Selected Prose, 1966–1978.* New York: W. W. Norton, 1979. Reads *Jane Eyre* as an archetypal portrait of a woman's successful struggle to resist patriarchal control.

Rigby, Elizabeth. "*Vanity Fair*—and *Jane Eyre.*" Unsigned review in the *Quarterly Review* 84 (December 1848/March 1849): 153–85. Reprinted in part in *Jane Eyre,* ed. Richard Dunn, 2nd edition, 440–43. An emblematic hostile contemporary review of *Jane Eyre* that found fault with the novel's spurning of gender and class conventions.

Showalter, Elaine. *A Literature of Their Own: British Women Novelists from Brontë to Lessing* (Princeton, N.J.: Princeton University Press, 1977). Showalter's argument about the novel by women roughly parallels the tripartite division of her argument about *Jane Eyre* (pp. 112–124, 139–141), which states that Bertha, along with Helen Burns, functions as a key aspect of Jane's threefold identity.

Spivak, Gayatri. "Three Women's Texts and a Critique of Imperialism." *Critical Inquiry* 12 (1985): 243–61. Briefly but effectively develops the imperial-

ist subtext of *Jane Eyre* and concludes that imperialist identity prevails
over feminist egalitarian scruples.

Woolf, Virginia. "*Jane Eyre* and *Wuthering Heights*." In Woolf, *The Common
Reader*. New York: Harcourt Brace Jovanovich, 1925, 219–27. Reprinted
in part in *Jane Eyre,* ed. Richard Dunn, 2nd edition, 455–57. An early
analysis, possibly inflected by her father Leslie Stephen's judgment,
which condemns Brontë's excessive emotionality.

Wyatt, Jean. "A Patriarch of One's Own: *Jane Eyre* and Romantic Love." *Tulsa
Studies in Women's Literature* 4 (1985): 199–216. Explores the archetypal
patterns to which female readers gravitate and explores their ideological
significance and their relationship to *Jane Eyre*'s enduring popularity.

SHIRLEY

Belkin, Roslyn. "Rejects of the Marketplace: Old Maids in Charlotte Brontë's
Shirley." *International Journal of Women's Studies* 4 (1981): 50–66. Belkin
focuses on Brontë's presentation of "old maids" as an "exploited group"
financially and socially in the novel's society (pp. 50–52).

Briggs, Asa. "Private and Social Themes in *Shirley*." *Brontë Society Transactions*
13 (1958): 203–19. Briggs states that the novel "is not concerned with
one theme but with a bundle of loosely connected—sometimes unconnected—themes. It lacks compactness and integration" (p. 206). Brontë
"was completely uninfluenced by political economy. . . . She concentrated on the human plight of the poor" (p. 215).

Dupras, Joseph A. "Charlotte Brontë's *Shirley* and Interpretive Engendering."
Papers on Language and Literature (1988): 301–16. According to Dupras,
Shirley uses "mastery" and "propriety" to determine how gendered roles
affect the protagonists' "virtues" as well as force the reader to question
the influence of his or her own gender roles on interpretation of the text.

Freeman, Janet. "Unity and Diversity in *Shirley*." *JEGP: Journal of English and
German Philology* (1988): 558–75. Freeman claims that *Shirley*'s unifying
principle can be found in the perception that reality "consists of surface
in relation to interior, of public *in relation to* private—and therefore that
penetration, whether mental or physical, is possible, even essential. In
Shirley, minds, like houses, like all the many versions of privacy in the
novel, are meant to be entered, just as faces, like Brontë's words, are
meant to be read" (p. 573).

Gubar, Susan. "The Genesis of Hunger According to *Shirley*." *Feminist Studies* 3
(1976): 5–21. Reprinted in Sandra M. Gilbert and Gubar, *The Madwoman in the Attic: The Woman Writer and the Nineteenth Century Literary
Imagination*. New Haven: Yale University Press, 1979. Also reprinted in
The Brontës: Modern Critical Views, edited by Harold Bloom. New York:
Chelsea House, 1987, 109–30. According to Gubar, the opening scene
of *Shirley,* with the complaining, greedy curates, contrasts the excesses of
the wealthy with the "hunger of the exploited." This hunger excludes the

exploited from a fulfilling life in English society. In *Shirley* Brontë examines the patriarchal economic and religious institutions, and she uses imagery of "imprisonment and starvation" to illustrate the destruction wrought by female confinement and submission and to explore how women are destroyed by traditional sex roles.

Kirkham, Margaret. "Reading the Brontës." In *Women Reading Women's Writing*, ed. Sue Roe. New York: St. Martin's Press, 1987. A discussion of the paired-heroine motif that Brontë inherited from Samuel Richardson, Austen, and Madame de Stael. For Roe, Shirley is "a Yorkshire version of the Rousseauist woman of genius" (p. 70).

Knies, Earl. "Art, Death, and the Composition of *Shirley*." *Victorian Newsletter* 28 (1968): 22–24. Typical of criticism produced during the 1960s, this article attempts to explain the novel's failure, and Brontë's supposed lack of artistic control, by focusing on her mourning for the deaths of her three siblings, all of whom died during her composition of the book.

Korg, Jacob. "The Problem of Unity in *Shirley*." *Nineteenth-Century Fiction* 12 (1957): 125–36. Korg argues that the novel's "narrative interest is almost entirely restricted to Caroline and her destiny, for she is the only figure who faces the task of choosing her way in life" (p. 135). He sees the novel's theme as "romantic egoism" and divides the characters into two groups: those who "choose to be guided by feeling" and those who "conform to custom or common sense" (pp. 126–27).

Langland, Elizabeth. "Dialogic Plots and Chameleon Narrators in Novels of Victorian Women Writers: The Example of Charlotte Brontë's *Shirley*." *Papers in Comparative Studies* 5 (1987): 23–37. By examining the influence of gender and gender-based experience on "the artist's creation of form", Langland hopes to illustrate how gender can disrupt traditional narrative unity by evoking conflict expressed as doubleness in women's fiction. She attempts to apply a poetics of women's fictions based on Sandra Gilbert's and Susan Gubar's notion of palimpsests and on Nancy Miller's ideas of "nongrammaticalities" or "implausibilities" in women's plots.

Lawson, Kate. "The Dissenting Voice: *Shirley*'s Vision of Women and Christianity." *SEL: Studies in English Literature* 29 (1989): 729–43. Lawson argues that *Shirley* "may be considered on one level, as her examination of the relationship of Dissent to orthodoxy, her consideration of the claims made by Protestants outside of the Church of England" (p. 729).

Lashgari, Deirdre. "What Some Women Can't Swallow: Hunger as Protest in Charlotte Brontë's *Shirley*." In *Disorderly Eaters: Texts in Self-Empowerment*. Edited by Lilian R. Furst and Peter W. Graham. University Park: Pennsylvania State University Press, 1992, 141–52. "Individual eating disorders in *Shirley* are portrayed as part of a much larger picture, in which a dysfunctional society starves women, literally and metaphorically, and women internalize that dis/order as self-starvation" (p. 141).

Reifel, Karen F. " 'And What Is Your Reading?': Self-Definition in Charlotte Brontë's *Shirley." Cahiers-Victoriens et Edouardiens* 34 (1991): 31–45. Karen Reifel believes that labor in *Shirley* occurs in the development of human relationship, and self-definition appears as a labor or work to find one's identity in existing social structures.

Shapiro, Arnold. "Public Themes and Private Lives: Social Themes in *Shirley." Papers on Language and Literature* 4 (1968): 74–84. Shapiro argues that the public and private themes in *Shirley* are, like the public and private lives of its central characters, unified by the theme of selfishness, which is defined as "the lack of sympathy between people," and reflected in the public economic crises and the characters who either adopt these values or become their victims.

The Marxist-Feminist Literature Collective. "Women's Writing: *Jane Eyre, Shirley, Villette, Aurora Leigh." Ideology and Consciousness* 3 (1978): 27–48. An early attempt to renew interest in *Shirley* as a novel by asserting that history is not simply a literary prop or static backdrop but actually a part of the action. They also argue that Brontë had not lost control of her formal literary structures, as so many earlier critics had claimed.

VILLETTE

DeLamotte, Eugenia. *Perils of the Night: A Feminist Study of Nineteenth-Century Gothic.* New York: Oxford University Press, 1990. Contains a chapter that analyzes the gothic residue—the phantom nun—in the novel.

Freeman, Janet. "Looking on at Life: Objectivity and Intimacy in *Villette." Philological Quarterly* 67 (1988), 481–511. An analysis of Lucy Snowe's emotional repression.

Gilbert, Sandra M., and Susan Gubar. "The Buried Life of Lucy Snowe." Chapter 12 of Gilbert and Gubar, *The Madwoman in the Attic: The Woman Writer and the Nineteenth-Century Literary Imagination.* New Haven: Yale University Press, 1979, 399–440.

Hoeveler, Diane Long. "The Obscured Eye: Visual Imagery in *Villette." Ball State University Forum* 19 (1978), 23–30. A psychological interpretation of the use of the "uncanny" in the novel.

Jacobus, Mary. "The Buried Letter: Feminism and Romanticism in *Villette.*" In *Women Writing and Writing About Women.* Ed. Mary Jacobus. London: Croon Helm, 1979, 42–60. An early feminist analysis of the novel.

Kazan, Francesca. "Heresy, the Image, and Description: Or, Picturing the Invisible: Charlotte Brontë's *Villette." Texas Studies in Literature and Language* 32 (1990), 543–66. Focuses on the visual displays and their connection to the theme of religious heresy throughout the novel.

Lawrence, Karen. "The Cypher: Disclosure and Reticence in *Villette." Nineteenth-Century Literature* 42, no. 4 (March 1988): 448–66. Lawrence argues that Lucy constructs herself as a "cypher" who refuses to explain herself even in her own autobiography.

Shuttleworth, Sally. "'The Surveillance of a Sleepless Eye': The Constitution of Neurosis in *Villette.*" In *One Culture: Essays in Literature and Science.* Ed. George Levine. Madison: University of Wisconsin Press, 1987, 313–35. A Foucauldian approach to the construction of female disease in the novel.

Silver, Brenda R. "The Reflecting Reader in *Villette.*" In *The Voyage In: Fictions of Female Development,* ed. Elizabeth Abel, Marianne Hirsch, and Elizabeth Langland. Boston: University of New England Press, 1983, 90–111. Reprinted in Gates, Barbara Timm, ed. *Critical Essays on Charlotte Brontë.* Boston: G. K. Hall, 1990, 287–305. Silver argues that Lucy's narrative manages to incite conventional readers to collude with more rebellious readers; by the novel's closure, these readers have united to create the community absent from Lucy's world.

Tayler, Irene. *Holy Ghosts: The Male Muses of Emily and Charlotte Brontë.* New York: Columbia University Press, 1990. Discusses M. Paul Emanuel as "the muse triumphant" in *Villette.*

Index

Alexander, Christine: as critic of Charlotte Brontë's juvenilia, 18; on poetry of Charlotte Brontë, 138; on visual imagination of Charlotte Brontë, 20

Allott, Miriam, 9

Angria: as African empire in Charlotte Brontë's juvenilia, 16, 21, 22, 35; Charlotte Brontë's letters and poetry as influenced by writing of saga with Branwell, 134, 141–42; contrasted to Haworth, 140; as influence on *The Professor*, 54; as radically polarized universe, 42; and relation to Charlotte Brontë's poetry, 138, 146, 148. See *also* juvenilia

anti-Catholicism, in *The Professor*, 41

Athenaeum, unsigned review of *The Professor* in, 34

Austen, Jane, contrasted with Charlotte Brontë, 18

Aylott and Jones, as publishers of Bell Brothers' 1846 volume of poetry, 35, 149

Barker, Juliet, as biographer of Charlotte Brontë, 14–15

Bayne, Peter, as champion of Emily over Charlotte Brontë, 8

Beer, Frances: as critic of juvenilia, 26, 28; as editor of Charlotte Brontë's juvenilia, 18–19

Bell, Acton, identity of, 1

Bell, Currer: identity of, 1; identity as author of *The Professor*, 36, 91; speculation about "his" identity, 57–60

Bell, Ellis, identity of, 1

Bell brothers, 1846 volume of poetry, 134–35, 141–42, 148

Benson, E. F., biographer of Charlotte Brontë, 2, 9

Bentley, Phyllis, 10

Blom, Margaret, as critic of *The Professor*, 46

Bonnell, Henry, 136

Brontë, Anne: author of *Agnes Grey*, 36; death of, 112, 143, 145, 153; as fictitious character in *Shirley*, 88; travels to London in 1848, 59

Brontë, Branwell: affair with Lydia Robinson, 148; as coauthor of Angrian saga, 24; compared to Ellen Nussey's brother, 149; death of, 112; as influence on Charlotte Brontë's writings, 9, 13, 14, 21–22; relation to Charlotte Brontë's poetry, 138–40, 146; soldiers as gift from his father, 23, 35; as source for cursing in *The Professor*, 40; as source for theme of imperialism in juvenilia, 79

Brontë, Charlotte: as aspiring visual artist, 20; biographical basis of her novels, 4; clinical depression in 1851, 112; composition of "Farewell to Angria," 31; composition of *The Poetaster*, 23, 138; death of, 155; defended *The Professor*, 34; emotionalism conditions her critical appraisal, 8; growing religious angst, 140; and Heger affair, 31; hysterical blindness, 151; letter about being buried alive, 148; letters of, 144–55; letters written to Heger by, 31; and London literary circles, 112; nearsightedness of, 20; nonconformity of, 3–4; pain expressed in letters, 148; paired with her sisters as a writer, 4; personality contrasted to Gaskell, 6; poetry of, 134–44; psychic pain in poetry, 141; reaction to marriage, 155; trance-like mode of composition, 19–20; travels to London in 1848, 59

Brontë, Elizabeth, death of, 7, 19, 63

Brontë, Emily: Charlotte Brontë's letter to, 148; and Charlotte Brontë's poetry, 143; death of, 112, 143, 145, 153; as fictitious character in *Shirley*, 88, 103–4; higher critical reputation

The Authors

Diane Long Hoeveler, associate professor of English and coordinator of the women's studies program at Marquette University, is the author of *Romantic Androgyny: The Women Within* (1990), coeditor of the MLA volume on *Approaches to Teaching "Jane Eyre"* (1993), and coauthor of *The Historical Dictionary of Feminism* (1996). She is also the author of *Gothic Feminism: The Professionalization of Gender from Charlotte Smith to the Brontës* (forthcoming, 1998) and coeditor of three forthcoming collections of essays on women writers, the gothic, and comparative romanticisms.

Lisa Jadwin is associate professor of English at St. John Fisher College in Rochester, New York. She received her Ph.D. from Princeton University in 1989. Her current research focuses on mid-century Victorian narrative, gender studies, and pedagogical theory and practice; her most recent book is a writing textbook addressing the role of cognition in composition.

The Editor

Herbert Sussman is professor of English at Northeastern University. His publications in Victorian literature include *Victorian Masculinities: Manhood and Masculine Poetics in Early Victorian Literature and Art; Fact into Figure: Typology in Carlyle, Ruskin, and the Pre-Raphaelite Brotherhood;* and *Victorians and the Machine: The Literary Response to Technology.*